Distillations

Distillations

Theory, Ethics, Affect

Mari Ruti

BLOOMSBURY ACADEMIC
NEW YORK • LONDON • OXFORD • NEW DELHI • SYDNEY

BLOOMSBURY ACADEMIC
Bloomsbury Publishing Inc
1385 Broadway, New York, NY 10018, USA
50 Bedford Square, London, WC1B 3DP, UK

BLOOMSBURY, BLOOMSBURY ACADEMIC and the Diana logo
are trademarks of Bloomsbury Publishing Plc

First published in the United States of America 2018

Cover design: Kerry Squires
Cover image © David Allan Brandt / Iconica / Getty Images

A catalog record for this book is available from the Library of Congress.

ISBN: HB: 978-1-5013-3379-8
PB: 978-1-5013-3378-1
ePDF: 978-1-5013-3382-8
eBook: 978-1-5013-3380-4

Typeset by Deanta Global Publishing Services, Chennai, India
Printed and bound in the United States of America

CONTENTS

ACKNOWLEDGMENTS

At Bloomsbury Press, I thank my incredible editor Haaris Naqvi for believing that a "distillation" of my recent thinking about theory, ethics, and affect was an idea worth pursuing. I am also grateful to Katherine De Chant, Monica Sukumar, and James Tupper for their diligence with the details of the production process.

In Toronto, I thank Philip Sayers for his flawless sentences, dazzling arguments, and invaluable contributions as my research assistant; Carson Hammond for his articulate emails and for graciously responding to my sporadic queries about all manner of minutia; Margeaux Feldman for her unique blend of bravery, intellect, and affective proficiency; Sheila Heti for being a true inspiration; Alexandra Gillespie for her unparalleled support; Michael Cobb for always being the first to congratulate; and Julia Cooper for having given me the idea that Alain Badiou may be mistaken in not considering suffering as an event: the influence of Julia's thoughtful dissertation on Chapter 6 of this book is undeniable and much appreciated.

At Harvard, Alice Jardine and Afsaneh Najmabadi have my profound gratitude for their unwavering faith in me. I also thank Michael Bronski, Caroline Light, Linda Schlossberg, and Phyllis Thompson for their professionalism coupled with kindness; Amy Parker for getting me across the border and countless other favors; Ana Iona for putting up with my frantic last-minute visits to the filing cabinet where I kept my teaching shoes; Kathy Richardson for her well-timed reassurance; Kacey Carter and Emma Childs for their astounding organizational skills; Jess and Steph Gauchel for being the best friends anyone could have; Jessica Bardsley, Mariya Chokova, Jovonna Jones, and Jackie Wang for appreciating theory as much as I do; Lev Asimow for keeping me on my toes with his encyclopedic mind; and the amazing students of my 2016 course "on love" for wading through Lacan's seminar on transference with me. From this course, a special thanks goes to Giora Ashkenazi, Lev Asimow, Delfina Martinez-Pandiani, Sage Moses, Megan Sims, and Karen Tocatly for their forbearance with my Lacanian neuroses.

In other parts of the academy, I thank Todd McGowan for always managing to change my mind; Amy Allen for being an intellectual kindred spirit; and Jennifer Friedlander, Henry Krips, Scott Krzych, and Hilary Neroni being the jolliest bunch of Lacanians under the sun.

None of the chapters of this book have appeared as chapters in my previous books. However, because this book was originally designed to be a collection of previously published work—a plan I abandoned midway through the writing process because too many new ideas kept cropping up—and because it attempts to rearticulate and streamline arguments that have preoccupied me for some time, there is inevitably some overlap between its first half and some of my previous books. I have done my best to flag this overlap for the sake of readers who are familiar with my earlier scholarship.

This overlap is most obvious in the first half of Chapter 1, which I originally gave as a lecture that was meant to summarize the arguments of *Between Levinas and Lacan: Self, Other, Ethics* (Bloomsbury Press, 2015). I thank the audiences at the University of Kentucky, Pomona College, and Sophia University (Tokyo, Japan) for their valuable feedback on that lecture, an augmented version of which was published in *Angelaki: Journal of the Theoretical Humanities* in 2015. The second half of this chapter—which displays a greater appreciation for Lacanian universalism than I had in 2015—consists of new material drawn from Paul Eisenstein and Todd McGowan's *Rupture: On the Emergence of the Political* and Sara Ahmed's *Willful Subjects*.

Chapter 2, which contains bits of an invited lecture presented at the Psychology and the Other conference in Boston, was published in *The Comparatist* in 2016. Chapter 3 in turn arises from a presentation written for a workshop on critical social theory and psychoanalysis at the New School. A revised version of this presentation was published in *Constellations* in 2016. I thank all three journals for the permission to include adaptations of these articles in this volume.

The last three chapters of this book have not been previously published, but they also began as talks. I presented the rudiments of Chapter 4 at the 2016 American Comparative Literature Association meeting; a section of Chapter 5 as an invited lecture at Duquesne University in 2017; and an early version of Chapter 6 at a meeting of the Association for the Psychoanalysis of Culture and Society some years ago. I thank the organizers and participants of these events for giving me a chance to discuss my work.

AUTHOR'S NOTE

This book contains no footnotes or endnotes, but it incorporates plenty of quotations. I have opted for the following simple system of identifying my sources: in cases where the book's bibliography lists only one text by a given author, the embedded reference merely provides the relevant page number; in cases where several texts by the same author are used, the embedded reference includes both the date of publication and the page number. In the latter cases, the date of publication is repeated at the beginning of every new paragraph in order to avoid any possibility of confusion. When the title of the text referred to is explicitly mentioned in the course of the argument, no publication date is provided. As is customary in the field, Lacan's seminars are identified by their original dates of delivery rather than by the dates of their English translations.

I refer to the subject—the individual—by the pronoun *it* in order to avoid unnecessary gendering. When the word *Other* is capitalized, it denotes the Lacanian symbolic order; when it is not capitalized, it denotes the intersubjective other (the other person).

Thank you for reading.

Introduction

This book distils—filters, purifies, refines, and condenses—ideas about theory, ethics, and affect that I have obsessively returned to in my recent scholarship. It offers a tightly knit collection of reflections about the general state of contemporary theory, posthumanist ethics, political resistance, subjectivity, agency, desire, trauma, suffering, and bad feelings such as anxiety. Because these reflections come on the heels of several books I have published on related topics, it is tempting to characterize them as a culmination of sorts, as a way to wrap up one phase of my research career. In some ways, this is exactly what they are. Or at least this is what I wanted them to be when I set out to compile them. However, it might be more accurate to describe them as a pool of themes that I have not been able to shake off because my position on them often goes against the grain of the dominant trends of my field: progressive critical theory, broadly understood.

My version of critical theory consists of a medley of Lacanian psychoanalysis, continental philosophy, affect theory, queer theory, and deconstructive feminism. These fields have routinely valorized antinormativity; celebrated subjective decentering; devised radical templates of political mutiny; and shunned reason, agency, and autonomy. In addition—with the notable exception of some prominent Lacanian political theorists whose arguments I will discuss in the chapters that follow—they have mostly passionately rejected universalism. In contrast, I have defended universalist ethics—or more precisely, an ethics that is historically specific and open to revision while nonetheless remaining universally binding. In addition, I have refused to embrace antinormativity without qualification; rejected nihilist accounts of subjective disintegration and self-shattering; criticized progressive theory's tendency to advance extreme models of rebellion that have little real-life applicability; and expressed a (guarded and careful) respect for reason, agency, and autonomy.

It has been difficult for me to come to terms with the fact that even though I was trained during the height of poststructuralism—and even though during those years of training I devoured deconstructive criticism with massive greediness—I have ended up endorsing points of view that the generation of American scholars, including some of my closest mentors, who made their names on poststructuralist theory and related fields would find incomprehensible. I have always known that the reasons for my hesitation in the face of some of the main ideals of posthumanist theory have nothing to do with a resistance to French theory: besides Freud and Nietzsche, there is nothing that I find more intellectually compelling. Moreover, the theory-phobia that currently characterizes much of the American academy enrages me because it renders (some) colleagues petty, hostile, and resentful, and because it prevents my graduate students from doing the kind of work that they would like to do.

The reasons for my bizarre blend of posthumanist theory and some seemingly more humanistic tendencies are idiosyncratic. Some of them arise from purely personal foundations, namely the lack of resources, security, and stability that characterized my formative years and that—in various inflections—has accompanied my life as an immigrant. Although things have recently shifted drastically for the better, reminders of previous trepidations, including concrete incidents at United States border checkpoints, still flare up on a regular basis. This makes it hard for me to sanction accounts of subjective decentering that promote the idea that courting insecurity and instability, and abandoning agency and autonomy, are the only way to remain an ethically laudable subject.

From a more theoretical viewpoint, I can name three reasons for the humanist streak in my posthumanist repertoire. First, despite my deep immersion in queer theory, I retain an appreciation for feminist theory that predates the rise of queer theory and that tended to place a greater accent on agency and autonomy than queer theory does. Along related lines, I am not as persuaded as many of my colleagues are by the idea that agency and autonomy are antithetical to transnational feminism. Second, my approach to psychoanalysis has always been attentive to its clinical goals, with the consequence that the rhetoric of self-pulverization favored by many posthumanist critics makes me apprehensive: who, after all, undergoes analysis in order to destroy themselves? Third, my interpretation of Lacanian theory—which has undoubtedly informed my thinking more than any other intellectual tradition—is more centered on the subject's "existential" viability and creativity than is customary in the field. Most significantly for the purposes of this book, I have finally, after many years of uneasiness, been persuaded by Lacanian political theorists who insist on the value of universalism instead of demanding, as most other progressive critics do, that we use the particular to dislodge the universal.

I admit that my relationship to the universalist strand of Lacanian theory remains ambivalent because the views of the thinkers who have most famously articulated it, namely Slavoj Žižek and Alain Badiou, are more or less impossible to reconcile with my endorsement of the reasons for which non-Lacanian progressive critics, including many feminists, have rejected universalist ethical and political models. The most obvious of these reasons is the recognition that the ideal of universalism has historically been used to exclude those who have been unable to claim a foothold under the banner of white masculinity. However, I have come to realize that the kind of universalism that progressive critics spurn bears little resemblance to the universalism that Lacanians advocate. Although I already had an inkling of this when I published my 2015 *Between Levinas and Lacan*, it is my recent exposure to the work of Paul Eisenstein and Todd McGowan that has clarified the matter for me in ways that convince me, both theoretically and ideologically.

As I illustrate in Chapter 1, Eisenstein and McGowan's universalism does not seek to marginalize but instead emerges from a place of marginalization. Žižek and Badiou have long attempted to make the same argument, but in part because they express their perspective through a virulent condemnation of multiculturalism, ethnic studies, queer theory, and feminism—which they regularly (but inaccurately) group under the questionable moniker of "identity politics"—their message has understandably gotten a cold reception from American progressive critics, myself included, who are sympathetic to these theoretical orientations. In contrast, even when Eisenstein and McGowan agree with Žižek and Badiou, they avoid the ideological provocations of the latter two thinkers, which is why their reasoning both persuades and sheds light on what the other two—in their more abrasive ways—have tried to articulate.

Here a note about vocabulary seems indispensable. The Lacanians I have named undoubtedly fall under the category of progressive (radical rather than liberal) theory. But because I need some way to distinguish between them and the rest of progressive theory (such as Butlerian ethics, feminist theory, and affect theory), I have reserved the term *progressive theory* for the latter. This distinction is not meant to be categorical, not the least because I am not alone in routinely crossing the divide between these fields. I therefore ask the reader to approach the term contextually, in the understanding that it is by necessity slippery. In the chapters that follow, it most often refers to theoretical currents influenced by affect theory, which, besides Lacanian theory, is the most important influence on the preoccupations of this book. Indeed, one of my aims is to explore the largely uncharted territory between Lacanian theory and affect theory, which are frequently pitted against each other as wholly discordant but which I believe can be brought into a productive dialogue.

Chapter 1 begins with an exploration of the divergent efforts of Judith Butler, Slavoj Žižek, and Alain Badiou to conceptualize a posthumanist, postmetaphysical ethics that would circumvent the pitfalls of Western liberal humanism yet still possess universal applicability. Butler approaches this task through her ethics of precarity, which posits vulnerability (injurability) as a foundation for a generalizable ethics of relationality in the Levinasian vein. Žižek and Badiou in turn ridicule the "victim mentality" of such an approach, employing instead a Lacanian perspective in order to build an event-based ethics in which a singular event—such as a sudden breakdown of the normative social order—carries the force of truth so strongly that it becomes universally applicable (or accepted).

After considering the strengths and weaknesses of both positions, and after concluding that Žižek and Badiou struggle to adequately address the hidden (white masculinist) particularity of their position, I outline key components of Eisenstein and McGowan's *Rupture* in order to illustrate how it is that the universal, from a Lacanian perspective (when properly expressed), manages to arise from a place of exclusion (deprivation and dispossession). In the course of my argument, I demonstrate that Eisenstein and McGowan have more in common with affect theorists such as Sara Ahmed than any of these critics might realize. Among other things, I show that Lacanian universalism is not necessarily incompatible with affect theoretical concerns about social inequality.

This convergence of concerns is easy to miss because Lacanian political theorists and affect theorists are working with such conflicting understandings of universalism that they keep speaking past each other. Where affect theorists, like most other non-Lacanian progressive critical theorists, associate universalism with fixed a priori norms promoted by Enlightenment rationalism, Lacanian political theorists believe that the universal leaps into existence from a rupture in the dominant political, economic, or social organization. The latter moreover believe that an authentic rupture, the type of rupture that truly expresses the universal, can only emerge from the outlook of those who have been violently cast out of the dominant order.

For Lacanian political theorists, a genuine universalism can never serve the interests of the powerful but must instead speak the language of those who have been banished from power. This in turn means that the universal is always historically specific and must be repeatedly rearticulated: we cannot assume that those who manage to make their way from a place of exclusion to one of inclusion will remain faithful to the universal that they themselves have helped bring into being; instead, it is those who remain excluded—or who become newly excluded due to shifts in the social order—that most truthfully represent the universal.

Chapter 2 argues that some of the main attitudes of contemporary progressive theory have become so predictable that they can be designated as the field's bad—automatic and therefore no longer sufficiently critical—habits. I discuss two habits that are so entrenched within progressive theory that one always knows ahead of time what a given critic will argue. The first of these habits is the tendency to leap from the (warranted) critique of the autonomous and sovereign subject of humanist metaphysics to the (in my view absurd) notion that the more thoroughly pulverized (destroyed and annihilated) the subject gets, the more "ethical" it will be. The logical conclusion of this position is that all efforts to establish a stable sense of self are fundamentally violent even when they represent an attempt to counter a traumatizing past. As much as I appreciate posthumanist theory's attempts to dismantle the humanist self, I am not willing to take the critique of reason, agency, and autonomy so far as to deny that there are situations where ritualistic calls for further subjective decentering make absolutely no sense.

The second of critical theory's bad habits that I analyze in this chapter follows directly from its valorization of subjective pulverization: this is the idea that radical antinormativity—a wholesale dismissal of normative ethics—constitutes the only adequate ethical stance. Even though I admit that there is some validity to this stance in the context of structural violence, I believe that progressive theory underestimates the degree to which normative judgments hover at the background of antinormative theories. In other words, the minute we hold values of any kind—the minute we, for example, want to oppose unfair social arrangements such as poverty, racism, or sexism—we have to have some grounds for holding them. As a result, there is no such thing as antinormativity without an underlying normativity. I propose that acknowledging this uncomfortable fact would increase the ethical relevance of progressive theory.

I end the chapter by positing that normative ethics do not need to be predicated on a (false) image of objective, eternal Truth in the same way as Enlightenment normative models were. Instead, deploying the insights about historically specific universal values developed in Chapter 1, I argue that posthumanist ethical norms should be universally valid at the same time as they remain open to renegotiation. In short, I propose that normative ethics does not need to be metaphysically grounded in order to be theoretically persuasive and politically useful.

I concede that normative ethics can adopt an oppressive (heteropatriarchal, racist, etc.) valence. And I understand that progressive critics reject such ethics because it is hard to dissociate from the Enlightenment humanism that such critics seek to defeat. Yet it seems necessary to admit that normative ethics—when utilized in a prudent manner that remains vigilant about its exclusionary tendencies—is frequently the best way to arbitrate between just and unjust actions.

Chapter 3 offers a more affirmative account of Lacanian theory than is customary among major thinkers in the field. I start the chapter with an appreciative sketch of McGowan's argument in *Capitalism and Desire: The Psychic Cost of Free Markets* regarding the manner in which capitalism takes advantage of the structure of desire by promoting the consumption of commodities as an (always illusory) solution to the alienating effects of the subject's lack-in-being. In vocabulary that in many ways echoes Berlant's notion of cruel optimism—of the kind of false optimism that hopes that things will eventually get better even when they are unlikely to do so—McGowan posits that the commodities that capitalism markets promise healing and future satisfaction without ever actually delivering on this promise. In order to conceptualize an alternative to this trap, McGowan—like Žižek, Badiou, and Lee Edelman—privileges the disruptive potential of the death drive (which does not care about objects) over the complacent ways in which desire fixates on and fetishizes objects. Essentially, McGowan suggests that if we could stop desiring objects, we would have no need for capitalism.

I welcome the main outlines of McGowan's argument, for I agree that capitalism remains operational in part because it offers a comforting fantasy of salvation in the form of an ever-proliferating array of commodities. Yet I also believe that the fixations of desire are not invariably complacent or socially conformist. For example, if we shift our attention from inanimate commodities to the people we desire, it becomes obvious that our desire sometimes fixates on "objects"—say, a lover who is not of the "right" race, gender, or religion—that are not culturally condoned, causing our estrangement from dominant society.

Along related lines, our melancholy fixation on a beloved person whom we have lost (perhaps due to death or abandonment) can paralyze us for long stretches of time in ways that impede our ability to carry out our usual (normative) social obligations; such a fixation can, for instance, hinder our ability to fully participate in the capitalist economy, which demands constant productivity and watchful alertness. Likewise, our desire's fixation of inanimate objects that hold no commercial value—such as a fraying piece of clothing, an ancient laptop, or a dented car that we obstinately cling to—can keep us from entering the cycle of consumption.

On the basis of these insights, I draw in the second half of this chapter on Lacan's seminar on ethics (*Seminar VII*) to demonstrate that ordinary objects can take on a special value whenever they seem to contain a trace of the Thing, the original (non)object that, according to Lacan, promises unmitigated jouissance. In other words, in contrast to many Lacanians who denigrate object cathexes as deceptive fantasy formations that keep us from confronting our lack, I am interested in the fact that Lacan analyzes desire as a matter of raising a mundane object to "the dignity of the Thing"—as a matter of refinding the sublimity of the lost Thing in a desired person. Simply put, if McGowan implies that worldly objects disappoint (because they are not the Thing), I propose that insofar as such objects (including people) transmit something about the singular glow of the treasured Thing—insofar as they contain a faint echo of this Thing—they manage to bring us partial satisfaction. This satisfaction, I argue, is more sustaining than the satisfaction promised (but ultimately not granted) by commodities.

This commentary regarding desire's capacity to raise a mundane object to the dignity of the Thing is perhaps the most consistent component of my Lacanian reflections since *The Singularity of Being: Lacan and the Immortal Within*, my first "Lacanian" book. I resurrect it here not only because I believe that it is one of the most misunderstood aspects of Lacanian theory but also because it allows me to speculate about why anxiety is arguably the dominant affective tone of contemporary Western society. Among other things, I am interested in Lacan's claim, in his seminar on transference (*Seminar VIII*), that desire functions as an antidote to anxiety.

I raise the possibility that anxiety in present-day Western society is heightened in part because the excess of objects, activities, and stimulation on offer in our consumer society is so pronounced that there is little space left for genuine desire. That is, because most concrete things (small things, not houses!) that we might desire are easily available to those who have the financial means to acquire them—like sexual gratification is easily available on online porn sites—the desire of contemporary subjects, particularly of privileged and middle-class subjects, is quenched before they get a chance to experience it.

If deprivileged subjects get anxious about making it to the next day (about surviving), privileged and middle-class subjects are presented with so many choices (ice-cream flavors, brands of wholegrain bread, or Google search options) that desire becomes intertwined with the anxiety of not knowing what to choose. Stated otherwise, one of the main problems of today's Western society is that the insistent chatter of its countless commercial lures drowns out the echo of the Thing, making it difficult for us to recognize the truth of our desire.

Chapter 4 continues my preoccupation with the ways in which major (male) Lacanians tend to valorize the disruptive valences of the death drive and to regard political resistance as a matter of suicidal acts (Žižek), derailing events (Badiou), antisocial self-shattering (Edelman), and violent ruptures (Eisenstein and McGowan). I juxtapose these approaches to the tendency of (mostly female) affect theorists to focus on tiny acts of everyday rebellion, the power of which seems to pale in comparison to the robust rhetoric of Lacanians, but which seem more grounded in the lived realities of everyday life (where antisocial acts of self-shattering and violent ruptures are arguably much less common than quotidian struggles to handle the daily grind).

For instance, although Berlant's theory of cruel optimism includes an attempt to grasp how some subjects—in instances where they manage to destroy the allure of cruel optimism—come to take some distance from normative narratives of the good life, she deliberately seeks to "dedramatize" this process, shying away from revolutionary formulations in favor of quieter accounts of resistance, such as depression, distraction, disengagement, and coasting along. I point out that, generally speaking, the tone of affect theory—which, like queer theory, tends to favor a rhetoric of bad feelings—is one of resignation rather than of rebellion. In other words, if Lacanians seek a radical break from Oppression (the big Other), affect theorists appear primarily interested in forging a livable life amidst circumstances that feel precarious. This chapter explores the pros and cons of these approaches, among other things trying to understand how they might enrich each other.

In this context, I examine the different levels of negativity (or negation) that Lacanians and affect theorists focus on, noting that while Lacanians are mostly interested in the subject's constitutive lack-in-being, affect theorists, though not unmindful of constitutive lack, are more interested in the myriad context-specific ways in which subjects—particularly deprivileged ones—can be wounded and traumatized. This disagreement about the level at which negativity "truly matters" leads to a whole host of other antagonisms. I propose that in reality there is no theoretical or practical reason to choose between these two levels, that it is entirely possible to analyze the effects of constitutive lack while remaining cognizant of the effects of context-specific negations (and vice versa).

Chapter 5 outlines the ways in which Lacanian political theorists—in this case Badiou, Žižek, and McGowan—conceptualize the event of love (one of Badiou's four truth events) as an experience in which transcendence meets with utter subjective derailment. In other words, Lacanian theorists emphasize the traumatizing aspects of love even when they acknowledge its inspiring dimensions. While they shun romance as a capitalist plot that draws the subject into a cycle of greedy commodification that extends to the desired other, they valorize love as the kind of rupture in the ordinary flow of life that forces the subject to reconfigure its entire existence.

It is once again McGowan who offers the most captivating account of this distinction between romance and love, illustrating that even though love is "never a good investment" (2016, 180)—even though it disrupts the subject's customary rhythm of life—it is nevertheless worth the trouble because it opens to what McGowan calls "a secular miracle" (187): a sliver of eternity in the midst of time. Indeed, it turns out that McGowan's argument about love comes close to the argument that I make in Chapter 3 about desire's ability to raise a mundane object to the dignity of the Thing. Our vocabularies may be different but our ideas are compatible.

The second half of this chapter provides an interpretation of Lacan's seminar on transference, focusing on Lacan's reading of Plato's *Symposium*, particularly his claim that Socrates may have been mistaken in rejecting the drunken confession of love that Alcibiades aims at him after crashing the symposium. On the one hand, Lacan argues that Alcibiades is clearly mistaken in falling into the snare of love's narcissistic illusions, demonstrating how the gleaming gems, the *agálmata*, that Alcibiades sees in Socrates are an invention of his fantasy life. Lacan hypothesizes that Socrates refuses to enter the game of love with Alcibiades because he recognizes this: Socrates knows that he does not possess the hidden treasure that Alcibiades finds in him; he knows that he is empty rather than brimming with riches. Lacan admits that on this level Socrates is right: too wise to allow himself to be duped by the narcissistic dimensions of love.

On the other hand, Lacan suggests that if Alcibiades is mistaken, so is Socrates, perhaps even more tragically so. This is because Socrates fails to see that it is through fantasy—through his ability to deposit a treasure in Socrates—that Alcibiades manages to raise him to the dignity of the Thing. That is, according to Lacan, Socrates does not recognize that the imaginary aspects of Alcibiades's desire do not preclude the possibility that there is something "real" about this desire, that it can touch the kernel of jouissance. After all, it is by locating a sublime glimmer in Socrates that Alcibiades renders

Socrates completely singular, and thus irreplaceable. On my reading of Lacan, Socrates is mistaken in walking away from this kind of love.

I begin the final chapter by wondering why Badiou does not view suffering as an event. If falling in love is an event that causes an unexpected tear in the fabric of everyday life, thereby irrevocably altering the subject's understanding of the world, why is suffering—the kind of pain that takes your breath away, causes you to miss your step, and leaves you completely altered—not an event of the same order? Why is the moment of stumbling upon what feels irreplaceable an event when the loss of the irreplaceable is not?

These queries run through the chapter in the context of my analysis of how Nietzsche and Freud, respectively, approach suffering, particularly the question of what one should do with suffering. At first glance, their perspectives appear incompatible, for where Nietzsche advocates forgetting (a deliberate brushing aside of pain), Freud advocates recollection (making the unconscious conscious). However, upon closer inspection, it becomes clear that both thinkers aim at the same goal, namely the overcoming of suffering in order to induce more dynamic modes of life. Yet both admit that this goal is often difficult, even impossible, to achieve. I propose that this difficulty of transcending suffering is precisely why we should—contra Badiou—consider it as a life-altering event.

For Badiou, betraying the event is an ethical failure of gigantic proportions. I speculate that this is perhaps the main reason that he does not classify suffering as an event: because suffering is something that we would all like to betray (leave behind) as expediently as possible, it does not accord with Badiou's schema of life-altering events that demand unwavering fidelity. However, Nietzsche and Freud demonstrate that fidelity is exactly what we, despite our best efforts to the contrary, usually bestow upon suffering. Yes, being in pain is the kind of event that we are desperate to betray. But frequently this proves impossible: the effects of trauma linger in ways that cannot be transcended and that over time reconfigure our entire manner of living. In this sense, suffering is an event that more often than not *cannot* be betrayed (no matter how much we would like to betray it). Consequently, it arguably *is* an event even in Badiou's sense, perhaps even the purest of such events. But one may need Nietzsche and Freud to perceive it as such.

1

The posthumanist universal: Between precarity and rebellion

In posthumanist theory, it is common to say that there is no self without the other—that the self owes its very existence to those who have facilitated its coming-into-being and who sustain its ongoing attempts to claim a foothold in the world. Human ontology, in other words, is inherently social so that it makes no sense to talk about the self as an autonomous entity who unilaterally acts on the world. Rather, the self—the human subject—is formed and maintained through its bonds to others, bonds that, among other things, make it susceptible to traumatization. This has tremendous repercussions for ethics, for if subjectivity is inherently relational, there is no way to envision it outside of ethics: the subject is implicated in ethics from the get-go, before it has developed a sense of who it is, let alone the capacity to make normative distinctions between right and wrong.

This way of envisioning subjectivity is one reason that Levinasian phenomenology has played such a crucial role in recent ethical theory, for Levinas sought to understand precisely the always already ethical inflection of ontology; he sought to grasp how ethics is built into the basic constitution of the subject—how ethics is something we engage in through our very act of taking up space in the world, through our very act of inhaling oxygen that is, consequently, not available to someone else.

For Levinas, every breath I take is a breath that the other cannot take. Not only do I owe my life to the other, but my existence can potentially diminish the other's chances of survival. This leads to an unconditional and asymmetrical ethical accountability that makes me answerable to the other regardless of how the other behaves. As Levinas states, "The fellow human being's existential adventure matters to the *I* more than its own, posing from the start the *I* as responsible for the being of the other" (xii–xiii). The other as face, as a site of human vulnerability, may incite my aggressive impulses, but it also calls me to an unqualified responsibility to *not* act on those impulses. The other as face is inviolable, and this is the case even when the face in question is uncanny or disturbing, and even—and this gets us to the heart of the topic of this chapter—when it threatens to hurt me. In Levinasian terms, I am responsible for the other as face even when the other seems altogether evil; as Levinas (reluctantly) concedes, even the executioner, even the Nazi guard, has a face (231).

The crisis of multiculturalism

How do we ethically relate to such a face—a face that seems to be out to injure, or even murder, us? This question has, during recent decades, in the aftermath of 9/11, the US-led war on terror, Guantánamo Bay, the conflicts of Iraq and Afghanistan, the Syrian refugee crisis, the visible resurgence of white nationalism in the Western world, President Trump's anti-immigration policies, police brutality against black American men, and so on, emerged as one of the biggest dilemmas of contemporary theory, destabilizing the tenets of the tolerant multiculturalism that many of us had learned to take for granted. Moreover, if it is Muslims, Syrian refugees, Mexicans, immigrants, feminists, transsexuals, and queers that threaten President Trump's followers, it is President Trump and the alt-right that threaten many of the rest of us, so that feeling endangered by the unnerving face of the other now appears like a general state of affairs rather than just the predicament of nationalist upholders of the white heteronormative establishment.

Multiculturalism—or even just respect for different points of view—works only as long as we can identify with the other, as long as this other possesses qualities, ideals, or values we can relate to; the other as face remains a relatively easy site of ethical accountability as long as it seems "human" in ways that correspond to our understanding of what it means to be a human being. But matters become complicated when the other—say, a suicide bomber, a white supremacist, or the president of the United States—no longer makes any sense to us.

Alain Badiou and Slavoj Žižek have long been among the most outspoken critics of multiculturalist ethics. Žižek in particular has alienated many Anglo-American progressive critics with his tirades against the "leftist-multiculturalist liberals who improvise endlessly on the motif of impossible universality" (2012, 831). Below I will outline some of Sara Ahmed's affect theoretical objections to Žižek and Badiou. But in the present context, what interest me are those of their insights that go some distance in diagnosing the failings of multiculturalism for us in useful ways. Badiou, for example, correctly asserts that the multiculturalist rhetoric of respecting differences usually falls apart the moment the other is *too* different, the moment the other is no longer the "good" other—the other with whom we can empathize because, on some fundamental level, it is just "like" us.

Within the multiculturalist paradigm, Badiou writes, "I respect differences, but only, of course, in so far as that which differs also respects, just as I do, the said differences. Just as there can be no 'freedom for the enemies of freedom,' so there can be no respect for those whose difference consists precisely in not respecting differences" (2001, 24). That is, the multiculturalist respect for differences applies only to those differences that are more or less compatible with the West's conception of liberal democracy and human rights. Any vigorously defended difference—any difference that deviates too drastically from the West's "humanistic" vision—is automatically deemed "barbaric," "totalitarian," or "terroristic." As Žižek sums up the matter, multiculturalism collapses the minute the other reveals itself as a "*faceless monster*" (2005, 185).

Badiou and Žižek both align the failings of multiculturalism with Levinasian ethics, implying that Levinas is not fully able to account for the more menacing aspects of the other. Žižek, for instance, reminds us of Lacan's assertion that the other is never just a symbolic or imaginary entity—someone we can safely relate to through processes of signification and narcissistic identification—but always also a terrifying, uncontrollable locus of jouissance. Against this backdrop, the Levinasian face, according to Žižek, functions as an ethical lure that seeks to gentrify the threat posed by the other by distracting us from the fact that, underneath the face, the other is radically unknowable. From Žižek's Lacanian standpoint, the Levinasian face is too placid, too reassuring. As Žižek asserts, "Levinas fails to include into the scope of 'human' . . . the *inhuman* itself: a dimension which eludes the face-to-face relationship" (2005, 158).

Even though there is some truth to this claim, it also confuses the issue, for Levinas actually does *not* depict the face as a site of straightforward identification. Rather, he describes it as "a being beyond all attributes" (33), as what escapes all the conceptual and perceptual categories that might allow us to reduce it to what is familiar to us. The face is a site of utter singularity, of utter self-sameness, which means that it by definition defeats our attempts to classify it. As Levinas explains, "It is this presence for me of a being identical to itself that I call the presence of the face" (33). Consequently, far from facilitating immediate empathy, the face alerts us to the limits of empathetic affinity, which is exactly why it, for Levinas, elicits unqualified responsibility—why Levinas believes that we are supposed to protect the other regardless of how this other appears to us, regardless of whether or not we experience the other's face as benevolent.

The idea that it is Levinas specifically who is responsible for the crisis of multiculturalism is also difficult to reconcile with the fact that thinkers deeply sympathetic to Levinas, most notably Judith Butler, have launched critiques of tolerant multiculturalism that are virtually identical to those of Badiou and Žižek. Like Badiou and Žižek, Butler (2004, 2005, 2009, 2012, 2013) condemns Western liberal notions of subjectivity, for such notions, in her view, cause us to perceive some faces as evil so that we can no longer find any grounds for identification, let alone for compassion. In other words, liberal concepts of subjectivity delimit our understanding of intelligible personhood so that when a particular face breaks our familiar frames of reference, when it violates our basic comprehension of how human beings are supposed to act, we suddenly suspend our ethical injunctions and give ourselves permission to wage violence in the name of self-defense.

Butler asserts that this is how some lives become grievable while others remain ungrievable, how we, for example, come to mourn the losses of 9/11, but not the ones of the anonymous Iraqis or Afghans killed by the US military. Her solution to this problem is to expand the horizon of who counts as a face. And her strategy for accomplishing this task is to make us more fully aware of shared human precariousness, of the vulnerability and injurability that connects everyone within the global community.

The ethical tensions of the face

We have here reached a difficult dilemma. We have returned, by the back door, to the problematic that Badiou raises, namely that, despite our rhetoric of respecting differences, it is difficult for us to respect those who refuse to do the same. If we resolve to do what Butler suggests and widen our horizon of who counts as a legitimate face, what do we do with the face of someone who in turn chooses to denigrate the faces of others? How do we respond to the face of the Christian or Islamic fundamentalist who shows contempt for the faces of women or gays? How do we meet the face of the racist who thinks that black faces are the devil?

The rise of Donald Trump and the alt-right has only augmented the stakes of these questions, for our current situation (2017) clearly demonstrates the ethical limits of Butler's reasoning. Those of us working on progressive theory might find it relatively easy to accept the idea that the Syrian refugee has a face in the Levinasian sense—a face that deserves our respect and protection. But we might find it harder to accept the same claim about the faces of alt-right ideologues. The latter might even cause us to suspect that Levinasian respect for the face might sometimes be overrated and that it might instead be better to heed Žižek's (2005) call to "smash" the other's face.

Butler's line of reasoning tells us that we cannot. Her Levinasian rejoinder is that each and every face is our ethical responsibility, and that we must avoid responding to aggression with aggression. Instead, we need to acknowledge the generalized precariousness of human life: the fact that the one thing we all have in common is that we are radically exposed to the world, impinged upon by social forces we cannot control, profoundly woundable and prone to suffering, as well as susceptible to destruction at the hands of others.

Butler of course admits that precariousness is unevenly distributed, that some lives are much more precarious than others. Indeed, the vast biopolitical and necropolitical power differentials of the world target some populations for precariousness while safeguarding others against it so that how we are positioned in relation to global, national, communal, or familial support systems determines how fragile our lives practically speaking are. But in principle, the *potential* for precariousness is something we share with each other, and it is this shared defenselessness that, for Butler, represents a valuable ethical opening in the sense that my recognition that the other is as woundable as I am offers a starting point for my ethical indignation, outrage, and horror in the face of any and all violence committed against the other.

On this view, I oppose injustice done to the other because on some level I can place myself in the other's position—because I perceive that, under different conditions, the oppression aimed at the other, or at least something akin to this oppression, could be aimed at me. Obviously, this dynamic only works to the degree that I am able to see the oppressed other in the first place, which is why Butler believes that it is crucial to revise the habitual frames of perception that I use to make sense of the world so as to increase the visibility of faces that usually remain invisible to me. This is why it is vital to humanize those faces that I am conditioned to interpret as somehow "inhuman" (or less than fully human).

Žižek's strategy is the exact opposite in the sense that ethics, in his opinion, calls for a radical *de*humanization of the subject—a move away from the face. According to Žižek, the problem with our ethical paradigms is that we are unable to abstract from the face in favor of impersonal justice. We keep focusing on the specifics of the face instead of applying the same neutral principles to everyone without exception. Because it is practically speaking impossible for us to consider all faces equally, justice cannot be a function of agitating for this or that face but rather of remembering "the faceless many left in shadow" (2005, 182). In a recent talk Žižek (2017) illustrated his point by arguing that it is not enough to help the Syrian refugees stuck at the European border; instead, the just thing to do would be to give equal attention to those left behind in Syria, for it is not necessarily the case that their predicament is any easier than that of the refugees.

Žižek proposes that justice begins when I recall the distant multitude that eludes my relational grasp. When justice prevails, everyone is equally my neighbor so that my "actual" neighbor is no more important to me than my "virtual" neighbor. While interpersonal empathy implies that I elevate the object of my concern over all others, justice demands the reverse: it asks that I set aside my inclination to grant a special status to those I know, identify with, feel compassion for, or even love. "This coldness *is* justice at its most elementary" (2005, 183), Žižek writes, for justice is a matter of transcending the fetish of the face so as to uphold the impartial letter of the law.

Along related lines, Badiou asserts that it is not respect for differences but rather a kind of studied indifference to them that founds ethics. As he boldly proposes, "The whole ethical predication based upon recognition of the other should be purely and simply abandoned. For the real question—and it is an extraordinarily difficult one—is much more that of *recognizing the Same*" (2001, 25). Since difference, infinite alterity, "is quite simply *what there is*" (25), ethics and politics alike need to be centered around what is valid for all of us. As Badiou sums up the matter, "Philosophically, if the other doesn't matter it is indeed because the difficulty lies on the side of the Same" (27).

The revival of universalism

What we have here is a clash between the Levinasians and the Lacanians, the defenders of the face and those who see the aesthetics of the face as a decoy that distracts us from impartial justice. While Butler wants us to stretch our frames of perception so that we are able to see everyone as a face, Žižek and Badiou want us to look past the face for the sake of justice. To some extent, this clash is artificially orchestrated by Žižek, who overlooks the fact that Levinas clearly distinguishes between ethics and justice, specifying that while ethics relates to the face, justice must dissociate itself from the idiosyncrasies of the face in order to arbitrate between the claims of different faces. But what most interests me is that, despite their obvious disagreements, both positions seem to be on a quest for a *universal* foundation for ethics. After all, whether we are looking to make every face count equally or to studiously ignore every face, we are striving for a general principle that levels distinctions between individuals. We are trying, in our divergent ways, to say that either everyone matters or no one does.

Universalism is having a renaissance. One reason I have taken the time to outline the ethical positions of Butler, Žižek, and Badiou is that I want to call attention to the enormity of the shift that has occurred in posthumanist theory. After decades of intense theorizing about differences, we are witnessing a resuscitation of the category of the Same: an attempt to figure out what unites human beings so as to determine a genuinely egalitarian starting point for ethics.

This trend is by no means limited to Butler, Žižek, and Badiou. For instance, Leo Bersani proposes in *Intimacies* (coauthored with Adam Phillips) that if we refused to approach others through the lens of their psychological particularity, or through categories such as race, ethnicity, gender, or nationality, we would discover that what is different about them is "merely the envelope of the more profound . . . part of themselves which is our sameness" (86). Likewise, neo-Marxist critics such as Ernesto Laclau, Michael Hardt, and Antonio Negri have retained an interest in universalist ethical and political models even though they are otherwise much less hostile to poststructuralism and multiculturalism—and the relativism that these approaches can imply—than Žižek and Badiou. Laclau, for example, has long investigated the processes of "hegemonization" through which the political claims of a particular social group—such as the workers—attain universal status so that everyone, and not just members of this group, recognizes the validity of these claims. Along related lines, Hardt and Negri argue that what they call "the experience of the common" is the only effective foundation of sociopolitical transformation. This experience of the common unifies people around a shared political goal in ways that allow them to transcend the particularities of their identity positions; it is a matter of a multitude of singularities coming together to form a new kind of universal—not the transcendent, metaphysical universal of Western rational humanism but a universal that is built from the bottom up, that is brought into existence by the collective action of individuals who are willing to push aside what divides them in order to access the power of what they have in common.

The neo-Marxist insistence on the possibility of universal ethical and political principles is hardly surprising. But Butler's endorsement of universalism perhaps is. As a matter of fact, it is clear that Butler herself feels ambivalent about this endorsement. On the one hand, Butler defends the universality of her ethics of precarity as follows: "Precariousness has to be grasped not simply as a feature of *this* or *that* life, but as a generalized condition whose very generality can be denied only by denying precariousness itself" (2009, 22). "The injunction to think precariousness in terms of equality," she continues, "emerges precisely from the irrefutable generalizability of this condition" (22). It is therefore the generalizability of precariousness that makes it a suitable foundation for a universal ethics of equality. As Butler asks, "From where might a principle emerge by which we vow to protect others from the kinds of violence we have suffered, if not from an apprehension of a common human vulnerability?" (2004, 30).

On the other hand, Butler takes pains to stress that she does not mean to "deny that vulnerability is differentiated, that it is allocated differentially across the globe" (2004, 31), with the consequence that it may be difficult to draw an easy analogy between one experience of vulnerability and another. Indeed, in her 2012 *Parting Ways*, Butler performs a somewhat unexpected retraction of her earlier rhetoric of generalizability by claiming that her emphasis on shared human precariousness is a matter of pluralization rather than universalization. Under pluralization, she writes, "Equal protection or, indeed, equality is not a principle that homogenizes those to whom it applies; rather, the commitment to equality is a commitment to the process of differentiation itself" (126).

One reason Butler hesitates is that it is difficult to defend universalism without raising the very specters of Enlightenment rationalism and Western imperialism that she has always sought to defeat. At the same time, it is impossible to deny that insofar as Levinasian ethics—the very ethics that Butler draws on to build her own ethical paradigm—relies on the notion of shared human precariousness, it is intrinsically universalist. It is true that Levinas replaces Enlightenment rationalism with relationality. But this arguably renders his vision *more* universalist than more metaphysically or epistemologically grounded approaches, for in the latter there is usually some hesitation about the reach, accuracy, and consistency of reason, whereas in Levinas, there is no way out, no excuse, no indecision (no possibility of questioning of the accuracy of one's approach) when it comes to ethical conduct.

If in, say, Kantian ethics, there is a great deal of analysis of how ethical conduct—or practical reason—can be corrupted by various "pathologies," such as personal interest or emotional ambiguity, in Levinasian ethics there is no space for falling short of the ethical injunction to place the other's well-being before our self-preservation, although, of course, we do constantly fail at this.

Nevertheless, Butler struggles to accept the universalist implications of her Levinasian approach. Speaking of suffering specifically, Butler maintains that, unlike universalization, pluralization recognizes that even though all of us are defenseless against suffering, any given experience of suffering is so unique that the attempt to draw analogies between various forms of suffering is bound to founder. If Butler's earlier work included a sustained effort to navigate the tension between universality and particularity, she now presents this tension as more or less insurmountable: "If we start with the presumption that one group's suffering is *like* another group's, we have not only assembled the groups into provisional monoliths—and so falsified them—but we have launched into a form of analogy building that *will invariably fail*" (2012, 128; emphasis added).

Butler's ambivalence about using the trope of universalism in *Parting Ways* is understandable, for in this text—which, among other things, stages a vehement critique of Israeli state policies against Palestinians—Butler is walking a tightrope between arguing, on the one hand, that the Jewish history of exile, violation, and dispossession should yield insight into the experiences of exile, violation, and dispossession of others, including the Palestinians, and insisting, on the other, that we should not conflate these two experiences. In other words, however critical Butler is of Israel's policies toward the Palestinians (and she is very critical), she wants to make absolutely sure that she cannot be accused of claiming that these policies are akin to Hitler's National Socialism; she does not want to imply that "Zionism is like Nazism or is its unconscious repetition with Palestinians standing in for the Jews" (29).

Drawing such an analogy, Butler notes, would "fail to consider the very different modes of subjugation, dispossession, and death-dealing that characterize National Socialism and political Zionism" (2012, 29). Instead, she wishes "to ask how certain kinds of principles might be extrapolated from one set of historical conditions to grasp another, a move that requires an act of political translation that refuses to assimilate the one experience to the other, and refuses as well the kind of particularism that would deny any possible way to articulate principles regarding, say, the rights of refugees on the basis of a comparative consideration of these and other instances of historical dispossession" (29–30).

Butler thus wants to avoid both the kind of universalism that levels distinctions and the kind of particularism that makes it impossible to compare experiences of violation. On the one hand, she—following Edward Said—urges Jews to draw upon their history of persecution and diaspora to build a sense of kinship with other persecuted and diasporic peoples, including the Palestinians; because the Jews have suffered so much hardship, she proposes, they may be capable of "ethical solidarity" toward others who have had comparable experiences (2012, 49). On the other, she specifies that it is important not to understand this convergence of experiences "as a form of strict analogy" (121).

Again, one can see why the context of Butler's discussion calls for such a disclaimer about strict analogies: she does not want to downplay the specificity of the Nazi genocide, yet she seeks to build a model of ethical responsibility that would recognize convergent modes of dispossession. She wishes to acknowledge that "there are historically specific modalities of catastrophe that cannot be measured or compared by any common or neutral standard" (2012, 29), yet she also strives to leap from one history of oppression to another. As she concludes, "In thinking about the history of the oppressed, it seems imperative to recognize that such a history can and does apply to any number of people in ways that are never strictly parallel and tend to disrupt easy analogies" (100). Butler, in short, aspires to translate convergent experiences of suffering into generalizable ethical edicts without thereby claiming that the experiences in question are equivalent.

The singular and the universal

I understand why Butler insists that histories of dispossession can be convergent without being equivalent. I agree with her resistance to the kind of universalization that would erase important distinctions. And I would never endorse an ethical model where one history of suffering would negate another, where the specificity of suffering would be lost. Yet there is also something implausible about Butler's attempt to replace universalization by pluralization, and particularly about her claim that, when it comes to experiences of suffering, analogies will "invariably fail." Given that the ability to draw analogies between different forms of suffering constitutes the very crux of her ethics of precarity, it is difficult to see how this ethics could survive the collapse of this ability. If anything, it seems that this collapse would instantly undermine the most radical potential of Butler's ethics, namely its ability to compete with other universalizing paradigms, including those derived from Enlightenment rationalism.

Butler's hesitation about universalism also does not seem theoretically necessary, for drawing an analogy does not cancel out the distinctiveness of the entities being compared. As she herself postulates in *Precarious Life* (published in 2004, eight years before *Parting Ways*), "When analogies are offered, they presuppose the separability of the terms that are compared. But any analogy also assumes a common ground for comparability, and in this case the analogy functions to a certain degree by functioning metonymically" (72).

Exactly. If I draw an analogy by saying that you and I both have two eyes, this does not mean that our eyes are therefore identical: my eyes will still be blue while yours will still be brown. But what is important is knowing that if someone throws acid in our eyes, we will both scream. Likewise, if I say that bodily vulnerability is something that you and I share, I do not mean to suggest that we experience this vulnerability in the same way.

A universalist ethics of precarity does not demand a similarity of experiences but merely that we are able to recognize points of contact between different experiences. Let us recall that even the most banal forms of universalism, such as the liberal rhetoric of "different but equal," do not ask that we all have the *same* experiences but merely that—as human beings—we have the capacity to recognize the correspondences, the often quite abstract resemblances, between different experiences. When it comes to suffering, for instance, universalism does not presume that my suffering is *like* yours but merely that I am able to draw a parallel between your suffering and mine.

In this sense, Butler's fear that universalization is *intrinsically* homogenizing seems misplaced, and in fact directly contradicts her own statements elsewhere in *Parting Ways*, such as the following: "It is only possible to struggle to alleviate the suffering of others if I am both motivated and dispossessed by my own suffering. It is this relation to the other that dispossesses me from any enclosed and self-referential notion of belonging" (127). Likewise, Butler explicitly posits that one history of suffering provides "the conditions of attunement to another such history," so that "one finds the condition of one's own life in the life of another where there is dependency and differentiation, proximity and violence" (130).

I have reservations about the idea that ethics should be based on something as utterly unreliable as my ability to be moved by the suffering of others. But if such an ethics is going to work at all, one must presuppose that the common experience of precariousness provides a grounds for translating from one experience to another in ways that open to a degree of universalization, that although each human life is unique, there is a kernel of sameness that makes identification (and thus indignation, outrage, and action) possible.

I am not saying that Butler does not recognize this, for she admits that one experience of suffering might reverberate with another experience of suffering in ethically significant ways. My point, rather, is that there is something perplexing about her vacillation between universalism and anti-universalism, and I suspect that this vacillation has to do with the tension between her poststructuralist antipathy toward universalization and the fact that her entire project in *Parting Ways* is predicated on her wish to move between different experiences of oppression in ways that are inherently universalizing. More specifically, her (repeatedly stated) aim is to derive a generalizable set of ethical principles from the Jewish heritage. As she writes, "It may seem to be a paradox to say that there is a Jewish route to the insight that equality must be secured for a population regardless of religious affiliation, but this is the consequence of a universalization that mobilizes an active trace of that formation with another, as well as a break with its original form" (18).

That specific ethical principles are derived from a specific cultural resource—in this case, the Jewish tradition—does not, Butler explains, "mean that they belong exclusively to [the] tradition from which they are derived" (2012, 3). She in fact suggests—and this will become significant in the second half of this chapter—that *only* principles that demonstrate applicability outside their tradition of origin are able to yield strong enough ethical and political principles to begin with, so that being able to depart from a given tradition is a precondition of ethical and political effectiveness. As she asserts,

"It would seem that other sorts of values and political aspirations did and do emerge in the light of the Nazi genocide, ones that seek to understand and forestall *all* forms of fascism and *all* efforts at coercive dispossession" (26; emphasis added).

Universalization is therefore built into the methodology and conceptual goals of Butler's text in ways that render the moments when she resorts to the rhetoric of anti-universalism wholly incongruous. I appreciate her persistent attention to singularity—her vigilant efforts to safeguard plurality, diversity, and difference against the homogenizing impulses of universalization—because this reminds us that even though precariousness is a universal condition of human life, it is always experienced in singular ways, and that there are consequently times when the temptation to compare two singularities augments rather than alleviates violence. Yet, as I have tried to show, Butler's overemphasis on the impossibility of drawing analogies at times threatens to undercut what is most inspired about her ethics, namely its universal reach.

Although I tend to be politically more aligned with Butler than with Žižek and Badiou, I believe that, theoretically speaking, Žižek and Badiou recognize something important that Butler struggles with, which is that there is no necessary contradiction between the singularity of experience and the universality of ethical principles—that the universal can, potentially at least, accommodate a multitude of singularities without subsuming them into a unitary whole. That said, I want to be careful to specify that I do not think that Žižek and Badiou have adequately thought through this relationship between the singular and the universal. For instance, they falsely assume that every singularity automatically has equal access to the universal. Žižek explains this perspective as follows: the singular "immediately participates in universality, since it breaks through the idea of a particular order. You can be a human immediately, without first being German, French, English, etc." (2009, 72) This is why, according to Žižek, "in every great philosopher there is the theme of the direct participation of singularity in universality, without the detour via particularities, cultures, nationalities, gender differences and so forth" (75).

In a different context, Žižek specifies that the Hegelian dialectical procedure that he favors "can be described as a direct jump from the singular to the universal, bypassing the mid-level of particularity" (2000, 239). The problem with these formulations should be obvious, namely that the majority of the world's people—women of all colors, nonwhite men, queer subjects, and so on—have historically been violently barred from the universal on the basis of their (supposed) particularity. Žižek and Badiou take it for granted that every singularity can claim an immediate membership in the universal. Yet nothing could be less true.

Let me try to state the matter succinctly. I think that Žižek and Badiou are on the right track in trying to revive a universalist ethics. They are also on the right track in recognizing, in a Lacanian vein, that the human is inevitably derailed by a kernel of the *inhuman* (the drives, jouissance, the unconscious)—so that what unites us, what makes us "same," is not something comfortably human(istic) but rather what causes us to be fundamentally out of joint with our so-called humanity. And I even have a degree of sympathy for their efforts to erect the singular as an antidote to the particularity of identity politics. The reason they want to go *directly* from the singular to the universal is that they see the focus on particular identity categories such as race, gender, sexuality, religion, or nationality as a "reactionary" political stance (2009, 75)—one that at best traps individuals in narrow and self-serving preoccupations, and at worst leads to the extreme violence of ethnic cleansings, religious fundamentalisms, and nationalist uprisings.

However, the problem with the reasoning of Žižek and Badiou is that it does not adequately distinguish between various identitarian movements, that it paints all forms of "identitarianism" as an unmitigated evil in ways that make it hard to differentiate between the Civil Rights Movement and National Socialism. Their approach leaves no space for historical specificity, nor does it show any awareness of the fact that if various people have historically taken shelter under the "particularism" of identity categories, it is precisely, as I just noted, because they have been *unable* to translate their version of singularity into the universal. If Butler's resistance to universalism is at times excessive, Žižek and Badiou's advocacy of it is too facile.

The victim versus the immortal

Žižek and Badiou's dismissal of the ways in which the particularities of subject position continue to matter cannot be divorced from their resistance to defining the human as a victim, as an entity marked by vulnerability and dispossession. In other words, what creates a chasm between Butler in the Levinasian faction on the one hand and Žižek and Badiou in the Lacanian faction on the other is Žižek and Badiou's vehement dismissal of the trope of precariousness—the very trope that is central to Butlerian ethics. Žižek has attacked Butler explicitly on this issue on several occasions, arguing that Butler's ethics "is an ethics of finitude, of making a virtue out of our very weakness, in other words, of elevating into the highest ethical value the respect for our very inability to act with full responsibility" (2005, 136). For Žižek, "Fragility alone does not account for ethics—the gaze of a tortured or wounded animal does not in itself make it an ethical subject" (2012, 828–29). What must be added to this fragility, Žižek claims, is an absolute fidelity to an "immortal Truth," for it is only such fidelity "that makes human vulnerability different from that of a wounded animal" (829). While it is not obvious where the truth in question comes from, its impact is unmistakable: it is "a principle for which, in clear and sometimes ridiculous contrast to its vulnerability and limitations, the subject is ready to put everything at stake" (829).

Putting everything at stake in "ridiculous contrast" to one's vulnerability and limitations is what the "act" in the Lacanian sense—in the sense that Žižek promotes it—consists of. Žižek's sliding from the impartial "coldness" of justice as what grounds justice "in the dimension of *universality* proper" (2005, 184) to an immortal truth for the sake of which the subject is willing to sacrifice everything is dizzying in part because the former seems to presume normative values whereas the latter strikes the subject with the kind of staggering force that ruptures its familiar coordinates of being, including, presumably, its normative conceptions of justice. This vacillation between normative ethics and its destruction is a theme that I will pick up in the next chapter. At this juncture, suffice it to note is that Žižek's commentary on the distinction between Butler's ethics of precarity and the subject's fidelity to an "immortal Truth" echoes Badiou's argument that to equate the human with the victim—to reduce the human to the fragility of its constitution—is to deny the rights of the "immortal."

The notion of immortality that Žižek and Badiou reference is (obviously) not meant to imply that we will not die but rather that we possess the capacity for transcendent, inspired acts—or what Badiou calls events. Badiou notoriously distinguishes between two levels of human existence. The first is the ordinary, everyday domain (what Badiou calls the "situation") organized around the pursuit of personal interests such as wealth, success, acclaim, happiness, or (normatively) rewarding relationships. The second is the exceptional domain of truth events—of moments when the subject is seized by an epiphanic vision so powerful that it is dislodged from its ordinary life (or "situation"). During such sudden surges of insight, the subject is able to perceive the world from an angle that is foreclosed by its customary mode of being.

Importantly for Badiou, the subject's ability to act in the name of the truth event is what brings it into being as a subject in the first place, so that, prior to the call of the event—and the subject's willingness to respond to this call—the subject in Badiou's sense does not exist. Such a subject of truth emerges when it is able, momentarily at least, to rise above its mundane interests in order to reach for something higher. In this sense, the realm of the truth event is by definition one of innovation: an unexpected occasion for something previously unimaginable to shatter the status quo and, as Badiou puts it, to forge the "possibility of the impossible" (2001, 39).

Badiou groups events into four categories: political events that accomplish genuine change, such as the Russian Revolution; scientific events that produce a major paradigm shift, such as the replacement of the worldview of Copernicus by that of Galileo; artistic events that generate new aesthetic standards, such as the emergence of Picasso's cubism; and amorous events that modify the coordinates of a person's life so that she cannot continue living as she lived prior to the event; after the amorous event, she has to account for the fact that another person—one who feels irreplaceable—has entered her universe. Of the four events, only the last—the event of love—is accessible to all of us, and even this one is not something that all of us experience, for Badiou is not talking about any old crush: he is referring to the kind of love that feels unequalled, the kind of majestic love that authors from Shakespeare to Tolstoy to Proust have attempted to capture on the page.

I will return to the amorous event in Chapter 5. For now, the point to underline is that, for Badiou, the event is an indication that something completely new and different has entered the world: the event is a "possibility in the name of which you act" (2013, 14). Unfortunately, the problem with the current neoliberal capitalist era is not just that it attempts to discredit past events—such as the event of communism—but also that it tries to prevent new events from taking place; it tries to convince us that the present order of things (the present "situation") is the only viable one. This ruse is easy to accomplish because the event, as I will discuss in greater detail in Chapter 4, is intrinsically derailing.

The event may open up a new possibility, even the possibility of flourishing, of living a fulfilled life—what Badiou depicts as "a life in which everything that could be experimented with . . . has been" (2013, 112). That is, the event may offer genuinely inspiring opportunities of reaching beyond the self in order to live for what is most sublime, most immortal; it may even come with an "affirmative feeling of a dilation" (130). But the price of such "an elevation to a different order," of such an experience of "exception and transgression" is upheaval, disruption, dislocation, indetermination, and not knowing where one is headed (133). One can see why our pragmatic, materialist era is not particularly conducive to such events.

Perhaps most significant for our purposes is the idea that the truth event is an ethical opportunity that allows the subject to pierce the canvas of the established order of things so as to identify what Badiou calls "the void" of the situation. Badiou derives his notion of the void from the Lacanian real, which explains why he sees it as a locus of antihegemonic insight: in the same manner that the real represents the internal limit, the internal stumbling block, to the symbolic order's fantasy of consistency and legitimacy, the void reveals the repressed irritant that makes the falsely coherent collective system (or "situation") struggle, malfunction, and sometimes fail.

The real (or the void) is intrinsic to the symbolic order (or situation)—to the hegemonic status quo—yet impossible to incorporate into the logic of this status quo. For both Žižek and Badiou, such an "extimate" element—an element that is at once intimate to the normative order and uncanny in its terms—is capable of tearing the fabric of this order, thereby fundamentally changing the rules of the game. From this tear in the social establishment—from the act or the event—arises an opening for an alternative politico-ethical vision, one that is not containable within its parameters. Indeed, the tear *is* the opening: the tear functions as a space within which something genuinely new can come into being.

At the same time, the tear (the real, the void) is absolutely necessary for the normative system's functioning. As Žižek maintains, social animosities frequently secretly structure the very reality that they appear to fissure. From this perspective, the tear that seems to impede the comfortable closure of a given social hegemony is in fact what ensures its perpetuation. What is so revolutionary about the event, then, is that it reveals that what might appear like a (mere) contingent obstacle to the system's smooth operation is in reality what ultimately guarantees its viability; it demonstrates that the obstacle in question is a systemic necessity without which the situation's "logic" would disintegrate. For example, it might suddenly become clear that the poor, the homeless, the "illegal" immigrants, the drug addicts, the rebellious intercity youth, the prostitutes, the gang members, and others who constitute the "void" (the invisible underside) of American society in fact facilitate the confident running of this society (its "business as usual"); they represent the deprivileged "stain" that perpetuates social privilege as one of the defining characteristics of the dominant ideology of what it means to be American.

In unveiling the void of a given situation, the truth event therefore creates an ethical opening, an occasion to see and do things differently. However, Badiou believes that when we categorize the human as a default victim, we effectively shut down the possibility of such events: we make it impossible for insights such as this, for new ways of interpreting things, to enter the world. We, as it were, sacrifice the rights of the immortal for those of the mortal, denying that it is only as something "other than a victim," something "other" than a (mere) mortal being, that man accedes to the status of ethical subjectivity; defining man as a victim, Badiou concludes, only ensures that "*he will indeed be held in contempt*" (2001, 12).

This is a rousing formulation, yet it is also somewhat awkward in implying that victimization is something that can be avoided or rejected at will. It may be that Badiou does not mean to vilify the victimized themselves but merely ethical models centered around the notion of victimization. But this distinction is not always easy to uphold, with the result that Badiou at times sounds as if he thought that some people "allow" themselves to be victimized whereas others (those we admire rather than hold in contempt) are strong enough to resist it. In this manner, he oversimplifies not only the realities of power but also the radical permeability of our bodies and psyches alike—the very permeability that Butler foregrounds.

Sara Ahmed's brick wall

Where does this leave us? I guess I would like Butler to acknowledge the universal scope of her ethics of precarity. And I would like Badiou and Žižek to admit that their version of universalism can easily slide into an aggravatingly predictable white masculinist identity politics—the kind of identity politics that hides its own particularist commitments by labeling everyone else as "particular." In other words, I would like Badiou and Žižek to admit that their universalism does not necessarily bypass the problems that have historically plagued Western humanistic models of universalism, otherwise known as Western parochialism.

Such parochialism is exactly what Ahmed, in *Willful Subjects*—a text that aspires to piece together what Ahmed calls a "willfulness archive" out of the experiences of those, such as feminists and racialized subjects, whom mainstream society has deemed excessively "willful" (troublesome, disorderly, anarchic, or stubborn)—accuses Žižek and Badiou of. In other words, Ahmed offers Lacanian universalism a resounding challenge by proposing that this universalism is plagued by a clandestine particularism that manages to conceal itself by translating white male particularity into the universal. The same accusation has been leveled against Enlightenment humanism by a whole slew of critics within feminist theory, ethnic studies, and postcolonial studies. However, Ahmed's critique is worth considering in the present context because it targets Lacanian universalism specifically.

Ahmed correctly points out that Žižek's repeated attacks on particularism—especially the particularism of multiculturalism—rest on an uninformed critique of identity politics. She takes Žižek to task for his "caricature of identity politics"—which maligns those who want to celebrate their particular identity, find their voice, or assert their "way of life"—by pointing out that perhaps "some have 'ways of life' because others have lives: some have to find voices because others are given voices; some have to assert their particulars because others have their particulars given a general expression" (2014, 160). Directing her critique to Badiou in turn, Ahmed writes:

> I could extend this critique to Badiou's formal universalism resting on set theory. If [my] book was read as a willful subject returning Badiou's address, it might say: "Hey, I am not part of your set!" We can use our particulars to challenge the very form of universality. . . . My argument extends over a century of feminist challenges to universalism. We have to keep up the challenge as the critiques of universalism do not seem to get through: I would describe universalism as a theoretical brick wall, which is to say, a wall that exists in the actual world of theory. . . . Note simply this: Žižek and Badiou do not need to create a "segment of identity politics" to guarantee their lecture tours. The universal is handy. (246)

The "theoretical brick wall" that Ahmed refers to is related to the experiential (real life) brick walls that deprivileged subjects find themselves up against on a daily basis; it is related to the analysis that Ahmed advances with regard to the dreadful fraying of life that ensues from repeatedly encountering the barriers of poverty, racism, sexism, homophobia, and other social inequalities, and from having to constantly undertake the tiresome effort "to keep up the signs of getting along," "to keep social surfaces shiny," in order to "adjust to an unjust world" (2014, 157). In other words, Ahmed believes that the theoretical message about the falseness of (white male) universalism that feminists and others have mounted for decades is not getting through—is not getting a fair hearing—because of the experiential brick walls that separate white male identity, understood as the universal, from all other identities, understood as the particular that never quite measures up to the universal. These experiential brick walls brand the voices of "the particular" insignificant in the eyes of the "universal" establishment, in this case the Lacanian establishment—and one must admit that there is such a thing, just like there is a Foucauldian establishment, a Deleuzian establishment, and a Butlerian establishment—comprised of critics such as Žižek and Badiou.

Ahmed makes her argument about the theoretical brick wall that separates the universally valid from the "merely particular" in the context of describing how deprivileged subjects are all too easily accused of willfulness (insubordination) when they are simply just trying to survive in an inegalitarian social world that places obstacles on their path. Drawing on William James—who in turn draws on M. Léon Dumont—Ahmed activates two striking metaphors for social privilege in institutional, including academic, settings: a well-worn garment and a well-functioning lock:

> Maybe an institution is like an old garment: it acquires the shape of those who tend to wear it, such that it becomes easier to wear if you have that shape. Privilege could be thought of in these terms: that which is wearing. Another of Dumont's examples is the reduction over time of the force required to work a locking mechanism. The more you use a mechanism, the less effort is required; repetition smoothes the passage of the key through the hole. James describes this reduction of force or effort as essential to the phenomenon of habituation. I would claim the lessening of effort is essential to the phenomenon of privilege. If less effort is required to unlock the door for the key that fits the lock, so too less effort is required to pass through an institution for bodies that fit. Social privilege is like an energy-saving device: less effort is required to pass through. No wonder that not to inherit privilege can be so "trying." Not to fit, or to fail to inhabit a norm, can often mean being charged with willfulness, whatever you say or do. (2014, 147–48)

The well-worn garment and the well-functioning lock signify the kind of universalism that functions by coding anyone who does not fit its mold—say, the mold of an institutional setting—as "particular." Whoever does not wear the garment easily, whoever seems to jam the lock, is excluded, ostracized, or marginalized in order to bolster the flourishing of those who look, think, and behave in the same way as those who have historically worn the garment or turned the key in the lock.

Ahmed argues convincingly that those who do not fit easily—those defined as particular in relation to a false universal that only becomes a universal by excluding those who do not fit easily—can become utterly exhausted because of having to repeatedly assert their right to belong: if social privilege is "an energy-saving device" that facilitates the capacity of those who possess it to pass through (and linger in) collective spaces, the lack of such privilege drains the subject because it demands a constant expenditure of energy; the deprivileged subject is forced to spend energy just to exist, to continue existing.

In this context, Ahmed gives the example of the transgendered having to repeatedly prompt others to use the appropriate pronouns, "of having to insist on what is automatically given to others" (2014, 149). And unfortunately, this wearisome (wearing) "having to insist" can be read by others as too insistent, too assertive, so that those who insist are seen to be too full of their own will, "not empty enough to be filled by the will of others" (154). This is why Ahmed posits that insistence—willfulness—can be a form of valuable (if exhausting) political labor, of refusing to stop talking when others would prefer you to shut up. "How often minority subjects are called assertive!" Ahmed exclaims: "In being called assertive we have to become assertive to meet the challenge of this call. . . . Just *being* is willful work for those whose being is not only supported by the general body, but deemed a threat to that body" (160).

But what is the universal?

As the misgivings I have expressed regarding Žižek and Badiou's arguments about universalism indicate, I think that Ahmed's critique of them is in some ways warranted. Among other things, I sympathize with Ahmed's frustration about the manner in which the charge of particularism—or identitarianism—can be used to silence those deemed unworthy of attention. Maggie Nelson puts her finger on this problem as follows: "Calling the speaker *identitarian* . . . serves as an efficient excuse not to listen to her, in which case the listener can resume his role as speaker. And then we can scamper off to yet another conference with a keynote by Jacques Rancière, Alain Badiou, Slavoj Žižek, at which we can meditate on Self and Other, grapple with radical difference, exalt the decisiveness of the Two, and shame the unsophisticated identitarians, all at the feet of yet another great white man pontificating from the podium, just as we've done for centuries" (54).

This is tiresome indeed. At the same time, in recent years of reading Lacanian political theory, I have come to see that if universalism persists as the kind of theoretical brick wall that Ahmed describes—a wall that keeps the two sides of the debate from getting through to each other—it is not because one side is reactionary and the other progressive but rather because their definitions of universalism are incompatible. Žižek's flippant provocations certainly do not help to dispel the confusion. However, nor is it theoretically sound to equate the version of universalism that Žižek and Badiou advocate with the violently exclusionary "general will" (2014, 246) that Ahmed regards as synonymous with universalism.

Even if Žižek and Badiou have not sufficiently considered the implications of their categorical rejection of particularism, it is important to recognize that their universalism has more in common with both Laclau's notion of hegemonization and Hardt and Negri's account of the kind of universalism that is built from the bottom up—that is based on the collaboration of individuals who are willing to set aside their differences in order to work toward a shared goal—than it does with an Enlightenment or a (more contemporary) liberal-democratic understanding of universalism. That is, their universalism has nothing to do with the kind of hegemonic big Other Universal that is imposed upon particulars from above but instead strives to grasp how the universal might emerge from a place of exclusion, that is, from the very place of deprivation and dispossession that Ahmed herself analyzes (and that she links to politically charged willful subjects). For Žižek and Badiou, it is exactly what is exiled from what Ahmed calls the general will—and what Žižek and Badiou call the symbolic order, the big Other, or the situation—that gives rise to the universal in its authentic sense.

This point is easy to miss—as I myself have done (see Ruti 2012, 2015b, 2017)—because of the facile rhetoric that Žižek and Badiou use about every singular being able to directly partake in the universal, not to mention because of their questionable rhetoric about victimization leading to contempt. But their commentary on how the universal, through the act or the event, arises from the real or the void clearly links the universal to the excluded. Žižek moreover refines the matter when he claims that a universalist ethics cannot be based on the denial of "the abyss of the Neighbor" (2012, 831).

According to Žižek, one of Lacan's lessons is the realization that it is the other as a monstrous, disturbing site of alien jouissance that concerns ethics more than—and here we return to the opening concerns of this chapter—the other as a benign face. That is, the most demanding task of ethics is to meet the other's jouissance without thereby spiraling into Levinasian masochism. As Žižek explains, "Lacan's option involves neither the aggressive thrust to annihilate the Other-Neighbor-Thing, nor its reversal into accepting the Other as the source of an unconditional ethical injunction" (2012, 828).

Given Ahmed's critique, it is also significant that Žižek proposes that a genuinely universalist ethics would take as its starting point those who are "part of no-part," "those who lack a determined place in the social totality, who are 'out of place' in it and as such directly stand for the universal dimension" (2012, 831). In other words, if for Ahmed those who are "part of no-part," or "out of place," embody the particular that can challenge (dislodge) the universal, for Žižek—and I would add, Badiou—the "part of no-part" is the foundation of the universal; the universal, from a Lacanian perspective, can only emerge from the "not-whole."

In elaborating on this point, Žižek unfortunately lapses into the conventional Marxist notion that only the proletariat can truly represent such a "part of no-part." Even if we use economic exploitation as the criterion of universality—as Žižek does—this "part of no-part" could be defined more inclusively, say, by acknowledging that racism, sexism, homophobia, transphobia, and other social inequalities can keep individuals underpaid and even prevent them from participating in the work force. This insight strikes at the core of my ongoing disagreement with Žižek and Badiou: their single-minded Marxism causes them to be callous toward those who have been marginalized for reasons other than economic—or at least for reasons that are not *merely* economic, such as race, gender, or sexuality.

Žižek and Badiou's Marxist blinders are precisely why they continue to (falsely) "particularize" (by accusations of "identitarianism") every marginalized identity category that cannot be "explained" solely by economic exploitation: their basic mistake is not being able to admit that those "otherwise" excluded can also function as the "part of no-part" that gives rise to the universal. This is why Ahmed's critique of them remains justified even if it does not sufficiently address the nuances of their understanding of universalism. Still, for me these nuances are decisive. They are why, despite the reservations that I have articulated regarding Žižek and Badiou's universalism, I in the final analysis agree with this universalism more than I agree with Ahmed's defense of particularism. I agree with Žižek and Badiou that a universalist ethics is necessary even in a posthumanist world, and that it is those who are "part of no-part" who on a fundamental level personify the void on the basis of which the ongoing negotiation of ethical norms should be undertaken.

Historically specific universalism

In *Rupture: On the Emergence of the Political*, Paul Eisenstein and Todd McGowan, arguing more capaciously (and therefore more convincingly) than Žižek and Badiou, illuminate the stakes of Lacanian universalism. Although they replicate Žižek and Badiou's basic insight that the universal can only emerge from a break from, a rupture in, the established order of things, they—as American-trained critics attentive to feminism and related fields—recognize that there are various social axes along which individuals or groups can be rendered "part of no-part." For this reason, I believe that their formulation can be used to begin to pull out some of the bricks from Ahmed's wall in order to create openings—apertures through which some light can shine through—that may in the long run facilitate productive dialogues across hitherto acrimonious disputes. This is because despite her opposition to the universal, Ahmed might not object to Eisenstein and McGowan's manner of conceptualizing it: "The universal is forged from the rupture with the ruling system, which is why Marx spends so much time talking about the political economists, why Wollstonecraft spends so much time talking about patriarchal society, and why Fanon spends so much time talking about the structures of colonialism. Universality resides in negating the oppression of what is" (82).

Eisenstein and McGowan's wording—that universality "resides in negating the oppression of what is"—echoes José Muñoz's claim that the world as it is currently configured "is not enough" (96), that we need to find a way to transcend the brutality of the present. It also echoes Lauren Berlant's condemnation of "the cruelty of the *now*" in the context of her analysis of how cruel optimism's false faith in a better future causes us to overlook what is unbearable about the present (2011, 28). In other words, Eisenstein and McGowan here seem to be on the same side of the theoretical (and ideological) brick wall that Ahmed describes as Muñoz, Berlant, and—I would propose—Ahmed herself: they view the universal that arises from a rupture in the oppressive status quo, a rupture that negates the reigning order of things, as a means to liberate what has been denigrated by this status quo.

This convergence of positions may initially be difficult to discern because, like Žižek, Eisenstein and McGowan trace their model of universality to Hegel. But a patient reading of their argument reveals a conceptual intersection where their version of Hegelian-Lacanian theory meets Ahmed's version of affect theory, for they advance the same critique of false universalism as Ahmed does. They point out that all Western philosophers prior to Hegel, from Plato to Kant, tried to locate the universal in fixed a priori rules that could not be challenged, and that were therefore impervious to change. Even the Kantian a priori—which needs to be brought into existence by rational deliberation—remains static in the sense that once it exists, it is supposed to always exist. Hegel, in contrast, associates universality with revolutionary change, with rupture or negation, in ways that allow the oppressed to carry the flag of the new—always historically specific—universal.

Eisenstein and McGowan explain that, for Hegel, universality emerges through historical revolutions so that different time periods have different universals. "This historicization of the universal," Eisenstein and McGowan specify, "forges a link between rupture and universality because the rupture in history represents the force that gives birth to the new universal" (73). In other words, it is the very historicity of the new universal that opens up the possibility of opposing the governing universals of a given social context. Furthermore, precisely because Eisenstein and McGowan do not regard universalism as being incompatible with historical specificity, they do not see any reason to abandon the ideal of universality in favor of particularism: if Ahmed wants to erase the hegemonic (static) universals of Western history—universals that are tainted by their association with imperialism, colonialism, racism, and sexism—by discarding the notion of universality altogether, Eisenstein and McGowan's Hegelian approach enables them to challenge hegemonic universals not by fleeing universality as such but rather by insisting on a new (less hegemonic) set of universals.

That said, Eisenstein and McGowan's historically specific universalism comes with a twist, for they emphasize that, for Hegel, a historical context never gives birth to its "own" universal in a straightforward way. Instead, the historically specific universal arises from the disjunction that exists between this historical context (the governing order of things) and the emergent universal that—by virtue of its connection to rupture (negation)—always stands in an antagonistic relationship to this context; because only a rupture from the old universal can produce a new universal, the new universal by necessity in some ways negates the old one. In other words, if a historical determinist would argue that the specificity of a historical context produces a specific kind of universal, Eisenstein and McGowan focus on how the universal comes into being from the antagonisms that underlie any given historical context.

This accent on antagonisms explains why Eisenstein and McGowan view their historicism as being discordant with Foucault's historicism. As Eisenstein and McGowan sum up the matter: "One of the amazing effects of reading an analysis by Michel Foucault is the awareness one arrives at that nothing escapes its context"; "In Foucault's conception, every law is the product of the situation that produces it, not an attempt to alter or transcend that situation" (166). In other words, according to Eisenstein and McGowan, Foucault's historicism makes it hard to conceptualize the kinds of acts, events, or ruptures that constitute a radical break from a given sociohistorical context. This in turn means that even though Foucault regards himself as a defender of singularity, he—in Eisenstein and McGowan's view at least—"actually remains at the level of the particular": "the effect of the historicism that his work spawned has been the widespread destruction of singularity" (167; 166).

Eisenstein and McGowan's condemnation of Foucault is therefore not aimed at Foucault's historicism per se but rather at his unwillingness to link the historical with the possibility of rupture, with the possibility of finding one's way out of the reigning status quo. In contrast, Eisenstein and McGowan, like Žižek and Badiou, believe in such a possibility for the simple reason that they think that there is no such thing as a historical context that is not haunted by antagonisms. Arguably, Foucault advanced the same idea when he proposed that there is no power without resistance, that every system of power generates its antagonisms. However, for Eisenstein and McGowan the rifts in the edifice of every historical context generate the possibility of the kind of radical break that seems more or less foreclosed in the Foucauldian model. Such rifts destabilize the hegemonic system in the same manner that the subject's lack-in-being destabilizes this subject, preventing its self-closure; by definition, every symbolic order, like every subject, remains non-self-identical and therefore vulnerable to the chaotic energies of what it excludes: the marginalized, the real, the void, lack—the excluded carries many names.

The radicalness of the universal

In her recent work, Amy Allen (2017) argues that the continual replacement of one historically specific universal by a new one does not necessarily represent progress; by returning to Adorno's skeptical version of Frankfurt School critical theory, she offers a persuasive critique of the ideal of progress that, say, Habermas (contra Adorno) believes is necessary if critical theory is to remain ethically and politically relevant. Eisenstein and McGowan's Hegelianism may at first glance seem to render them more amenable to the ideal of progress than Allen is. But it turns out that they are also highly suspicious of progress narratives, including accounts of subjective or collective (political) redemption. They for instance concede that most emergent universals over time become coopted by conservative forces so that what begins as a revolutionary rupture may well end up becoming a new oppressive status quo. This is why, unlike Badiou, who hopes that a new, more egalitarian social order might arise from rupture (the event), Eisenstein and McGowan believe that it is only by respecting and sustaining the unruliness of the rupture that it is possible to prevent its ossification into a repressive social hegemony.

Let me restate the matter as follows. On the one hand, it is easy to see how Eisenstein and McGowan's notion of rupture mirrors Badiou's notion of the event in the sense that, as I have shown, Badiou regards the event as a sudden moment of change that reveals a hitherto concealed fissure (negativity, void, or lack) in the façade of the hegemonic situation; from this perspective, Eisenstein and McGowan are merely giving Badiou's event a new name: rupture. But on the other, if for Badiou what is important is the new order of things that emerges from the event—which is why his philosophy tends to have an affirmative, even inspirational tinge—Eisenstein and McGowan place the emphasis on unresolvable antagonisms.

Eisenstein and McGowan write: "Each time that one attempts to ground a system of thought or a social order on a universal, the contradictions that beset positive universality reveal the untenable status of this grounding. In Hegel's thought, there is a universality of negation that cannot be translated into any positive form" (74). In this sense, any new universal is automatically vulnerable to the pressures of antagonistic forces that are clamoring for its undoing, for yet another set of universal values. This does not mean that no enduring universal values are possible. But it does mean that these values need to constantly justify themselves in relation to newly ignited antagonisms; they need to prove their continued validity against relentless questioning.

Recall that Hegel associates the universal value of freedom with the slave's ability to question his or her situation. The master in the Hegelian master-slave dialectic remains complacently embedded in his or her situation for the simple reason that this situation accommodates him or her exactly in the manner that Ahmed expresses through her metaphors of the well-worn garment and the well-functioning lock; the master's situation does not offer any resistance because it manages to suppress the slave's animosity. But the slave cannot be indefinitely contained. He or she finds his or her situation unbearable and therefore seeks to break free from it; he or she begins to question the master's system, and from this questioning arises the universal value of freedom. It is easy to see how Eisenstein and McGowan leap from this Hegelian seedling to an analysis of revolutionary moments as ones that bring into being a new set of universals, and how it is the excluded—the fracture in the governing situation—that becomes the lever for the emergence of the new universal.

For Eisenstein and McGowan, there cannot be a revolutionary rupture that serves the powerful, that serves those who wear the garment or turn the key effortlessly. This is why it is not the French or American revolutions that, for Eisenstein and McGowan, represent rupture (and therefore universality) at its purest, but rather the Haitian Revolution. The French and American revolutions all too rapidly reverted to a celebration of national and cultural particularity, which—as we will see shortly—Eisenstein and McGowan, like Žižek and Badiou, regard as one of the main adversaries of genuine universality. The Haitian Revolution, in contrast, dissociated the ideals of the French Revolution (freedom, equality, and solidarity) from their original locus of expression, thereby proving their universal validity. In other words, the Haitian Revolution illustrated that universal values are not—cannot be—connected to a specific national or cultural context.

As Eisenstein and McGowan reason, "The fact that the revolutionaries of Haiti take up universals already articulated in France does not lessen the importance of their revolution, it magnifies it": "In a time dominated by seemingly infinite assertions of cultural particularity as the ultimate horizon of thought, the Haitian Revolution stands as a reminder that universality has the power to trump the particularity of culture. The people of Haiti did not revolt in the name of this particularity but for the sake of the universal" (79, 80). That is, for Eisenstein and McGowan, the Haitian Revolution is "the great event in modernity" because it "punctuates the spirit of the French Revolution by attesting to the nullity of cultural difference in the face of the universality of rupture" (79, 80).

It is noteworthy that Eisenstein and McGowan's argument parallels the one that Butler attempts to make regarding the Jewish heritage, namely that universal values should be applicable to contexts other than their place of origin. But where Butler backs away from the implications of her vision by resurrecting the particular in ways that, in my view, compromise the radicalness of her ethics, Eisenstein and McGowan hold their course, defending their version of the universal against all assaults by the particular. This is a bold move because their renunciation of particularity, including national and cultural particularity, obviously counters progressive theoretical models from multiculturalism to affect theory that, like Ahmed, defend the particular against the universal. What interests me are the ramifications of this move.

For most of non-Lacanian (and non-Marxist) progressive theory—and here I remind the reader of the artificial distinction that I created in the introduction between Lacanian theory and the rest of progressive theory—the universal stands for the conservative and the particular stands for the radical: the universal represents the oppressive status quo that the particular contests. This vision is so prominent in non-Lacanian progressive theory that it is virtually impossible to defend universalism without instantly being categorized as a proponent of traditional (or neoliberal) values. In this theoretical climate, what is so fascinating about Eisenstein and McGowan's model—and here they do once again follow Žižek and Badiou even if this may be somewhat difficult to discern—is that it reverses this assessment: for Eisenstein and McGowan, it is the particular that is conservative and the universal that is radical. This is because, as I have shown, they associate the universal with a rupture arising from the antagonisms that the excluded (those who cannot easily wear the garment or turn the key) introduce into the normative status quo.

If, for Eisenstein and McGowan, there is no such thing as a (genuine) rupture that serves the powerful, that serves conservative values, it is because conservatism by definition aspires to stabilize both identities and values. In contrast, rupture, in whatever form it takes, does not permit the sense of security—material or psychic—that conservatism seeks. A rupture is a traumatic cut that cannot be sutured into a new status quo. As Eisenstein and McGowan explain:

> The rupture is always a traumatic cut. Though the rupture gives birth to political values like freedom and equality, it does so through disconnecting individuals from the bonds of tradition through which they receive a sense of identity and belonging. To remain within the rupture is to exist without the security of a place in the world. One is traumatically cut adrift, and even the solidarity one experiences with other subjects does not provide the assurance of a collective identity. It is a solidarity of isolated and singular subjects who have no home with which to identify or to strive for. We find value only through the embrace of trauma. The values worth fighting for are the ones that would also destroy us. (36)

Eisenstein and McGowan connect rupture to the trauma of losing the bonds of tradition that allow the subject to obtain a sense of identity and belonging. The universal cuts the cords of tradition, sets the subject adrift, and bars it from any secure connection to a collectivity. This does not mean that it cannot forge solidarity with others. But this is a solidarity that is not based on a shared platform of identity. It is a coalitional solidarity of "isolated and singular subjects who have no home with which to identify or to strive for."

Breaking with tradition, culture, and custom

Eisenstein and McGowan here do what Žižek and Badiou also attempt to do: they jump directly from the singular to the universal by bypassing the particular. They envision revolt as a definitive break from sociohistorical context that allows the universal to defeat the particular, including the particularity of tradition, culture, or custom. I reckon that it might be challenging for progressive critics in affect theory, queer theory, feminist theory, ethnic studies, and postcolonial studies to accept this jump. At the same time, I hope that living in President Trump's America, an America built on a xenophobic rejection of ideals, such as the ideal of the equality of all people, that—let's admit it (see Chapter 2)—for many of us carry universal validity, makes it easier to see the radical edge of Lacanian universalism.

Trump's America reveals that the nationalist (and militarist) celebration of American exceptionalism, the valorization of the particularity of social identity and belonging, can be enormously repressive. Most non-Lacanian progressive critics would of course admit this: they would acknowledge the dangers of particularist claims of the "blood and soil" variety, the kinds of claims that founded Nazi Germany and that we are witnessing in Trump's America. At the same time, they tend to hedge their bets regarding particularity by arguing that how the chips fall depends on the nature of the particularity in question, so that the defense of oppressive particularity, such as American exceptionalism, is terrible whereas the defense of oppressed particularity, such as non-Western cultural practices, is laudable. In contrast, Eisenstein and McGowan take a firmer stand: for them, the particular is intrinsically conformist. It ties people to tradition, culture, and custom in ways that make it impossible for them to embrace values such as freedom, equality, and solidarity—values that, in Eisenstein and McGowan's view (and, admittedly, in my own) *should* be universally accepted.

I know that this is a difficult argument to defend against progressive critics of universalism because these critics view the values in question as hegemonic for the simple reason that they seem to originate in a specific place and time that falsely claims that status of the universal: the Western Enlightenment and its liberal-democratic legacies. In other words, if many progressive critics remain suspicious of both universalism and singularity, it is because the former smacks of Western metaphysics and colonial exploitation whereas the latter arouses the specters of individualism, arrogance, and heroism. The particular, in contrast, appears to offer much-needed resources for finding a footing in the world and for (potentially) building some momentum for collective action.

There are therefore both convergences and divergences in the visions of Eisenstein and McGowan on the one hand and non-Lacanian progressive critics on the other. The biggest convergence has to do with the fact that even though Eisenstein and McGowan defend universalism in ways that critics such as Ahmed might find unpalatable, their vision is ultimately harmonious with progressive theory's understanding of coalitional politics as a means for those who have been "particularized" (barred from the universal) to work together. Such a coalitional politics is not built around identity categories but rather around shared experiences of marginalization. Indeed, although non-Lacanian critics do not usually express the matter in this manner, I would say that the very possibility of fashioning a coalition around commonalities of exclusion implies that there is something "universal" about exclusion, that even if it takes vastly different forms—even if it "particularizes" each subject in specific ways—it still contains a kernel of generalizable material, psychic, and affective gravity.

I have tried to demonstrate that on this issue Eisenstein and McGowan's reasoning is not very different from the reasoning of those non-Lacanian progressive critics who advocate coalitional politics as an alternative to a straightforward version of identity politics. In both instances, excessive adherence to the particularity of identity positions and dreams of seamless belonging is seen as problematic. In this context, it might once again help to think about the "particularized" that progressive critics such as Ahmed talk about as being equivalent to the "part of no-part" that Lacanians talk about: the main difference is that if progressive critics would like to see those who are "part of no-part" retain their particularity even as they band together to obliterate the false universal that has particularized them in the first place, Lacanians would like to see those who are "part of no-part" defeat the false universal by insisting that their very exclusion opens to more a genuine universality.

Lacanian political theorists have little patience with the particular because they believe that it leads to conservatism (to attempts to preserve the social status quo) regardless of the context in which it is valorized. Stated differently, they believe that capitulating to the seductions of the particular—the allure of tradition, culture, and custom—would be a mistake because it would in the final analysis only bolster the ability of the dominant symbolic order to continue excluding those who do not easily wear the garment or turn the key. This is why—and this is one of the main divergences between Lacanian political theorists and other progressive critics—Lacanian political theorists categorically condemn the hegemony of tradition, culture, and custom in instances where (and here my wording reveals a personal prejudice of mine) other progressive critics tend to lose their nerve.

Consider the fact that contemporary feminist theory often wavers in its defense of gender equality whenever it is forced to confront the complexities of tradition, culture, and custom: critics who have (rightly) spent decades condemning heteropatriarchy in Western contexts can sometimes become oddly apologetic of it when it takes place in non-Western contexts. The reason for this is obvious: Western (or Western-based) critics do not want to perpetuate imperialist agendas by imposing "Western" ideals of equality and freedom on cultures that (supposedly) are not premised on these values. Yet the retreat from these values results in situations where so-called feminists are selling women down the river in order to defend—apologize for—cultural practices that are clearly heteropatriarchal; they end up siding with the male elites of non-Western societies rather than with those women (and men) who would like to see heteropatriarchy collapse.

This is one of the biggest dilemmas of contemporary (transnational) feminism: "respect" for tradition, culture, and custom has arguably neutralized feminism's capacity to advocate for gender equality to the extent that it is sometimes hard to know where feminism ends and the apology for heteropatriarchy begins. Critiques of imperialism, racism, poverty, and other social inequalities are of course an essential part of contemporary feminism. But when these critiques override the critique of gender inequality out of reverence for cultural "particularity," it feels that other progressive agendas have become more urgent than feminism. This in itself may not be a problem: there are many progressive agendas besides feminism that are worth promoting. But when culturalist justifications of heteropatriarchy become a part of such agendas, I am not sure that it is still possible to talk about feminism.

In this context, note also that Lacanian political theorists view the break from context that defeats the particular—including the particularity of tradition, culture, and custom—as worth defending because it releases not just the universal but also the singular: it allows the singular to thrive in its singularity without domesticating it under the umbrella of the particular, without forcing it into the shackles of particularity imposed by tradition, culture, and custom.

Unlike some other progressive critics, I do not regard this privileging of the singular as a matter of embracing the fragmentation and displacement that neoliberal capitalism thrives on. Certainly this is always a danger, but it seems to me that many individuals—women, queers, and other marginalized individuals—rattle the chains of tradition, culture, and custom not so that they can enter the neoliberal market of transient labor but rather because they find these chains oppressive: too tight for comfort. In addition, we are all familiar with the justified vexation of those who are asked to showcase the "particularity" of femaleness, queerness, blackness, Asianness, Arabness, and so on, for the benefit of those who assume that a visible membership in a given identity category automatically connects one to that category. In such cases, the defense of singularity—of one's right to break ties with the identity category that the rest of the world asks one to embody—seems more radical than the defense of particularism.

Granted, Eisenstein and McGowan admit that even the Haitian Revolution eventually lost its transformative edge. In addition, like Badiou, they admit the possibility of totalitarian incidents that masquerade as universal ruptures. However, ultimately such totalitarian incidents reveal their reactionary inflection precisely because they so rapidly fall back on the comforts of particularity, of tradition, culture, and custom (e.g., nationalism of the "blood and soil" variety). This is why Lacanian political theorists root for the (genuine) universal as what can shelter and foster the singular, for the break from the particularity of context that allows the singular to relate directly to the universal.

Consider, finally, that even if the denigration of context-specific particularity that Eisenstein and McGowan express seems to pit them against Ahmed's defense of particularity, Ahmed may have her own way of depicting the type of rupture that they view as the hallmark of being able to break with one's context. After all, one version of Ahmed's concept of a willful subject is a defiant subject who stops on its tracks, who refuses to participate, and perhaps even *snaps*. Ahmed gives the example of a feminist who becomes so fed up with the repetitious disparagements of heteropatriarchy that she simply just loses it. As Ahmed posits, for such a feminist there is "a breaking point, when it is 'too much' and what did not seem possible becomes necessary. She fights back; she speaks out. . . . No wonder that leaving a situation of violence can feel like a snap: a bond of fate has indeed been broken" (2014, 155).

Here we find not just the kind of rupture that Eisenstein and McGowan advocate but also an obvious resonance with what Badiou calls "the possibility of the impossible." Ahmed clearly characterizes "the feminist killjoy"—a figure that she repeatedly uses in her work—as a willful subject who abruptly breaks ties with her context, who, for instance, flies off the handle in a sudden expression of rage. Regarding such a killjoy, Ahmed writes:

> She is assumed not only to cause her own breakage but to break the thread of a social connection (a history enacted as judgment: feminism as self-breakage). A willfulness archive does include broken threads; it is full of scenes of breakage. Feminists can be filled with the content of their disagreement: when we are no longer willingly helpful we are judged as willfully unhelpful. Perhaps being no longer willingly helpful simply refers to the condition of not being willing. Feminists are often judged as willful women because we are unwilling to participate in sexist culture; more than that, we are willing to critique the very requirement that women be willing. To be unwilling to participate is to have too much will. . . . Feminism: a history of disagreeable women! (2014, 154)

Feminist killjoys—sometimes, as Ahmed notes, called *haggards*—are "disagreeable women" who are not willing to remain willing to participate in sexist culture and who are consequently judged to be too willful: not being willing participants, according to the reasoning of dominant culture, amounts to being excessively willful. Such feminist killjoys, Ahmed specifies, live "in proximity to a nerve" (153). They "ruin the atmosphere" (152). And they smash pots and jugs, thereby severing the threads of social connection that heteropatriarchy asks them to respect. In this manner, they arguably break with their sociohistorical context in exactly the same way as Eisenstein and McGowan's revolutionaries do. As Ahmed puts it, "Perhaps the slow time of endurance can only be ended by a sudden movement" (155).

I cannot imagine a better example of the assertion of singularity than this.

It feels fitting to conclude this chapter with a statement that many progressive critics may find audacious: when it comes to the values of freedom, equality, and solidarity, I do not care about where they originated; whether they are the brainchild of Confucius, Immanuel Kant, Audre Lorde, or someone else really smart does not much matter to me. And I am not convinced that France or the United States—the places that are usually credited with the birth of these values—have any special claim to them. If anything, both countries have betrayed them in the most obvious manner conceivable. What is important to me is that these values seem worth upholding regardless of setting.

2

The bad habits of critical theory: On the rigid rituals of thought

Progressive critical theory—defined here loosely as a combination of Lacanian psychoanalysis, continental philosophy, poststructuralism, Marxism, cultural studies, and deconstructive feminist and queer theory—has been relentlessly dismissive of habits, particularly of habits of thought that organize social collectivities. Such habits have, often correctly, been aligned with outmoded traditions, ideological complacency, persistent inequalities, authoritarian governance, and the lack of imagination. Moreover, faithful to Nietzsche's proclamation that so-called truths are merely metaphors that have become habitual, that have managed to camouflage their fictitious origins, critical theory has meticulously questioned all taken-for-granted forms of judgment, meaning, and action; it has been so thoroughly suspicious of the propensity of ideas to congeal into rigid, lifeless configurations that it has rejected everything systematic and centralized, that is, everything that smacks of the habitual.

This explains in part why critical theory has long been characterized by what Eve Sedgwick diagnosed as a paranoid hermeneutics of suspicion: an interpretative practice that distrusts the surface of things, actively digs for hegemonic intent, and flees from all surprises because the worst that could happen would be for the critic to be duped by ideology. This paranoid attitude—as

Sedgwick herself emphasized—has generated some of the most thrilling critical work of recent decades, the kind of work that has interrogated the foundations of subjectivity, agency, meaning, and ethics. Yet it has arguably also produced a new set of entrenched habits of thought that curtail critical theory's capacity to remain genuinely critical.

In this chapter, I want to consider two attitudes that have become so predictable in contemporary critical theory that it seems legitimate to label them as the field's bad—distracted and therefore largely unreflexive—habits. The first of these habits is the tendency to leap from the (justified) critique of the autonomous and sovereign subject of humanist metaphysics to the (in my opinion preposterous) notion that all efforts at subjective recentering should be discouraged, that, indeed, the more thoroughly pulverized the subject gets, the more "ethical" it will be. The second bad habit is the logical outcome of this pulverization of the subject, namely the idea that radical antinormativity—the blanket rejection of the kind of normative ethics that makes judgments about right and wrong—constitutes an adequate ethical stance.

Regarding the latter of these habits, I admit to a degree of admiration. I have written extensively, and mostly sympathetically, about the Lacanian-Žižekian ethics of the real, Alain Badiou's ethics of the event, and queer theory's ethics of antisocial negativity, all of which start from the premise that antinormativity is the only effective antidote to our society's corrupt normativity (see Ruti 2015b, 2017). As a response to structural violence, this claim—which on some level hearkens back to Benjamin's notion of divine violence—is difficult to contest. Yet it underestimates the degree to which normative judgments hover at the background of antinormative theories. Simply put, the minute we hold values of any kind, we have to have some grounds for holding them.

Let us assume that I want to argue—as I do in "real" life—that racism, sexism, homophobia, and economic inequality are oppressive (i.e., wrong). On what basis do I posit this? On the basis of norms that I have come to accept as valid. To the extent that antinormative theories deny this basic insight, they cannot even begin to approach the core of contemporary ethical dilemmas.

As my discussion of Eisenstein and McGowan in the previous chapter implies, I am not interested in resurrecting an ahistorical, transcendent system of normative ethics that would be metaphysically grounded: the Enlightenment notion of universal values is not what I am after. Rather, I believe that inasmuch as we are willing to entertain Eisenstein and McGowan's argument that the universal arises contextually—or more precisely, that the universal as a liberatory force emerges from a rupture that defeats an oppressive context—it should be possible for us to conceptualize historically specific values that nevertheless become universally (and normatively) binding. In the second half of this chapter, I will consider the possibility of such historically specific normative values. The first half of the chapter explains why I think that the habitual slaying of the humanist subject represents a theoretical dead end.

Before I get started, I want to note that the two ideals of critical theory I have named—the pulverization of the subject and radical antinormativity—suffer from the additional problem of being more or less untenable as real-life politico-ethical choices. In *Edgework*, Wendy Brown states: "As a meaning-making enterprise, theory depicts a world that does not quite exist, that is not quite the world we inhabit. But this is theory's incomparable value, not its failure. Theory does not simply decipher the meanings of the world but recodes and rearranges them in order to reveal something about the meanings and incoherencies that we live with. To do this revelatory and speculative work, theory must work to one side of direct referents" (80). Fair enough. I concur that critical theory should not necessarily be expected to reflect the concerns of real life, that it should be allowed to work "to one side of direct referents"; I agree that the task of theory is to reinvent the world rather than to merely describe its existing—impoverished—forms. Yet there is, for me, a difference between theorizing that provides alternatives to lives as they are currently lived and theorizing that sounds like empty rhetoric about visions that are entirely unlivable.

Hyperbolic accounts of the politico-ethical benefits of subjective pulverization and radical antinormativity veer toward the latter, which is why my levelheaded response to them tends to be, "If we aren't going do this, what's the point of talking about it?" Nor am I willing to endorse Brown's assertion that "theory is never 'accurate' or 'wrong'" (80). I think that when theory calcifies into semiautomatic rituals that remind me of the Freudian repetition compulsion, it is on the "wrong" track in the sense that such rituals prevent the emergence of fresh interpretative avenues. Freud described the repetition compulsion as a form of habitual, mechanical behavior that defines the individual's entire modality of being, that—essentially—gives rise to her psychic and affective destiny. Something similar could be said to happen with critical theory when it starts to say exactly what one expects it to say.

Slaying the humanist subject

Admittedly, my disappointment at the mind-numbing regularity with which critical theory undertakes the ritual of slaying the humanist subject may be idiosyncratic, due to too many decades of reading Lacan, Derrida, Deleuze, and Levinas. Furthermore, my annoyance at my ability to forecast the advent of the obligatory sentence denouncing the arrogance of this subject does not arise from my love of the said subject—I am well aware of its historical, ethical, and political failings—but rather from my sense that by now this sentence is thrown into texts quite indiscriminately in order to justify all manner of dubious arguments.

This is why I was tired of reading the sentence by the late 1990s. But its allure continues to captivate major thinkers in the field. Consider, for instance, Jack Halberstam's 2011 *The Queer Art of Failure*. In this text, which is otherwise both insightful and entertaining, Halberstam undertakes the questionable task of redefining feminism as a matter of "feminine" masochism, passivity, submission, and sacrifice, going as far as to claim that self-cutting "is a feminist aesthetic proper to the project of female unbecoming" (135). Beyond the shock value of this statement, one might ask how it is that a heteropatriarchal nightmare gets turned into a queer feminist ideal. The answer is the expected: the need to destroy Western feminism's "humanistic investment in both the female subject and the fantasy of an active, autonomous, and self-activating individualism" (129).

Western feminism's complicated and beleaguered history is here reduced to the struggle to become one of the guys by upholding the fantasy of an active, autonomous, and self-activating individualism. What this caricature brushes under the rug is that heteropatriarchy has consistently asked female subjects to fail at this very fantasy, to offer a "feminine," passive, and non-agentic counterpart to the "masculine," active, and agentic subject. In this sense, "the project of female unbecoming" is hardly a new deconstructive invention but rather the status quo of heteropatriarchy.

In establishing the foundations for his new feminism—what he calls "shadow feminism"—Halberstam relies on the work of Saba Mahmood and Gayatri Spivak, who have challenged the idea that (Western) feminists should invariably promote (non-Western) female agency. In itself, this critique is justified. But Halberstam pursues it to a place that the other two thinkers might hesitate to endorse. Mahmood, for example, writes in the preface to her analysis of the Egyptian women's piety movement—which Halberstam draws on—that her "point is not that the program of ethical self-cultivation pursued by the piety movement is 'good' or conducive to establishing relations of gender equality, or that it should be adopted by progressives, liberals, feminists, and others" (xii). Likewise, I doubt that Spivak's objective in asking Western feminists to consider the complex reasons for which Indian widows might choose to commit suttee rather than to agitate for "autonomy" was to argue that feminists should model themselves after such widows.

Halberstam, in contrast, uses the ideal of "feminine" masochism, passivity, submission, and sacrifice *prescriptively*, suggesting that in order to be "good"—genuinely progressive rather than merely liberal—political subjects, feminists must be masochistic, passive, submissive, and sacrificing. In other words, rather than merely describing the psychic and affective phenomenon of abjection, Halberstam elevates abjection into a politico-ethical *goal*, implying that any feminist who aspires to agency instead is not a "real" feminist but merely a puppet of the hegemonic system that produces dreams of arrogant individualism.

The autonomous and sovereign humanist subject was a philosophical abstraction, a theoretical fiction. It is questionable that even Descartes experienced himself as fully autonomous and sovereign. Most people I know certainly do not. This is why I have long wondered what critical theory is attacking when it attacks this figure: what is the ghost in the mirror that elicits the wrath of critics who presumably know full well that most people look nothing like this figure, that, in contrast, many, and certainly the socially marginalized, are engaged in an exhausting struggle to gain a modicum of what feels like autonomy and sovereignty.

Indeed, even those who most vehemently champion the fiction of autonomy and sovereignty can—as Judith Gurewich does in relation to President Trump—usually be shown to be motivated by deep insecurity and paranoia. I do not deny that this fiction can wreak havoc in the world when it is coupled with power: it can generate immense violence. But nevertheless it is an abstraction that does not accurately communicate the degree to which human subjectivity is built upon unsteady foundations: out of joint, off-center, fractured, driven by unconscious motivations, derailed by irrational impulses, and so on. One might even argue that the reason Trump manages to inflict so much damage is not because he is autonomous and sovereign but because his inability to control his irrationality is much less developed than that of the average person. That is, he would benefit from a dose of rationality (which critical theory maligns as the hallmark of the excessively autonomous and sovereign subject but the lack of which in today's global politics is arguably a source of a great deal of brutality).

My more general point here is that critical theory assumes that it is the fiction of the autonomous and sovereign subject, rather than the more psychoanalytic version of the decentered and deeply irrational subject that it *itself* believes in, that represents the reality of subjects outside the domain of critical theory (the reality of subjects in the real world). In other words, even though critical theory's own understanding of the subject suggests that the subject is never autonomous and sovereign (is never the master of its own house, to paraphrase Freud), its critiques of "the subject" routinely assume the opposite about the subjects they attempt to analyze.

My question is: Where are the autonomous and sovereign subjects that critical theory admonishes? Why is it that those within the folds of critical theory so obviously lack autonomy and sovereignty but that "the subject" in the world—the subject that critical theory routinely aims its rage at—seems to be full of autonomy and sovereignty? Otherwise stated, it rattles me when statements about the need to annihilate "the subject" are indiscriminately deployed in contexts that bear little resemblance to the original (metaphysical) target, in the context of subjects who are already fraying around the edges.

When Lacan, Derrida, Deleuze, and Levinas criticize the Man of Metaphysics, they have a point; when Halberstam applies the same critique to feminism, he misses the point. And he is not alone:

critical theory's crusade to demolish "the subject" has long annoyed those (more "humanistic") feminists, antiracists, and others who understand that the world is filled with people who are already so dispossessed, so devoid of agency, that the attempt to crush the last hint of it comes across as a bit obscene. Likewise with some of the darling ideals of poststructuralism: fragmentation, disintegration, decentering, disunity, fluidity, mobility, and volatility. Although it made perfect sense for French poststructuralists to use these ideals to dismantle the rational, unitary, and stable humanist subject, they cannot possibly be translated into all-purpose blueprints for living for the simple reason that many individuals already lead such precarious lives that asking them to endure even greater levels of disintegration merely adds insult to the injury.

In this context, it is instructive to pay attention to efforts to break the cycle of repetition. For example, in *Terrorist Assemblages*, Jasbir Puar criticizes Western queer theory's tendency to equate queerness with unruly subversiveness and transgressiveness, noting that this tendency gives the impression that Western queer subjects are the most liberated subjects in the world, that no one else is free to quite the same degree. In this manner, queerness indexes freedom from norms, customs, and constraints of any kind, becoming "an elite cosmopolitan formulation contingent upon various regimes of mobility" (22).

Puar thus recognizes the problematic nature of the trope of queer mobility in relation to individuals who, for financial or other practical reasons, are unable to live up to the ideals of this trope. Yet ultimately even she cannot resist the siren song of this trope, for she ends her analysis with an enthusiastic celebration of Deleuzian-Guattarian fluidity, promoting a rhizomal model of "assemblage" as the kind of ever-mobile and chaotic mesh of energies that effectively pulverizes the subject. Puar in fact goes as far as to elevate the suicide bomber—whose "identity" is, literally, blown to pieces—to an icon of such an assemblage, asserting that "self-annihilation is the ultimate form of resistance" (216).

Why? Predictably, it is because we need to take down the autonomous and sovereign subject. The suicide bomber, Puar suggests, is the epitome of antihumanist rebellion: "The dynamite strapped onto the body of a suicide bomber is not merely an appendage or prosthetic; the intimacy of weapon with body reorients the assumed spatial integrity (coherence and concreteness) and individuality of the body" (217). The dissolution of subjectivity that poststructuralist, particularly Deleuzian-Guattarian, theory has for decades promoted as a politico-ethical goal becomes, in this vision, concretized in the image of splattered blood, muscle, tissue, and bone fragments.

Is the subject precarious or arrogant?

Similar, if less drastic, moments of ambivalence are easy to find in recent critical theory. For example, in *Dispossession*, Judith Butler acknowledges the awkwardness of calling for the dispossession of those who have already been dispossessed—stripped of agency—yet cannot keep herself from valorizing dispossession as the cornerstone of her "politics of the performative." Generally speaking, one of the most consistent components of Butler's thinking since her 1997 *The Psychic Life of Power* has been the effort to discredit the autonomous and sovereign subject, initially through a Foucauldian analysis of how hegemonic power divests the subject of agency and later through a Levinasian analysis of how agency, or even any attempt to center the self, is not only impossible but also intrinsically *evil*. As she states in *Giving an Account of Oneself*, there can be "no recentering of the subject without unleashing unacceptable sadism and cruelty" (77). According to Butler, the only remedy to such sadism and cruelty is to remain "decentered," at a distance from the kind of "unbridled cruelty . . . in which the self seeks to separate from its constitutive sociality and annihilate the other" (77).

I agree that self-assertion can take place at the expense of others. And I agree that the fantasy of autonomy and sovereignty can promote contempt not only for others but also for alternative, more relational modalities of being. But I am not convinced that the subject who seeks to recenter itself is *automatically* sadistic and cruel, driven to annihilate the other. For disempowered subjects—subjects who have been robbed of autonomy, violated, abjected, humiliated, or otherwise traumatized—acts of recentering can be the only way to survive. Presumably Butler knows this. Yet her allegiance to the ritual of slaying the humanist subject—of contesting "sovereign notions of the subject" (2004, 9), critiquing "the ontology of individualism" (2012, 9), and so on—makes it virtually impossible for her to relax the rhetoric that tells us that dispossession is an ethical virtue whereas self-possession, in all of its forms, spells instant ethical failure.

Butler's stance also illustrates the paradox I identified above: On the one hand, her Foucauldian account of the ways in which the subject is divested of agency and her Levinasian account of the ways in which the subject's relational ontology renders it intrinsically precarious (impinged upon by the other, exposed to the violence of the other, etc.) assume that the subject is immensely fragile. On the other hand, she regularly undertakes the project of taking down the autonomous and sovereign subject. What is the logic behind this? What are the mechanisms through which the fragile subject—the subject who is barely able to defend itself against the aggression of the big Other and the interpersonal other alike—turns into an arrogant one? Or is the assumption that the world is divided into two entirely different subjects: the fragile ones and the arrogant ones?

In Butler's Levinasian theory, the subject is not only subjected to hegemonic power but also mortified by the hostile grids of sociality that surround it. In her words, because I am "acted upon unilaterally from the outside," I am "not only persecuted but besieged, occupied": "That which persecutes me brings me into being," "animates me into ontology at the moment of persecution" (2005, 89). To "be" a subject, for Butler, is to be dislocated by otherness. As she states: "If I am confounded by you, then you are already of me, and I am nowhere without you. I cannot muster the 'we' except by finding the way in which I am tied to 'you,' by trying to translate but finding that my own language must break up and yield if I am to know you. You are what I gain through this disorientation and loss. This is how the human comes into being, again and again, as that which we have yet to know" (2004, 49). The "human" here is the name for the disorientation and loss that results from being "broken" (persecuted, besieged, occupied) by the other; it is the signifier for the fact that I am, from the start, mired in otherness for the simple reason that my relation to the other is what "I" am.

The basic idea here is that because we start our lives in a state of utter dependence on others, "a formation in passivity" constitutes our prehistory: we are acted upon by others prior to any possibility of being able to act on our own, and "this scene is persecutory because it is unwilled and unchosen" (2005, 86). In this manner, Butler follows Levinas in positing that because the other inhabits my being, intrudes into my ontology, during the coming-into-being of my subjectivity, being "persecuted" by the other is the precondition of this subjectivity; I literally do not exist without the persecuting other. How is it, then, that "the subject" under constant attack is suddenly arrogant—too centered, agentic, and individualistic?

It seems reasonable to assume that most subjects are both precarious and agentic, woundable and to some degree autonomous. And it may be that some subjects—due to circumstantial factors such as unequal power relations or painful personal histories—are more precarious than others. But I do not think that it is theoretically consistent to deem "the subject" (in the abstract) wholly precarious, as Butler essentially does, only to then accuse it of being too arrogant (as Butler also does). Most importantly, once subjective empowerment has been declared inherently problematic—or unethical, as it is in Butler—it becomes difficult to advocate the empowerment of disempowered subjects.

Why do we want to kill the subject?

This is the dilemma that Lynne Huffer discovers between her 2010 *Mad for Foucault* and her 2013 *Are the Lips a Grave?*, with the result that—and this is laudable—she revises her theory. In *Mad for Foucault*, Huffer accuses prominent poststructuralists, including Butler, of not going far enough in their deconstruction of the subject. For instance, with regard to Butler's early theory of performativity, Huffer maintains that insofar as this theory relies on a Hegelian logic of negation, reversal, and sublation, it fails to do away with the subject, merely enacting the kind of "negation of negation" by which a new positivity is installed; the Butlerian performative subject, Huffer stresses, may not be a normative subject but it is nevertheless a subject. As Huffer sums up the matter, "With performativity, the subject is not undone but rebelliously remade: she is a joker, a trickster, a sassy artist who operates in the camp mode of ironic subversion" (132).

To this stealthy perseverance of the subject, Huffer, following the early Foucault—the Foucault of the *History of Madness*—juxtaposes a process of desubjectivation: the utter draining away of the subject, including the last remains of the psyche. Desubjectivation, Huffer proposes, moves "the subject away from himself (or his dialectical negation) toward the place of anonymity that is the promise of the subject's undoing" (2010, 129). In more visceral terms, desubjectivation—as Huffer puts it—enacts "the terrifying disintegration of the face in madness: Nietzsche's lifeless eyes, his corpselike body" (131).

This formulation gives me pause. *Why do we want this degree of subjective disintegration?* Why do we want Nietzsche's lifeless eyes, his corpselike body? Did even Nietzsche want these? Personally, I would prefer Nietzsche's overactive mind (his psyche); I would prefer Nietzsche before his tragic descent into madness, the Nietzsche who sought to become the poet of his life. My sense is that we—posthumanist critics—are so used to reading the types of pronouncements that Huffer makes about the need to destroy the subject that it is easy for us to glide over them without much resistance, with a distracted "yes, yes, of course we want the subject dead." Yet stopping for just a moment reveals that things are perhaps not quite so straightforward.

I recently had a graduate student who, in her master's thesis, wanted to reduce the subject to its digestive track. Her response to my query about *why* she wished to accomplish this extraordinary feat was to give me the usual litany of the crimes of the Enlightenment subject: too autonomous, too sovereign, too agentic, too masterful, too transparent, too moralistic, and so on. Fine. But even if we accept this abstraction, what makes the alternative of condensing the complexity of human experience to digestion more desirable, ethically or otherwise?

Huffer's reasoning about wanting to obliterate the subject, and particularly the psyche, is more sophisticated, arising from the Nietzschean view that the psyche cannot be dissociated from the hegemonic morality that is responsible for bringing it into being. Still, would not a subject without a psychic life be a fairly lackluster one? Do we not need the psyche to make meaning, relate to others, and devise the kinds of affective histories that allow us to experience ourselves as semicoherent creatures? And is the psyche not capable of taking a measure of critical distance from the very social forces that have fashioned it? It seems to me that if it were not, there would be no self-reflexivity or social change.

I noted above that Huffer's critique of Butler targets Butler's early theory of performativity. Had Huffer focused on Butler's (2004, 2005, 2009, 2012, 2013) later Levinasian ethics of precarity instead, she would have been forced to acknowledge that her outlook regarding the utter mortification of the subject as a politico-ethical goal shares a great deal with Butler's idealization of dispossession, decentering, and other modalities of self-undoing. Both Huffer (of *Mad for Foucault*) and Butler, like Halberstam in his own way, imply that the only "proper" (ethically acceptable) way to be a subject is to model oneself after a severely traumatized subject.

However, in *Are the Lips a Grave?*, Huffer reconsiders her stance because she realizes that the destruction of the subject leads not only to the erasure of the self but also to the erasure of the other, including the other who has already been erased by various collective inequalities; the other, after all, is also a self. More specifically, Huffer draws on the work of José Muñoz and Roderick Ferguson to argue that "the standpoint epistemology" of these critics of color "gives epistemic and moral authority to the experiential truths of a coherent subject in ways that are in tension with Foucauldian desubjectivation" (16).

The emphasis that Muñoz and Ferguson place on the desubjectivating impact of various empirical, historically specific forms of marginalization—an emphasis that causes them to advocate "critical resubjectivation" rather than further desubjectivation—serves as a wake-up call of sorts for Huffer, who now remarks that she understands why these critics strive "to reclaim subjectivity" rather than to agitate for its demise (2013, 16). As a consequence, Huffer calls for a model of ethics that "puts the autonomous status of the sovereign humanist subject into question without shattering subjectivity altogether"; she wishes to rethink "the antifoundationalist claims of postmodernism together with the ethical dimensions of intersubjectivity" (60).

This is a conclusion I can accept, for it admits that the subject who seeks to survive its traumatization is not invariably following a path of breadcrumbs back to the masterful humanist subject; it admits that the autonomous and sovereign subject can be questioned without thereby shattering the subject altogether, without pretending that any of us could live in a state of absolute bodily, psychic, and affective disintegration (desubjectivation) for longer than a fleeting moment (such as a moment of orgasmic jouissance or cataclysmic pain).

I also appreciate Huffer's perspective because her call to think postmodern antifoundationalism together with "the ethical dimensions of intersubjectivity" sidesteps the second of the bad habits of critical theory I want to examine: the notion that radical antinormativity—the flat rejection of normative judgments—represents a sufficient, and perhaps the only *truly* political, ethical stance. As Huffer correctly notes, "To simply shatter [the] subject—and along with it, morality—is to ignore the first burden of a nonviolent practice: the acknowledgement of harms, including, most importantly, the constitutive exclusion or forgetting of the other" (2013, 44).

Huffer thus concedes that desubjectivation valorizes the subject's (solipsistic) self-shattering to such an extent that it disregards an essential component of ethics, which is that ethics needs to respond to intersubjective harms, including the harm caused by the exclusion or forgetting of the other; that is, *ethics needs normative content in addition to antinormative rebellion.* This is why Huffer ends up asking for a theory that recognizes the decentered status of the subject without losing track of the fact that most subjects retain enough self-consistency to be capable of relationality and that with relationality comes ethical responsibility.

The rewards of antinormativity

Many critical theorists categorically reject the ideal of normative content, instead opting for antinormative rebellion. Due to Marxist qualms regarding dominant ideology, Foucauldian analyses of biopolitics as a form of control that infiltrates the deepest recesses of our being, poststructuralist misgivings about organized structures of all kinds, postcolonial interrogations of Western imperialism and global capitalism, and feminist and queer critiques of racist heteronormativity, critical theory tend to suspect that normative ethics, and particularly rights-based ethics, ultimately always serves the interests of the dominant establishment.

This perspective has generated legitimate—and frequently inspiring—calls for comprehensive social change. At the same time, as I mentioned at the beginning of this chapter, it cannot avoid the fact that its antinormativity remains haunted by a clandestine normativity. For example, every denunciation of rights on some level depends on an alternative definition of rights so that critics who, say, reject bourgeois rights, such as the right to own property, may simultaneously demand the "right" to global equality and general flourishing. In other words, the idea that ethics has something to do with the "right" to lead a certain kind of life—in this instance, a life free of oppression—seems conceptually inescapable.

In itself, this lingering of normativity is not a problem: I support the (normative) ideal of global equality and general flourishing. But what *is* problematic is critical theory's disavowal of its investment in normative judgments, its attempt to pretend that antinormative destructiveness—the kind of destructiveness that either arises from, or results in, the pulverization of "the subject"—represents a satisfactory ethical stance. This is the cause of my disagreement with Huffer's ethics of desubjectivation in *Mad for Foucault*. And it is the cause of my (partial) disagreement with Lacanians who promote various versions of "subjective destitution," defined as the act of exiting the symbolic order through a suicidal plunge into the jouissance of the real.

Like Foucauldian-Hufferian desubjectivation, Lacanian subjective destitution entails the death of the socially viable self in the sense that the subject, momentarily at least, ceases to care about the big Other's mandates: the subject liberates itself from the coercive decrees of the collectivity by discarding its symbolic supports—by, effectively, disappearing into the whirlpool of jouissance. Žižek's ethics of the real and Lee Edelman's queer antisociality are perhaps the best-known examples of this approach. Badiou's ethics of the event goes some way in the same direction but ultimately steps back from the unqualified embrace of negativity that characterizes the thinking of Žižek and Edelman, with the consequence that it opens the door to normative ethics in ways that I will discuss at the end of this chapter. But first I want to briefly consider both the rewards and the pitfalls of Lacanian antinormativity (in the hope that doing so will shed some light on the rewards and the pitfalls of antinormativity as such).

Perhaps the most satisfying component of Lacanian antinormativity is the vehement *No!* it utters to the hegemonic demands of the social order, as Edelman famously does in *No Future*. I have admitted (see Ruti 2015b, 2017) that such a *No!* can bring relief to subjects who experience their encounters with the symbolic establishment as tyrannical or wounding: not giving a damn about what the Other wants can be liberating for those who have been subjected to the unjust laws of this Other.

This is why Lacan views Antigone—who defies Creon's prohibition against burying her brother Polyneces—as a quintessential ethical actor. Antigone's defiance costs her everything, including her life, but it also frees her from the constraints of Creon's version of the big Other. As Lacan states, "When she explains to Creon what she has done, Antigone affirms the advent of the absolute individual with the phrase 'That's how it is because that's how it is'" (1959–1960, 278). Essentially, Lacan suggests that Antigone as an "absolute individual"—as a subject whose desire is nonnegotiable (a theme I will discuss in the next chapter)—comes into being as a result of her willingness to forgo her symbolic viability for the sake of her act of defiance (her act in the "real," as it were).

One can see why this approach is appealing to Žižek, who views the symbolic order as so hopelessly corrupt, so overrun by the economic and political interests of global capitalism, that the only tolerable form of ethical intervention is a radical act of negation that demolishes the very foundations of this order. One can also see why it is appealing to Edelman, who analyzes the ways in which mainstream culture equates queerness with death, destruction, and the demise of social respectability to such an extent that the only effective politico-ethical option is to embrace this very characterization, to become the very force of negativity that normative society always already expects one to be.

Whether the enemy is capitalism (Žižek) or "reproductive futurism" (Edelman), Lacanian antinormativity brings a welcome clear-sightedness about the mechanisms of false hope that sustain these hegemonic formations, rendering us aware of the ways in which we are tricked into patiently waiting for improvements that are unlikely to ever arrive. Lauren Berlant labels such patience "cruel optimism": the stubborn, irrational belief that social arrangements and ways of life that hurt us will one day pay off and make us happy. Berlant specifies that "a relation of cruel optimism" exists when something we desire is in reality an impediment to our flourishing (2011, 1).

Berlant has a degree of sympathy for this predicament because she recognizes that hopefulness about the future can, particularly for marginalized subjects, be a precondition of surviving the harshness of the present; to the extent that cruel optimism can feel life-sustaining even as it causes suffering, that it provides the kinds of fantasies of eventual victory that allow injured subjects to keep on living despite the obstacles they face, it—as Berlant succinctly concludes—may be "better than none at all" (2011, 16). In contrast, the Lacanian hardline, the line adopted by Žižek and Edelman, utters a passionate *fuck this!* to cruel optimism; it tells us to lose our patience in the face of social oppression, to discard the fantasies that keep us attached to wounding modalities of desire.

Cleansing the plate

This way of putting things foregrounds one of the main strengths of Lacanian antinormativity: its conviction—discussed in the previous chapter—that it is possible to accomplish what Butler has long asserted is psychically and affectively impossible, namely to reject our socio-psychic context, particularly our wounded attachment to our own subjection. Both in her early Foucauldian theory of how we are formed in relation to power and in her later Levinasian formulation of the primacy of the other—including the persecuting intimate other—in our subjective formation, Butler's emphasis lies on the difficulty of discarding, later in life, the impact of the injurious components of subjectivation. This is why she maintains that, on a fundamental level, we always remain invested in our own injury. Žižek, in turn, insists that Lacanian negativity offers a way out.

Žižek responds to Butler's Levinasian formulation of formative injury as follows: "Lacan's position is thus that being exposed/overwhelmed, caught in a cobweb of preexisting conditions, is *not* incompatible with radical autonomy. Of course, I cannot undo the substantial weight of the context into which I am thrown; of course, I cannot penetrate the opaque background of my being; but what I can do is, in an act of negativity, 'cleanse the plate,' draw a line, exempt myself, step outside of the symbolic in a 'suicidal' gesture of a radical act—what Freud called 'death drive' and what German Idealism called 'radical negativity'" (2005, 140).

Žižek is here reacting to Butler's claim that the socially determined, partially opaque nature of subjectivity divests us of agency. Butler believes that our inability to control the collective symbolic field into which we are inserted—along with our inability to access the murky history of our own formation—renders us partially incomprehensible to ourselves and therefore inherently incapable of autonomy. Žižek, in contrast, believes that being caught in the cobweb of preexisting social conditions is not incompatible with radical autonomy, the kind of "autonomy" that Antigone, according to Lacan, exhibits. That we cannot master the collective context into which we are thrown is a given, Žižek concedes, as is our inability to retrace the obscure, partially unconscious history of our own formation. But this does not consign us to an unbreakable attachment to collective structures of power, for we always retain the freedom to reject our predicament. As Žižek elaborates, "Even when the entire positive content of my psyche is ultimately impenetrable, the margin of my freedom is that I can say No! to any positive element that I encounter" (2005, 140). That is, I can refuse to obey the demands of hegemonic sociality.

Lacanian antinormativity offers a powerful counterpoint to the Butlerian perspective, the early Foucauldian version of which suggests that we are so thoroughly permeated by social power that the best we can do is to negotiate with this power through subversive processes of reiteration and resignification, and the later Levinasian version of which suggests that our subjectivity is so profoundly marked by constitutive sociality, by the (often wounding) imprint of the other, that the very notion of autonomy is nonsensical. It also offers a counterpoint to Butler's tendency to follow Levinas in elevating the other to such a sacrosanct status that the other essentially cannot do wrong. This tendency is apparent, for example, when Butler argues, in the context of discussing normative judgments aimed at those who have damaged others, that "condemnation is very often an act that not only 'gives up on' the one condemned but seeks to inflict a violence upon the condemned in the name of 'ethics'" (2005, 46).

Butler here deems the violence of judgment—of normative ethics—to be as bad as (and perhaps even worse than) the violence of the act that is being judged, specifying that "it may be that only through an experience of the other under conditions of suspended judgment do we finally become capable of an ethical reflection on the humanity of the other, even when that other has sought to annihilate humanity" (2005, 45). This implies that when we judge another person, even one who has "sought to annihilate humanity," we cease to be ethical; judgment, as Butler concludes, "turns the moralist into a murderer" (49).

Like Huffer's valorization of Nietzsche's dead eyes, this formulation gives me pause, for it suggests that there is literally nothing that a person might do that can be judged to be normatively unacceptable. In other words, because Butler's Levinasian ethics places no normative limits on the behavior of the victimizer—because it starts from the premise that we are responsible for the other regardless of how brutally this other behaves—it arguably makes an unreasonable demand on the victimized: it shifts the ethical burden wholly from the victimizer to the victim, so that ethics no longer assesses the actions of the victimizer but rather the responses of the victim. As Butler asserts, "Our responsibility is heightened once we have been subjected to the violence of others" (2004, 16). Consider also the following statement: "The responsibility that I must take for the Other proceeds directly from being persecuted and outraged by that Other. Thus there is violence in the relation from the start: I am claimed by the other against my will, and my responsibility for the Other emerges from this subjection" (2012, 59).

Admittedly, within Butler's theory, my "subjection" to the persecuting and outraging other is first and foremost ontological, having to do with my irreversibly relational bodily, psychic, and affective constitution. But the step from this primordial state of affairs to more tangible inflections of subjection is short—too short in my opinion—in the sense that Butler, following Levinas, reminds us that "precisely the Other who persecutes me has a face" (2005, 90). This in turn explains why "I cannot disavow my relation to the Other, regardless of what the Other does, regardless of what I might will" (91). Responsibility, in this account, is "not a matter of cultivating a will, but of making use of an unwilled susceptibility as a resource for becoming responsive to the Other": "Whatever the Other has done, the Other still makes an ethical demand upon me, has a 'face' to which I am obliged to respond" (91).

I understand why Butler's Levinasian ethics represents an effective decentering of the Enlightenment subject. But does it not swing too far to the other extreme, making a virtue out of masochism? According to Butler, ethical responsibility entails a kind of unwilling of the will so that I can accept my "unwilled susceptibility" to the other as the basis of my responsibility for this other. That is, it is precisely insofar as the other claims me "against my will" that I am responsible for it. This in turn implies that I become an ethical failure the minute I attempt to regain a degree of agency, autonomy, or empowerment. How did Butler—one of progressive theory's most notorious defenders of the marginalized—end up here?

The failings of relationality

It seems to me that Butler overestimates the degree to which relationality can found ethics. In other words, although I agree with Huffer (and Butler) that ethics needs to *address* relationality, I am not persuaded that relationality offers a sufficiently reliable *foundation* for it. More specifically, it seems to me that Butler's attempt to derive ethics from my recognition that the other is just as precarious, just as vulnerable to injury as I am, results in a play of mutual recognitions where too many things can go wrong. For instance, I agree with the assessment of Žižek and Badiou (see Chapter 1) that such an injunction to honor the "humanity" of the other falls apart the moment the other no longer appears fully human. We have learned that Butler's response is to try to expand the domain of the recognizably human, so that everyone is equally included. Yet her own analysis of hegemonic power implies that this is a doomed endeavor insofar as one of the effects of this power—of necropolitics—is to render some people "inhuman" so as to make them more easily expendable.

If everyone adopted the Levinasian stance of absolute respect for the other, the world would be a better place. But given that this is not the reality we live in, Butler's call to revere the other regardless of how this other behaves comes across as a recipe for intolerable tolerance (tolerance that stretches too far). The lack of normative limits in her theory, as in Levinasian ethics, makes it hard to avoid the conclusion that I am supposed to actively sustain those who hurt me, and that this is the case regardless of whether they are sexists, racists, neo-Nazis, or homophobic religious fundamentalists.

Norms of social conduct keep me from throwing stones (or worse) through the windows of such people, which is why I think that such norms, and the penalties that result from a noncompliance with them, are not an entirely unreasonable foundation for ethics. This is not to say that I fail to recognize the oppressiveness of norms that bolster mainstream morality, such as dominant norms of gender and sexuality. In other words, I am not arguing that critical theory should (uncritically) stop interrogating the hegemonic foundations of normative ethics—far from it. I am merely asserting that the attempt to replace normative ethics by something as vague as "relationality" will not work for the simple reason that my reverence for the other as face founders as soon as I perceive the brutality of the face I confront.

Sometimes—as Butler argues—the perceived brutality of the other is a fantasy, an ideological effect of unequal power relations. But this is not invariably the case: sometimes the other does actually act brutally. Even though I have argued that the autonomous and sovereign subject is a theoretical fiction, I do not deny that there are people who commit atrocious acts, who could not care less about the precariousness of others: the lack of complete autonomy and sovereignty does not keep people from acting violently; indeed, sometimes it is this very lack that triggers aggression. Attempting to neutralize this aggression by embracing my "unwilled susceptibility" to the other quickly becomes an unbearable burden. Instead of being a matter of ethics, it is a matter of self-harm.

Butler's relational ethical model also overlooks the fact that the individuals who facilitated my formative (relational) coming-into-being are not necessarily the same as those I interact with as an adult. Surely there is a distinction between the idea that I am inhabited by an ontological otherness that I cannot denounce—that I only have a self to the extent that I partake in structures of intersubjectivity—and the idea that I cannot sever my connection to *specific* others who injure me. I may owe an existential debt to those who have over the years made my life viable. But does this condemn me to an indiscriminate patience with each and every person I encounter irrespective of any normative considerations?

Butler's ethics reproduces not only the Levinasian ideal of nonnegotiable responsibility for the other but also Derrida's (2001) view that ethics entails forgiving the unforgiveable. In contrast, the Lacanian alternative, though not being open to normative ethics either, reminds us that the other frequently functions as an avatar for the hegemonic injunctions of the big Other; the Lacanian rejoinder to Butlerian ethics is to insist that relationality is not necessarily any more pure, any more devoid of violent power struggles, than any other domain of human life.

On this point, I find myself in agreement with the Lacanians. I do not believe in the purity of either relationality or relational ethics. Furthermore, if Butler believes that I would rather sustain wounded psychic attachments than risk losing my relational bonds—that the recognition granted by the Other (or by an array of others who represent the Other) is so important to me that I am willing to harm myself to prolong it—I believe that there are circumstances where I am perfectly capable of cutting my connection to others who injure me, of uttering the *No!* that Žižek and Edelman advocate, even if this means risking the symbolically intelligible underpinnings of my life. I moreover do not for one minute believe that cutting my connection to wounding others renders me an ethical failure.

Butler's relentless relationality obviously cannot be dissociated from the compulsion to defeat the autonomous and sovereign subject that I discussed in the first half of this chapter: relationality has, for Butler, come to function as the lever that dislodges this hubris-filled subject from its throne not merely by revealing the degree to which otherness is constitutive of subjectivity—the degree to which autonomy and sovereignty are undercut by formative social bonds—but also the degree to which the primacy of the other defines the ethical. Though I do not disagree with Butler about the inherently relational nature of subjectivity, I think that her abhorrence of the autonomous and sovereign subject leads her, on the one hand, to downplay aspects of human life that presuppose agency and self-responsibility, and on the other, to exaggerate the merits of vulnerability, dependence, and attachment.

What I find counterproductive about Butler's approach is that, instead of acknowledging that concepts such as autonomy, rationality, self-possession, and normative limits are ambiguous, open to context-specific interpretations and deployments, she draws uncompromising binaries along the lines of autonomy bad, relationality good; rationality bad, opacity good; self-possession bad, dispossession good; normative ethics bad, the ethics of precarity good, and so on. This propensity for dichotomous thinking—which critics such as Lacan, Derrida, Barthes, and Kristeva managed to resist—is what leads to the idea that autonomy, rationality, self-possession, and normative limits are invariably horrendous. In contrast, I want to argue that they can be horrendous in some situations, and in some inflections, yet productive in other situations, and in other inflections.

Moreover, when it comes to relationality specifically, it seems to me that Butler inadvertently participates in our culture's habitual (and uncritical) celebration of its (supposedly) unquestionable value, implying that even bad relationality is better than no relationality. Although Butler is not a proponent of the kind of heteronormative relationality that Michael Cobb criticizes in *Single*—where he notes that, within our cultural imaginary, coupledom is supposed to "end our tragic twists and turns, nullifying all the bad feelings of misunderstanding and misconnection that preceded it" (13)—on some level she does appear to believe in the inherently remedial nature of relationality. I do not mean to suggest that Butler believes that relationality is benign. Quite the opposite, her tendency to portray the other as intrinsically persecuting makes it hard for her to conceptualize mutually enabling relationality. In Butler's theoretical universe, relationality is usually dangerous, likely to result in damage of some kind. Yet somewhat paradoxically, this does not keep her from presenting relationality as an indisputable good, as something we should all aspire to.

Cobb proposes that in our society "you're not allowed to be without love"; love is "not merely an activity one adds to a list of things that have to get done in this life . . . but life itself" (18). One could say the same about Butler's Levinasian attitude toward relationality: we are simply just not allowed to be without it; any attempt to sever relational bonds, even deeply detrimental ones, turns us into ethical monsters. This may be my main disagreement with Butler: if she suggests that relationality is an unmitigated virtue, I believe—and this is related to Žižek's statement, quoted above, about cleansing the plate by drawing a line—that in rejecting damaging relationships I "choose" my aliveness over the suffocating entanglements of traumatizing relationality.

The problems of antinormativity

My misgivings about Butler's relational ethics, however, do not mean that I find the Lacanian antisocial alternative straightforwardly palatable. If Butler overvalorizes relationality, Žižek notoriously veers in the opposite direction of inflating the benefits of antisociality, as does Edelman when he asserts that the death-driven queer "forsakes *all* causes, *all* social action, *all* responsibility for a better tomorrow or for the perfection of social forms. Against the promise of such an activism, he performs, instead, an act: the act of repudiating the social" (2004, 101).

Edelman has been taken to task for his adamant antisociality by those who, like Butler, view relationality as an ethical given (see, for instance, Muñoz 2009). My own disagreement with it—as well as with the antisociality of Žižek—is more technical in the sense that I believe that both critics miss something fundamental about Lacan's ethics of the real, which is that while this ethics is always counterhegemonic, it is not necessarily antisocial (let alone antirelational). Simply put, Antigone acts against the Other (Creon's system) but not against the other (Polyneces). Generally speaking, I can imagine individuals undertaking destructive, counterhegemonic acts on behalf of intersubjective ties that they deem important.

Žižek and Edelman overlook this component of Lacanian ethics because they focus on the self-shattering jouissance of the subject who destroys is social viability. In contrast, I would place a greater emphasis on the reasons for which the subject engages in self-annihilating acts. It may be that sometimes these reasons have nothing to do with intersubjective ties. But other times, such ties may form the background of the subject's compulsion to act in ways that, from the perspective of the dominant social order, may seem absolutely insane.

Butler neglects this nuance when she objects to the ethics of the real on the basis of her assumption that it contains "individualistic" undertones, that it "fortifies the deciding 'I,' sometimes at the expense of relationality itself" (2009, 183). In this manner, Butler concludes that the ethics of the real is antithetical to relationality. Unfortunately, Žižek and Edelman do the same, albeit not because they, like Butler, want to defend relationality. Rather, they prefer to ignore it altogether, with the consequence that they run into the problem that Huffer identifies in the context of Foucauldian desubjectivation, namely that there is something odd about an ethical paradigm that leaves the other behind, that, effectively, renders the other irrelevant.

If Butler sees relationality everywhere, Žižek and Edelman tend to pretend that it plays no role in human life, including ethics. On the one hand, Butler is mistaken in suggesting that the Lacanian act "fortifies the deciding 'I,'" for Lacan associates the act with social suicide rather than with "individualism" in the humanist sense. Differently stated, there is no "deciding I" who actively chooses to undertake the act; instead, the act overtakes the subject—compels it to act against its own survival—to such an extent that it loses its symbolic supports. If Antigone is an "absolute individual," it is not because she is an autonomous and sovereign subject, but rather because she is no longer subjected to Creon's edicts for the simple reason that she has stepped outside the boundaries of socially intelligible subjectivity.

On the other hand, it is undeniable that the outlook of Žižek and Edelman is profoundly solipsistic. Indeed, inasmuch as the subject of Lacanian antinormative ethics is a subject of pure jouissance, it is incapable of relationality. Badiou (2012) inadvertently reveals this reality when he observes that Lacan's oft-quoted claim that "there is no sexual relation" (*Il n'y a pas de rapport sexuel*) does not mean—as it has frequently been taken to mean—that there is an unbridgeable gap between men and women in heterosexual relationships but rather that, at the (fleeting) moment of jouissance, there is no "relation" whatsoever to another person; orgasmic jouissance, in short, neutralizes intersubjective capacity.

While Lacan recognized that antinormative acts of defiance, such as Antigone's act, might be motivated by relational bonds that the subject feels driven to defend regardless of consequences, Žižek and Edelman shift their attention to the devastating impact of the act so forcefully that antisociality itself, rather than the possible reasons for this antisociality, becomes the point of ethics: (self-) destructiveness *as such*—destructiveness that cannot be traced back to any desire for justice (for the other)—gets elevated to the pinnacle of ethical action. In this vision, the psychotic becomes the template for ethical subjectivity (which is why Žižekian-Edelmanian antisociality is closer to Deleuzian-Guattarian schizophrenia than the former critics might care to admit).

If Butler's Levinasianism guides her to indulge the other to such a degree as to leave no space for condemning this other even when it has acted viciously, Žižekian-Edelmanian antisociality leads to the equation of destructiveness with the ethical. If Butler dissolves the distinction between right and wrong by forgiving even the unforgivable, Lacanian antinormativity dissolves it by turning one version of the unforgiveable—groundless, senseless violence—into an ideal. In both cases, the result is the kind of relativism that makes no distinction between just and unjust behavior—that is, precisely, an ethics without any normative content. Yet as I have suggested, an ethics with no conception of normative limits is hypocritical in obfuscating its own normative commitments.

The flight from normative ethics cannot but be inspired by normative commitments. Among the critics I have named, Edelman perhaps comes closest to pure antinormativity in the sense that his analysis confirms that he truly "forsakes *all* causes, *all* social action, *all* responsibility for a better tomorrow or for the perfection of social forms"; Edelman's cause, in a way, is to have no cause. But even this is a politico-ethical vision of sorts; even Edelman's extreme articulation of antinormativity carries a furtive normative message about the kind of life that is worth living. Still, Edelman asserts his antinormative stance consistently, without indulging the temptation to create enclaves of normativity within otherwise antinormative paradigms that both Žižek and Butler succumb to.

Posthumanist ethical aporias

We saw in the last chapter that Žižek vacillates between idealizing Lacanian antisociality and promoting a quasi-Kantian vision of formal, impersonal justice that abstracts from the face in order to apply the same neutral principles to everyone without exception. In other words, Žižek attempts to endorse the Lacanian ethics of the real while munching on his Kantian cake too. Žižek's Hegelian analysis of universal values arising from the predicament of those who are "part of no-part"—also discussed in the last chapter—complicates the picture even further. In the end, it may thus be impossible to determine exactly where Žižekian ethics resides. But it seems fair to say that even he does not steadily hold the Lacanian antinormative line: a normative vision of justice lingers at the background of his theorizing, especially when it comes to his condemnation of global capitalism.

Butler in turn strives to replace a rights-based ethics by a Levinasian relational approach while simultaneously having her equal rights (liberal normative ethics) on the side. Indeed, the impossibility of discarding normative judgments in the context of real-life ethical dilemmas is illustrated by the fact that Butler's resistance to them—even ones derived from the Enlightenment—dissipates in the context of her critique of Israeli state violence against Palestinians, for she argues that Palestinians have the right to have basic rights, such as the right not to be dispossessed of land, due to their membership in the global human community. Regarding Palestine's claim "to the lands that rightfully are its own," Butler writes: "One could formulate the right in light of international law or on the basis of moral and political arguments that may or may not be framed within a specific version of the nation-state" (2012, 205). I happen to agree with this stance: I also think that Palestinians should have basic human rights regardless of whether or not they belong to a nation-state. Yet there is nothing about Butler's Levinasian ethical vision that supports her sudden turn to the kind of liberal rights-based cosmopolitanism that can be traced, through Arendt, all the way back to Kant.

If Butler stayed faithful to her Levinasian approach, she would not be calling for equal rights for Palestinians but rather saying that self-preservation should not be a priority for them, that, if anything, there might be something unethical about their quest for sovereignty and self-determination. Butler makes a valiant effort to prove that her cosmopolitanism is not the same as that of Kant by proposing that it is precarity rather than the integrity of the autonomous and sovereign self that is the foundation for equal rights. But this does not change the fact that, in this instance, she falls back on the very system of Enlightenment morality that she has spent much of her career criticizing, so that all of a sudden equal rights are indispensable (2012, 205–16).

One could of course argue that the Enlightenment does not own the ideal of equal rights, that it is possible to think about equal rights beyond their humanistic context, as Derrida does when he claims that "what remains irreducible to any deconstruction" is "an idea of justice—which we distinguish from law or right and even from human rights—and an idea of democracy—which we distinguish from its current concept and from its determined predicates today" (2006, 74). But Derrida's elusive definition of justice and democracy is not what Butler is working with when she, in a Kantian vein, calls for international law that recognizes the rights of individuals not on the basis of their attachment to nation states but rather on the basis of their humanity.

It seems to me that, theoretically speaking, Butler cannot have it both ways. If she wants to define ethics in the Levinasian vein as a matter of conjuring away all rights to self-protection, then she cannot turn around and return those rights to the Palestinians out of political exigency. If some victims are supposed to honor the faces of their victimizers to the point of compromising their own welfare, this must be the case with all victims. That is, if Butler is going to recoil from any mention of the Enlightenment, as she consistently does, she cannot use its ideals whenever these happen to suit her political purposes.

Butler is not alone in engaging in such theoretical waffling: even the most virulent critics of Enlightenment-inspired rights-based ethics tend to resort to the ideal of rights when their backs, ethically or politically speaking, truly are against the wall. After all, it is difficult to argue against "rights" such as equality, freedom, solidarity, reciprocity, and democratic process. Sometimes progressive critics try to resolve this dilemma by placing the word *radical* in front of concepts such as democracy. I appreciate this attempt to distinguish between false and true democracy (or false and true equality, etc.), for there is no doubt that most existing "democratic" systems fall far from the ideals of democracy. Nevertheless, this strategy does not go far enough in addressing the suppressed presence of normative judgments in nominally antinormative theories, with the result that such theories resort to normative ethics in a slapdash manner, whenever the situation calls for it. More specifically, they often disavow ethics of the "liberal-humanist" denomination while simultaneously keeping such ethics in their back pocket for times when their progressive alternative falters.

I do not think that this inconsistency is a matter of callous theoretical (or ideological) opportunism. Instead, it is the logical outcome of what I have argued all along, namely that an ethics without any normative content is ultimately unsustainable. It is of course possible that some empirical situations profit from a Levinasian approach, others from a Lacanian one, and yet others are best dealt with Kantian normativity. I accept that there is room in critical analysis for more than one ethical paradigm. But when I see critics (implicitly) using a paradigm, such as Kantian normativity, that they have explicitly denounced, I sense that their thinking is frustrated by unresolved aporias. This is why I believe that the knee-jerk rejection of normative ethics by progressive critical theory constitutes one of its worst habits: it leads to too many embarrassing theoretical contradictions for the simple reason that, at the end of the day, an ethics without a way of judging the difference between right and wrong is impracticable.

A genuine relativist might not care. But a relativist with a heart of gold—the kind of relativist who, despite her relativism, wants social justice—cannot but care in the sense that behind her antinormativity (or postnormativity) lurk normative views about the good, fair, and just. In a way, the situation is almost humorous: progressive critical theory's habit of slamming normative ethics as an unacceptable liberal-humanist habit of thought is so stubborn that it cannot allow itself the conceptual luxury of trying to figure out how it might be possible—to return to Huffer's wording—to consider posthumanist antifoundationalism "together with the ethical dimensions of intersubjectivity." In the same way that critical theory finds it difficult to admit that the demise of the autonomous and sovereign humanist subject does not deprive humans of *all* autonomy and sovereignty—and that there may in fact be situations where a measure of autonomy and sovereignty is essential for psychic and affective survival—it finds it difficult to admit that normative ethics could be detached from its metaphysical origins; it finds it difficult to admit that normative judgments could be context specific without thereby being worthless.

I understand that for many progressive critics, normative ethics is by definition associated with hegemonic power, particularly with the brutal exclusions of Enlightenment rationalism. Yet this is not the only way to think about normative limits, for many of the ones that enjoy a great deal of global support—such as the idea that genocide is a crime—have emerged, in part at least, from our prior experiences with collective atrocities. I think that it would be intellectually dishonest to assert that these atrocities are so drastically different from each other that they cannot support any universally applicable ethical principles.

The most hardcore of relativists are likely to object by pointing out that even basic human rights edicts can be traced back to the European Enlightenment, and that they merely function as a flimsy smokescreen for Western economic, political, and military interests. I do not deny that the latter is sometimes true (see Ruti 2015b). But this is far from being the whole story. While there certainly are normative limits that we need to criticize and transgress, there are others that we need to endorse and refine. As Dominick LaCapra points out, there are some normative limits "you might want to place in question, some you may want to reform, and others you may want to test critically and perhaps validate" (154). That is, not all normative limits are diabolical: there are some that are by far the best (or even the only) way to check the abuses of power.

I am willing to risk saying that there are some ethical principles—say, the conviction that all human beings, regardless of race, ethnicity, religion, nationality, gender, and sexuality, are equal—that are worth defending independently of context. I am not saying that one culture should violently impose them on another. And it is clear that there is no country in the world that in reality respects the idea that all humans beings are equal, even if some, most notably the United States, pay lip service to it. But this does not diminish the value of this principle. Once again—as I argued at the end of the last chapter—where it originated seems secondary to me; what matters is its content, its normative weight.

The historicity of normative ethics

It also seems vital to shed the notion that normative ethics by definition aspires to metaphysical foundations (the purity of reason). To be sure, there are plenty of academics in Anglo-American philosophy departments who still hunt for such foundations. But the rest of us understand that normative limits are always historically specific and open to renegotiation, reassessment, and revision. This historicity does not render these limits inconsequential but in fact makes them more dynamic.

As Amy Allen proposes, any set of normative limits is by necessity "our historical a priori," yet rejecting such limits wholesale "would mean surrendering intelligibility" (2008, 35). Allen grants that any given historically specific a priori can take hegemonic forms, so that we need to remain cautious about the constitutive exclusions (say, the exclusion of women, or the exclusion of racialized subjects) that norms all too often rely on. At the same time, as Allen sums up the matter, "We have no choice . . . but to start from where we are" (35).

Allen's insight arises in part from her intricate interpretation of Foucault as a thinker who, despite being tremendously critical of the oppressive ways in which reason had been deployed in the course of Western history, did not reject rationality as altogether useless. More specifically, Allen (2013) demonstrates that if Foucault wanted us to subject the history of reason to a relentless critique, it was not because he was interested in replacing reason with unreason but because he wanted to work his way into a less repressive, less tyrannical version of reason. That is, although reason for Foucault was invariably contaminated by its context, by disciplinary power, this "impurity" also left it open to modification. As Foucault states,

"If critical thought itself has a function—and, even more specifically, if philosophy has a function within critical thought—it is precisely to accept this sort of spiral, this sort of revolving door of rationality that refers us to its necessity, to its indispensability, and, at the same time, to its intrinsic dangers" (2000, 358).

Reason can be dangerous but it is also indispensable. The failings of Enlightenment reason are irrefutable. But this does not mean that reason has no legitimate role to play in human life (don't most of us use it on a daily basis?), that there is no possibility of arriving at a less objectionable variety of reason.

In *Adorno on Politics After Auschwitz*, Gary Mullen makes a related argument by analyzing Adorno's distinction between instrumental and critical reason. Mullen clarifies the political stakes of Adorno's philosophy by dispelling some of the most common misconceptions about Adorno's (supposed) retreat from politics and his (supposed) nihilism, pessimism, and irrationalism. Most importantly for our purposes, Mullen shows that, contrary to what many of Adorno's critics—including Habermas—have argued, Adorno did not want to do away with reason. Instead, like Foucault, he wanted reason to become critical of itself and humble about its history in order to transcend the instrumentalist and hugely violent tenor it had taken in the West, culminating in Auschwitz.

According to Adorno (as interpreted by Mullen), the problem with instrumentalist reason—scientific reason, cold "bourgeois reason"—is that it has severed its connection to the body, the senses, affect, pleasure, and lived experience, particularly suffering; instrumentalist reason, in short, serves death rather than life. Mullen claims that Adorno wanted to correct this by replacing instrumentalist reason with critical reason; he wanted to reconnect reason with its social context, with "the context of human needs, longings, and hopes" so that it could "renew its potential as a voice of criticism" (9–10). As Mullen explains: "Adorno dedicated his life to restoring the relationship between reason and human freedom. His work is both a testament to the fragility of the bond between reason and freedom, and an endeavor to repair reason so that it can again speak on behalf of human emancipation. Adorno's project is nothing less than the effort to recover the critical potential of reason—a potential which was lost through the formalization and abstraction of reason from the details and complex interactions of social life" (9).

Adorno therefore wanted reason to be a matter of critical thinking, self-reflexivity, and unremitting questioning. He wanted to undo the numbing effects of what he referred to as "the administered society"—a society governed by the type of instrumentalist reason that resulted in Auschwitz—by rejoining reason with "the details and complex interactions of social life." That is, Adorno wanted reason to be embodied, attentive to the nuances of lived experience, and serving the needs of emancipation rather than oppression. This is a very different undertaking from simply trying to destroy reason.

My point is that reason (like related concepts such as autonomy, sovereignty, freedom, and agency) is not frozen in time, incapable of being rethought along lines that are less filled with destructive hubris than the instrumentalist ethos of the Enlightenment and its (neo)liberal inheritors. Both Foucault and Adorno interrogated the limits of instrumentalist reason while at the same time leaving open the possibility that reason could take less hegemonic forms. The same could be said about the attempts of Lacan, Derrida, and Kristeva to question dominant modes of autonomy, sovereignty, freedom, and agency. This fact is frequently lost in Anglo-American critical theory, which seems more invested in burning these concepts on the stake than in reawakening their more humane, capacious potentialities.

This eagerness to destroy rather than to rethink is not unrelated to critical theory's reluctance to admit that normative ethics can be historically specific yet essential for the functioning of social collectivities. Interestingly, Žižek seems to gesture toward a recognition of the value of normative ethics when he argues—thereby notably deviating from his usual critical stance regarding human rights—that even though we must acknowledge that human rights discourses privilege Western individualistic values, we should not make the mistake of thinking that they are "*directly and only* capitalist ideological masks for domination and exploitation" (2012, 1005).

Žižek goes as far as to assert that making this mistake would be even "more dangerous" than the opposite one of accepting human rights as an instance of value-free universality (2012, 1005). This is because, Žižek continues, "formal freedom"—which human rights, like other rights-based systems of justice, presumably aspires toward (even if it usually falls short of this goal)—"is *the only form of appearance (or potential site) of actual freedom*"

(1006). In other words, freedom cannot become actual without the envelope of formal freedom, which is why Žižek concludes that "if one prematurely abolishes 'formal' freedom, one loses also (the potential of) actual freedom" (1006).

Badiou's ethics of the event

These statements are somewhat difficult to reconcile with Žižek's overall Marxist-Lacanian orientation. But they may not be entirely incompatible with the attempt that—as I demonstrated in the previous chapter—Žižek, Badiou, Eisenstein, and McGowan make to envision a context-specific universalism, for this type of universalism opens to a context-specific model of normative limits in the sense that any emerging universal by definition gives rise to an emerging set of normative limits (or basic values). The Lacanian premises of these thinkers are obviously very different from Allen's more Foucauldian approach. And as I have shown, Žižek himself is a strong champion of antinormative ethics. Nevertheless, I believe that the notion of a historically specific universalism almost automatically implies the possibility of historically specific normative values.

This possibility is most obvious in Badiou's theory because while Žižek, Eisenstein, and McGowan place the accent on the disarray of antagonisms (the real, rupture), essentially asking us to embrace this disarray, Badiou's event is meant to bring a new social order into existence. From Žižek's viewpoint, this is the main failing of Badiou's theory. The difference between the visions of these two thinkers is that whereas Žižek views the ethical act (the tear in the fabric of the symbolic order) as a moment of negativity that destroys the social status quo without necessarily replacing it with a new one, Badiou sees the event as an opportunity to create a new collectivity that is prepared to translate the event's message—whether political, scientific, artistic, or amorous—into a new status quo through its prolonged fidelity. In other words, while Žižek is (for the most part) content to celebrate destruction, Badiou portrays the event as the starting point for a new collectivity formed around a cause that everyone involved agrees merits their loyalty.

Another way to state the distinction between Badiou and Žižek is to call attention to the contrasting status of truth in their formulations: if the event for Badiou reveals a truth that can be named and incorporated into the new social order that (potentially, through the subject's fidelity to the event) arises from the ashes of the event, Žižek maintains that the immortal truth that leaps forth from the subject's act of negativity has no positive content but, rather, signifies the failure of meaning as such. That is, while Badiou views the void that generates the event as containing some sort of legitimate meaning, Žižek views it in a more strictly Lacanian vein, as the "real" of the situation, as an insurmountable impediment to the legitimatization of meaning.

This is why Žižek consistently accuses Badiou of downplaying the negative, destructive force of the event. As Žižek writes, "This, then, is the ultimate difference between Badiou and Lacan: Badiou's starting point is an affirmative project and the fidelity to it; while, for Lacan, the primordial fact is that of negativity (ontologically, the impossibility of the One being One)" (2012, 836). For Žižek, "naming" the event, as Badiou aspires to do, merely establishes a new hegemony—one that seeks to suppress the disruptive force of negativity percolating beneath every social order (as it also percolates beneath every "coherent" subjectivity).

On some level, Žižek's critique of Badiou's desire to translate the negativity of the event into "an affirmative project" is valid. Eisenstein and McGowan, who value the idea of dwelling within the rupture, and who recognize that every rupture runs the risk of eventually turning into a new oppressive status quo, might agree with Žižek. At the same time, there is something to be said for the fact that Badiou's ethics of the event explicitly strives to negotiate the tension between antinormativity and the need for normative ethics that I have foregrounded. Badiou is at least *trying* to tackle the problematic of normativity in a postmetaphysical world; he is making an effort to envision how the spontaneous (and profoundly antinormative) moment of the event might get filtered into norms that everyone can, at least for the time being, agree upon.

This effort is not without its difficulties. Recall that at the core of Badiou's model, we find an insight akin to Ernesto Laclau's account of hegemonization: any given situation can potentially, through the event, produce a generic truth that everyone comes to recognize as valid. Such a truth—by naming the void of the situation at hand—arises from the idiosyncratic logic of this situation, yet once in place, it applies to everyone equally. This is how Badiou's ethics manages to be universalist without being tied to ahistorical normative limits.

However, the problem is obvious: Badiou gives us no way to ensure that the ethical principle that arises from a given situation is able to transcend the power differentials of that situation; there is no way to safeguard against the fact that some people will find it easier than others to name the void of the situation and therefore also the parameters of the ethics that this situation is supposed to generate. Badiou's event presupposes that participants will arrive at a shared truth through a miraculous galvanization of their passions. Ethics becomes a matter of the kind of quasi-theological (Kierkegaardian) leap of faith that is not grounded in anything besides personal commitment. What matters is the strength of conviction and the capacity to rally others behind this conviction, with the consequence that those with powerful or charismatic personalities are likely to overpower more timid ones.

The second problem with Badiou's ethics of the event is that the subject of truth that the event brings into being is arguably a walking contradiction: hell-bent on destroying the previous status quo—the previous "situation"—yet simultaneously willing to defend a new status quo without even a hint of hesitation. More concretely speaking, the subject of a political event wants to topple the previous political system in order to build a new one, the subject of the scientific event wants to discredit the previous scientific paradigm in order to advance a new one, the subject of the artistic event wants to break the rules of previous artistic practices in order to create a new practice, and—somewhat incongruously—the subject of the amorous event wants to transcend a previous relationship (or state of nonrelationship) in order to devote itself to a new one.

To be sure, Badiou emphasizes that a new event does not necessarily erase the "eventness" of previous events, so that Galileo does not neutralize the value of Copernicus, Picasso does not neutralize the value of Rembrandt, and my new lover does not neutralize the value of my old one. Nonetheless, it would be difficult to deny that the new event in some ways pushes previous ones into oblivion. For instance, if my new lover were not able to replace my old one as a site of psychic and affective cathexis, I might as well stay with the old one. Likewise, it seems clear that, for Badiou, a political event such as the Russian Revolution represents a decisive improvement in the overall state of world affairs (rather than just one political event among others). This implies that the new status quo that the event generates, in some instances at least, is superior to the one it replaces. But on what basis is this decided?

The answer, once again, seems to ride on the blazing impact of the event, on the sheer impossibility of refuting the validity of its message. In a way, the unpremeditated, passion-driven formation of the norms that arise from the event is Badiou's solution to the tendency to associate the normative with the rigidly habitual: the new norms that leap into existence from the event appear more legitimate than the status quo of the social establishment because they have not had time to congeal into hegemonic configurations. However, this does not solve the problem that the event explicitly solicits the kind of fidelity that aims to transform the spontaneous truth revealed by the event into new habits of thought.

Badiou is emphatically not asking the subject to question the truthfulness of the event at every turn. Instead, the event requires such unconditional faithfulness that, as Badiou (2001) himself admits, it can be difficult to tell the difference between the demands made by the event on the one hand and ones made by a dictator on the other. This is why it can be impossible to distinguish between a genuine event and a simulacrum such as Nazi Germany until after the fact. Consequently, it is entirely possible that norms that seem to emerge spontaneously, that seem to counter the habitual normative edicts of the status quo, end up being more oppressive than the status quo they replace. What, then, is the distinction between the (good) norms born from the event and the (bad) norms that govern mainstream society, particularly if the latter were once inspired by an event of some kind, such as the French Revolution?

Badiou's context-specific ethics is therefore not a perfect solution. It still lacks sufficient normative foundations: it lacks a clear distinction between right and wrong. But like Allen's more Foucauldian approach, it recognizes that even a postmetaphysical world cannot operate without values. Likewise, like Allen's "historical a priori," it holds open the possibility of the kind of continual revision of norms that, according to Allen, is the only way to guarantee that our ethical systems do not congeal into an oppressive status quo. It does not clearly answer the question of how to sustain this process of revision over time. But nor can I. It seems to me that the ability to keep revising collective norms is one of the major challenges—perhaps *the* challenge—of genuine democracy: a task at which most actually existing democracies fail miserably. Because revision of this kind cannot be divorced from volatility and social disorder, most democracies seek to curtail it. But they can only do so at the cost of true democracy.

This may be why critical theory tends to associate true democracy with the lack of normative limits. But I would argue that this merely inadvertently plays right into the hands of neoliberal capitalism in the sense that capitalism, like antinormativity, despises limits. It thrives in the absence of constraints. For this reason, the self-absorbed neoliberal individual who is used to an endless array of existential possibilities, and who does not like limitations on her freedom—including her freedom to choose her hair color, breakfast cereal, video game, and mode of exercise—may be perfectly happy with the idea that she should not be beholden to norms that might in some way hinder her ability to move about the world without restriction. From this viewpoint, normative ethics could be argued to war against the neoliberal capitalist ethos of unmitigated choice, perhaps even decentering the neoliberal subject by introducing within its being "alien" elements (norms) that it experiences as constraining.

Arguably, the effect of normative ethics is to render the subject secondary (rather than autonomous and sovereign in the humanist sense): the subject is expected to respect the values of such ethics regardless of its self-serving interests. The Kantian categorical imperative, for instance, starts from the premise that how the subject feels—whether it, for example, regards a given norm as a threat to its capacity to experience pleasure—is completely irrelevant to ethical deliberation. We all know that separating ethics from feeling is a tall order. But the relevant point here is that, from a Kantian perspective, antinormativity comes across as too convenient, even self-centered and narcissistic, which is why it could easily be interpreted as a *symptom* of the very neoliberal system that critical theory condemns.

I am not advocating a return to Kantianism. But it seems to me that if critical theory wishes to remain genuinely critical, it needs to rethink its condemnation of normative ethics. On the one hand, this condemnation is constitutive of critical theory in the sense that this theory aspires to reveal the tyrannical underbelly of the norms that we have been taught to take for granted; it is impossible to envision a critical theory that is not on some level hostile to received forms of ethical deliberation. On the other, rejecting normative ethics wholesale denies the normativity that can be detected beneath even the most radical pronouncements of antinormativity.

This is why I lean toward the stance of context-specific (historically grounded) normativity that Allen advocates and that Badiou, in his own way, gestures toward. Such a stance is messy because it demands that we remain vigilant about repeatedly distinguishing between habits of thought that have become, or are in danger of becoming, oppressive and others that might—for the time being at least—be conducive to the advancement of social justice and global flourishing. But the messiness of the approach does not cancel out the likelihood that it may be our best option, our most agile means of navigating the terrain between antifoundationalism and normative ethics.

My objective in this chapter has been to illustrate that critical theory needs to develop a comparable vigilance regarding the distinction between stagnant habits of thought and useful (vitality-preserving) critical tendencies, that critical theory, in short, is not immune to ossified bad habits. The categorical rejection of normative ethics is one of these. The related demonization, independently of context, of autonomy and sovereignty is another. I have attempted to show that both of these bad habits have unfortunate consequences. Breaking these habits, in contrast, would release critical theory from some of its repetition compulsions, thereby allowing us to begin to conceptualize what it might mean to be a subject beyond the autonomous and sovereign subject of humanist metaphysics, and moreover, what it might mean to think about normativity beyond the exclusionary ethical models that the fiction of this subject produced.

3

Why some things matter more than others:

A Lacanian explanation

Progressive critical theory—defined here in the same way as in the previous chapter, namely as a mixture of Lacanian psychoanalysis, continental philosophy, poststructuralism, Marxism, cultural studies, and feminist and queer theory—is chronically suspicious of our (potentially normative, potentially complacent) investments in various goals, ideals, objects, and aspirations. This hermeneutics of suspicion regarding the contours of our desire is hardly surprising, given that many of the most prominent precursors of critical theory were explicitly wary of mainstream society's capacity to interpellate desire into hegemonic manifestations: Althusser explained how we come to desire the ideological structures of dominant society; the Frankfurt School analyzed the ways in which the culture industry causes us to desire what capitalism wants us to desire; Barthes revealed the power of cultural mythologies over our psychic lives; and Foucault illustrated the manner in which biopolitical conditioning produces the parameters of our subjectivity. No wonder, then, that contemporary theory does not trust that our desire is in fact *ours*.

To be sure, thinkers from Georges Bataille to recent queer theorists have appreciated, and sometimes even overstated, the radical potential of desire, often celebrating desire's capacity to wreak havoc with the coherent organization of individual and collective life alike. At the same time, much of progressive theory, particularly its Marxist denomination, has taken a more cynical perspective on desire, viewing it as largely antithetical to the world-changing ambitions of critical inquiry. This more cynical approach—which usually amounts to one form or another of ideology critique—has been particularly appropriate in the context of analyses of neoliberal capitalism as a system that generates the desire for a very particular version of the good life, a version that places an emphasis on the individual's willingness to exert herself in order to reap the benefits of consumer culture, make a diligent effort to improve herself, aspire to be a "balanced" person with equally "balanced" relationships, and—importantly for the smooth functioning of the system—smile her way through hardship.

Lacan offers ample support for this line of thought, for he acknowledges that desire tends to follow normative pathways, that our desire often cannot be dissociated from the desire of the big Other. However, my aim in this chapter is to demonstrate the ways in which Lacan complicates the conclusions of ideology critique by revealing that our desire can also be far too idiosyncratic, far too unpredictable to be instrumentalizable in terms of our society's dominant values. For instance, the fixations of our desire frequently war against the neocapitalist creed of efficiency and high productivity, sometimes paralyzing us to the extent that we cannot even perform the routine tasks of everyday life, let alone "accomplish" things in the sense that this creed demands. Alternatively, our desire can attach itself to objects, including people, that mainstream society deems worthless. At times such enigmatic cathexes even thwart our culture's ethos of consumerism by focusing our attention on a particular object to such a degree that we become uninterested in all other objects: insofar as a special object outshines all others, it ruptures the logic of capitalism that asks us to glide from one object to the next without hesitation.

Such instances of "irrational" desire are difficult to account for in the vocabulary of ideology critique. In contrast, Lacan offers a rich theory of why some things matter to us more than others, why there may even be some things in the world that we experience as more or less irreplaceable. In the pages that follow, I will outline some of Lacan's reasoning in order to argue that our desire is not always misguided, that some of the things we cathect to actually deserve our faithfulness, and that it is consequently possible to think of desire as an ethical—and perhaps even a political—force.

My argument proceeds in three steps. First, I offer a snapshot of contemporary theory's (warranted) reservations regarding desire, focusing on critiques of neoliberal capitalism. Second, I summarize recent Lacanian accounts that, despite Lacan's own appreciation for desire (which I will get to in the third step of my argument), privilege the drive over desire as a way of breaking capitalism's hold on our psyches. Such arguments imply that if it is the case that capitalism is inconceivable without objects of desire, the most effective way to defeat capitalism is to neutralize—or at least to mitigate—the force of desire, to replace desire's future-oriented cadence by the immediacy of the drive as a force that does not require external objects for its satisfaction but rather attains this satisfaction from its own relentless movement.

The culmination of this perspective is Lee Edelman's notorious valorization of the death drive as the core of a defiant queer ethics. Yet in categorically rejecting desire, this outlook falls into the difficulty I just mentioned, namely the inability to account for the fact that our desire is not *invariably* normative or ethically compromised. To address this problem, the final sections of this chapter—and this is the third step of the argument I referred to above—work toward a Lacanian ethics of desire that clarifies why the fixations of our desire sometimes—not always, but sometimes—promote the kind of loyalty to cherished objects, including other people, that it would be a mistake to betray. In essence, I propose that there are times when we should trust our desire, when the hermeneutics of suspicion is the wrong attitude to cultivate. At the same time, I consider the ways in which consumer culture's tendency to diffuse our desire across too many objects can generate anxiety as the dominant affective tone of contemporary culture.

The hermeneutics of suspicion

Given that I am operating with a broader definition of critical theory than those who associate the term with the Frankfurt School specifically, it may be useful to begin by noting that contemporary theory's hermeneutics of suspicion regarding the contours of our desire is among the most obvious ways in which the spirit of the

Frankfurt School persists in progressive critiques of neoliberal society, for these critiques—whether explicitly or implicitly—adopt Adorno's conviction that the culture industry conditions our desire to such an extent that whenever we want anything, we are likely to replicate normative modes of life.

I discussed progressive critiques of neoliberal society in detail in *The Ethics of Opting Out*, so here I merely provide a succinct overview of some of the most influential arguments of the recent decade. For instance, arguing from an affect theoretical perspective, Sara Ahmed proposes that the dominant happiness scripts of our society guide us to a very particular vision of the good life, one replete with fantasies of financial security, individual fulfillment, married monogamy, and unmitigated overall satisfaction. As Ahmed states, "There is no doubt that the affective repertoire of happiness gives us images of a certain kind of life, a life that has certain things and does certain things" (2010, 90). This repertoire effectively blocks other repertoires before we even get a chance to imagine what it would be like to pursue them, thereby giving us a very precise education in how we are supposed to desire.

Ahmed observes that our investment in our culture's dominant happiness scripts can be so strong that when a given script—say, the script that tells us that marriage will heal the wounds of prior romantic disappointments—does not deliver what it promises, we do not think of questioning the script itself but instead assume that somehow we have failed to live it out correctly. When we have been invested in the notion that a certain kind of life is the happy life, it can be very difficult for us to admit that this life has not made us happy; it can be difficult to admit that our faith in a particular happiness script has led us astray. As Ahmed explains, "It is hard labor just to recognize sadness and disappointment, when you are living a life that is meant to be happy but just isn't, which is meant to be full, but feels empty" (2010, 75).

Lauren Berlant reasons along related (affect theoretical) lines when she asserts that many of us are caught up in cruel optimism: the unwavering conviction that scenes of desire—social arrangements, emotional patterns, comforting objects, intimate scenarios, and so on—that repeatedly wound us will eventually pay off and make us happy. Cruel optimism implies that the very things that we most ardently desire are in reality an impediment to our flourishing in the sense that they cause us to hope against hope that things will in the end get better even when they are extremely unlikely to do so. In Berlant's words, "The compulsion to repeat a toxic optimism can suture someone or a world to a cramped and unimaginative space of committed replication, *just in case* it will be different" (2011, 259).

As Berlant explains, cruel optimism is hard to discard because even when it undermines us, it provides us with a sense of subjective continuity, of "what it means to keep on living on and to look forward to being in the world" (2011, 24). In the last chapter, I noted that Berlant recognizes that cruel optimism may be better than no optimism in situations where people's survival depends on their ability to trust that things will ultimately somehow work out. However, she simultaneously calls attention to the treacherous nature of "the 'technologies of patience' that enable a concept of the *later* to suspend questions about the cruelty of the *now*" (16; 28).

Barbara Ehrenreich in turn analyzes the ways in which an optimistic attitude toward scenes of desire has come to define American culture to such an extent that many Americans believe that they can attract good things to their lives by the sheer force of positive thinking; they have an almost boundless faith in their ability to prosper, achieve their goals, bring about miraculous reversals of fortune, and beat the odds of illness even when their chances of doing so are slim. The insidious underside of this mentality, Ehrenreich stresses, is that "there is no excuse for failure": the flipside of our society's sugarcoated attitude of cheerfulness is "a harsh insistence on personal responsibility, meaning that while capitalism produces some people's success through other people's failures, the ideology of positive thinking insists that success depends upon working hard and failure is always your own doing" (8).

Ahmed, Berlant, and Ehrenreich all suggest that our habitual patterns of desire support our sense of subjective viability, our sense of belonging in the world, to such a degree that they can be impossible to discard even when they are not in the least bit good for us. As Berlant posits, to the extent that we value the idea of a "dependable life," "a life that does not have to keep being reinvented," we can come "to misrecognize the bad life as a good one" (2011, 170; 174).

At the same time, our relationship to the scenes of desire that buttress our subjectivity can be ambivalent for the simple reason that our culture gives us conflicting messages about satisfaction. As Slavoj Žižek, arguing from a more Marxist-Lacanian viewpoint than Ahmed, Berlant, and Ehrenreich, emphasizes, our society is governed by the imperative to enjoy (rather than by the more traditional imperative to curtail enjoyment), so that—whether the focus is on sexual performance, professional achievement, or spiritual awakening—we are besieged by "the superego injunction 'Enjoy!'" (2005, 152). Neoliberal society censures nothing: we are urged to enjoy and consume—enjoy because we consume—as much as possible. However, because we know that the profusion of the various "enjoyments" on offer in our culture—from drugs, alcohol, cigarettes, and french fries to video games, fast cars, and unprotected sex—can harm us, we can simultaneously become a bit paranoid about our satisfactions.

This is why Alenka Zupančič characterizes the double bind of contemporary life in Western societies as follows: "on the one hand, the imperative 'Enjoy!,' and, on the other, the reminder that we are also constantly bombarded with: 'Enjoyment can kill you!,' 'Enjoy!—but be aware that enjoyment can kill you'" (68). This is how we end up in the bizarre bind of feeling apprehensive about the very patterns of desire that situate us in the world. This may in turn explain why our desire tends to be displaced onto the future, why it tends to crystallize around fantasies of a better future that cause us to repeatedly exert ourselves even when past experience has shown us that our exertions are unlikely to bring us the satisfaction we crave.

Our neoliberal culture of positive thinking—and here again, in order to take a shortcut, I reproduce an argument from *The Ethics of Opting Out*—assures us that personal fulfillment is attainable through ambition, striving, and calculated risks; that there is no obstacle that cannot be overcome by perseverance; that effort will invariably be rewarded; and that dissatisfaction is merely a temporary state, often just a stepping stone to satisfaction. It is not for nothing that one of the most enduring elements of American cultural mythology is the idea that Americans are a resilient people, capable of bouncing back from any difficulty, setback, or defeat. As this mythology would have it, hindrances are mere fleeting impediments. Even better, they are blessings in disguise in the sense that they strengthen our character, thereby making us more capable of leaping over the next hurdle that appears on our path.

Consider what happens when a catastrophe strikes, either on the personal or collective level. We are encouraged to mourn our losses as quickly as possible, to get back on our feet, to brush ourselves off, and to get "back to business." While ostentatious demonstrations of grief may at times be actively elicited as proof of our humanness—of the goodness of our souls and the generosity of our spirits—prolonged periods of paralyzing grief are unacceptable because they render us incapable of participating in the life of the economy, either as producers or consumers. The kind of depression that drives us to the mall may be worth something; but the kind of debilitating sadness that drives us to our darkened bedroom is not. In this sense, our society approaches grief with the same uncompromising efficiency as it approaches most other aspects of life: we are supposed to deal with it as expediently as we can so that we can get back to work.

Work, of course, is imperative. Besides its relentless cheerfulness, neoliberal culture is defined by a hard-nosed pragmatism. It wants us to work harder, faster, longer, and better. It valorizes productivity and good performance. And it asks us to maximize the functioning of our minds and bodies alike so that we can lead happy, healthy, balanced, and well-adjusted lives. As Foucault already claimed in *The Birth of Biopolitics*, neoliberal capitalism transforms the human being into a miniature economic enterprise—what Foucault called *homo economicus*—driven by the logic of input and output, effort and profit. This utilitarianism characterizes life under neoliberal capitalism to such a degree that people tend to measure their worth primarily by pragmatic criteria of accomplishments. Even those who fail to live up to the expectations of this system are impacted by it in the sense that the glossy version of the good life it promises becomes a goal that they reach for even when it repeatedly eludes them.

This system exploits human adaptability: the ability to endure instability and repeated disappointment. By selling us the fantasy of eventual happiness—happiness that seems to await just around the corner but that repeatedly eludes us—it causes us to pursue one goal after another, one consumer item after another, in the hope that we will one day arrive at the end of frustration. Neoliberal capitalism is psychically appealing, and hence economically lucrative, because it plays into the basic structure of desire by promising that it can replace a state of scarcity by a state of satiated abundance.

What may be harder to discern is that the system produces the very scarcity that it proffers to help us transcend. Indeed, without this production of lack—without this ability to make us feel that something is missing from our lives (yet surely attainable in the future)—the system would quickly collapse, for if we ever reached a state of complete contentment, our desire would come to an end, and with it, our conviction that the new products we see advertised might add something to the quality of our lives. This is why, despite appearances, neoliberal capitalism thrives on the perpetuation of lack—frequently experienced as a vague anxiety about losing what we already have—more than on the generation of excess even as its excesses threaten to drown us in waste. Its genius is to generate the very lack that the seductive objects it manufactures—objects that are meticulously designed to sparkle brightly enough to mesmerize us—promise to fill.

When satisfaction dissatisfies

This insight about capitalism's ability to produce the very lack it promises to fill is Todd McGowan's starting point in *Capitalism and Desire*. If Lacan theorized subjectivity as a complex interplay of lack and desire, McGowan argues that capitalism knows how to intensify our desire by intensifying our sense of lack. In other words, capitalism exploits the ontological lack that (according to Lacan) founds subjectivity—and that forces all of us to grapple with alienation as an integral part of the human condition—by actively fanning our awareness of deprivation while simultaneously (seemingly) offering a solution to this deprivation. In a way, the more excess capitalism produces, the more deprived we feel for the simple reason that none of us are able to "enjoy" everything at once. As McGowan quips, "Just when one imagines it's safe to return to the supermarket without finding a new form of potato chip, Lays invents the wavy, fat-free chip flavored with sea salt" (144).

One might express the predicament of the capitalist subject—particularly of the affluent or middle-class subject but the point can in certain instances be relevant even to those with low incomes—as follows: at the moment when this subject enjoys a specific flavor of potato chips, it fantasizes about another flavor that might bring even more satisfaction, with the result that, instead of being fully satisfied with the chips it consumes, it experiences a tinge of deprivation. This is the quandary of the child at an ice-cream parlor who is distracted from the pleasure of savoring her enormous chocolate fudge sundae by the sight of an even bigger one at the next table. This is one way in which capitalism perpetuates the logic of cruel optimism so that, in McGowan's words, "As subjects of capitalism, we are constantly on the edge of having our desire realized, but never reach the point of realization": "Capitalism offers the promise of belonging with every commodity . . . but the subject can never buy the perfect commodity, or enough of them, to unlock the secret of belonging" (2016, 11; 21). In this sense, "capitalist subjects experience satisfaction itself as dissatisfying, which enables them to simultaneously enjoy themselves and believe wholeheartedly that a more complete enjoyment exists just around the corner, embodied in the newest commodity" (11).

Capitalist subjects experience their satisfaction as dissatisfying; they feel cheated of enjoyment at the very moment of enjoyment. Yet they trust that enjoyment will eventually find its way into their lives. And to secure this enjoyment, to guarantee their sense of "belonging," they study the desire of the big Other. As McGowan explains:

> This focus on the desire of the Other creates subjects who dedicate themselves to the interpretation of this desire. They spend their time reading fashion magazines, learning about the lives of Hollywood stars, or following the movements of famous sports figures. All of these activities that capitalist society fosters have as their goal interpreting the desire of the Other so that the subjects engaged in this interpretative process can solve the problem of desire. . . . The subject does not simply settle for the desire of the Other or betray its own desire by adopting that of the Other. To the contrary, the subject's own desire derives from its interpretation of the desire of the Other. (2016, 42)

The subject thus turns to the big Other for guidance on what and how it should desire: the Other seems to hold the key to the enigma of desire, with the consequence that its desire becomes the subject's desire. The subject of course believes that its desire is entirely original and genuine. But this is an illusion because, as McGowan states, "The image of the desiring Other kick-starts the desire of the subject" (42).

In making this argument, McGowan acknowledges that the capitalist subject's (self-diagnosed) "deprivation" frequently hides much more severe forms of oppression, so that, for example, the dissatisfaction of the Western child at the ice-cream parlor must always be placed in the context of the exploitation of non-Western children (and adults) whose cheap labor fills the coffers of corporate capitalism. That is, in focusing on capitalism's power to feed the Western subject's gluttony for ever greater levels of consumption, McGowan does not mean to overlook global (or domestic) inequalities but merely to explain the logic of future satisfaction that renders capitalism so difficult to resist (even by those who bear the brunt of its brutality).

McGowan asserts that even progressive theories that aim to undermine capitalism routinely end up replicating its logic by envisioning a future with no lack, scarcity, limitation, or regulation, so that Marxism promises the end of alienation, psychoanalysis promises the lifting of repression, and Derrida promises "democracy to come." According to McGowan, even Foucault—who certainly recognizes that capitalism generates desire as much as it curbs it—ends up asserting that we need to liberate our "bodies and pleasures" from capitalism's grip. As McGowan postulates with regard to Foucault, "This is the key point: power doesn't permit the free movement of bodies and deprives them of the pleasure that they are capable of experiencing. Critique or revolution then fights against this restriction. Though Foucault rejects the terms *repression* and *desire*, his replacements—*power* and *bodies*—perform precisely the same roles" (2016, 10). That is, although Foucault rejects the repressive hypothesis, he still, in McGowan's assessment, believes that power (or capitalism) "blocks or dams up what would otherwise flow freely" (10). This is why McGowan concludes that Foucault "does not mark a new epoch in the history of the critique of capitalism" (10).

For McGowan, progressive theory's quest for a better future represents a theoretico-political dead end because it merely bolsters one of the main illusions of capitalism. Obviously, as my analysis of Eisenstein and McGowan's *Rupture* in Chapter 1 revealed, McGowan wants social justice. But as we also learned, he does not believe in the possibility of a harmonious future, a future devoid of antagonisms. If anything, antagonisms are what, in McGowan's view, keep the social establishment from fossilizing into repressive permutations; dwelling within the rupture in the sense that he and

Eisenstein promote is more or less the antithesis of comfortable (and thus complacent) satisfaction.

It is therefore not surprising that McGowan proposes that rather than agitating for higher levels of satisfaction, we should learn to recognize the satisfaction we already possess. If capitalism seeks to convince us that with the right commodities we might be able to transcend the barriers that keep us from fulfilling our desire, McGowan argues that the last thing we need is more desire (or the toppling of the barriers to desire). Essentially, McGowan suggests that the only effective antidote to capitalism is to discard the image of ourselves as subjects of deprivation so that we can discern that we are already satisfied enough. As he expresses the matter, "If we recognized that we obtained satisfaction from the failure to obtain the perfect commodity rather than from a wholly successful purchase, we would be freed from the psychic appeal of capitalism" (2016, 14). If the "promise of a better future is the foundation of the capitalist structure," McGowan adds, "the revolutionary act"—the anticapitalist act—"is simply the recognition that capitalism already produces the satisfaction that it promises" (13).

When dissatisfaction satisfies

What does this mean? McGowan hypothesizes that the solution to capitalism's hold on us would be to recognize that our satisfaction does not arise from the objects we pursue but rather from the repetition of our quest for the perfect object; the very fact that each new object disappoints us—thereby forcing us to repeat our hunt for an object that promises gratification—is what satisfies us, so that capitalism, counterintuitively enough, provides satisfaction in the guise on dissatisfaction. In other words, the repetition of our pursuit of objects alleviates the trauma of subjectivity—the fact that subjectivity is founded on lack—by offering us the fantasy that there exists an object in the world that will put an end to the search. And paradoxically, it is the fact that the system never delivers what it promises that gives us satisfaction. The failure of satisfaction—dissatisfaction—is what, according to McGowan, ultimately satisfies us. It is just that we usually fail to see that it is the repeated disappointment of our quest for the object rather than the object itself that satisfies us.

McGowan's analysis of capitalism is a brilliant elaboration of the basic Lacanian idea that the psychoanalytic "cure" consists of acknowledging that there is no cure, that human subjectivity arises from the kind of lack that cannot be sutured no matter how desperately or diligently we try to do so. For Lacan, it is the acceptance of this lack—of castration—that provides the opening to something that could be called a meaningful life. In my previous work (see Ruti 2009, 2012, 2015b, 2017), I have often argued that it is precisely this lack that gives us everything that is worth living for in the sense that, without it, we would have no reason to reach out into the world in search of things (and here I am not talking about commodities but goals, ideals, activities, creative preoccupations, and loved people) that might appease our sense of alienation. Indeed, if we lost our lack, we would also lose our subjectivity, for subjectivity, in Lacanian terms, is nothing but this lack.

In a recent classroom discussion, after one student—understandably frustrated by the bleakness of the Lacanian vision—asked why Lacan's ontology of constitutive lack is a valid way to characterize subjectivity, I explained the matter as follows: when, during a run in a beautiful area of Cape Cod, I turn a corner and suddenly the ocean opens in front of me, turquoise and turbulent, I feel exhilarated but also sad because I know that I will not always be around to witness this stunning scene; I feel a sting of loss even as I feel pure joy. I assume that if a cat, squirrel, or chipmunk arrives at the same spot on the path, they will not experience the same combination of joy and loss. It is the fact that my joy cannot be dissociated from loss that renders me human (which, as we will see in the next chapter, does not make me superior to other animals but merely different from them).

McGowan extends this insight to propose that the only way to escape the allure of capitalism is to admit that, as human beings, the only thing that can truly satisfy us is our dissatisfaction: our repeated encounter with our lack, mortality, deficiency, alienation, and woundability. In other words, if we understood that the sealing of our lack—which is what capitalism promises—would turn us into the equivalent of a chipmunk, we might stop trying to look for objects (consumer goods) that promise to plug the void of our being; we, in short, would cease to need consumer capitalism.

A more palatable way to explain the matter may be to suggest, as McGowan also does, that subjects who reject the fantasy of a fully satisfying object cease to look for it and instead "content themselves with outmoded objects and recognize the satisfaction embodied in the object's failure to realize their desire"; such subjects "see their satisfaction in the object's inadequacy" (2016, 40). In Chapter 5, I will illustrate how this scenario plays itself out in the context of the amorous event, why McGowan believes that the lover finds the beloved satisfying precisely to the extent that the latter remains inadequate. At the present juncture, the crucial point is that in this scenario—which is rare in the context of commodity capitalism but which anticipates some of what I am about to say about Lacan's ethics of desire—the subject acknowledges that there exists no commodity that can satisfy it more than the imperfect one it already enjoys.

In *Enjoying What We Don't Have*, McGowan approaches the ideas that I have outlined by focusing on the Lacanian drive as a force that does not seek satisfaction in objects but rather attains it from the lack of objects. Unlike desire, which pursues objects for its satisfaction, the drive bypasses objects, getting its satisfaction (jouissance) from its dissatisfaction, from its incessant failure to reach its goal. In this sense, the satisfaction of the drive arises from the sheer doggedness of its movement, from the mindless repetition of its trajectory. This is why McGowan claims that the satisfaction of the drive in the final analysis consists of enjoying what it does not have: the drive enjoys by enjoying "nothing" (the lack of an object).

This line of thinking has led other Lacanians with more antisocial predilections than McGowan, such as Žižek and Edelman, to theorize the destructive jouissance of the drive as a subversive force that allows the subject to decathect itself from the cruelly optimistic happiness scripts of normative society. This insight underpins the notion of the Lacanian "act" that I have already talked about, and that is often depicted as a suicidal plunge into the jouissance of the real, such as Žižek's advocacy of divine (Benjaminian messianic) violence or Edelman's analysis of the queer as a figure of death-driven negativity.

In Chapter 1, we learned that McGowan courts this notion of the act with his theory of rupture. But in the two texts that I have discussed in this chapter—*Capitalism and Desire* and *Enjoying What We Don't Have*—he is less interested in radical acts of defiance than in the idea that the subject who has no need for objects or who has little need for new objects—because it deems its old objects satisfying enough—also has little need for capitalism. As

I have sought to demonstrate, McGowan is convinced that when we acknowledge that the consumption of objects does not in reality yield the satisfaction it promises, when we learn to enjoy "what we don't have," we automatically thwart the foundations of capitalism.

McGowan's position is elegantly simple and convincing to those of us, such as myself, who have chosen to lead relatively "minimalist" lifestyles centered less on accumulation than on avoiding the burdens of "owning things." This attitude can be taken to problematic lengths, as happens in anorexia, where the subject seeks to forgo the consumption of objects altogether. But there is no doubt that a degree of independence from objects brings a degree of freedom: as the Stoics already recognized, when we do not rely on objects for our satisfaction, the external world loses much of its power to disappoint—dissatisfy—us.

However, this formulation also highlights the main shortcoming of this perspective, which is that it fails to adequately distinguish between objects that do not merit our cathexis and others that do: it implies that desire is intrinsically erroneous and politically regressive, that our objects of desire are invariably tainted by (capitalist) normativity, and that not wanting is automatically more progressive than wanting. McGowan partially sidesteps this problem by insisting on the value of the imperfect object, on the idea that what elicits "genuine" desire is an object that is inadequate (lacking). In this way, McGowan's stance provides a contrast to the more radical one of (for instance) Edelman, who juxtaposes the drive-centered queer to the desire-centered structure of heteronormative futurism in ways that suggest that queerness compromised by any hint of desire is queerness compromised *tout court* (see Ruti 2017).

I will return to some of the details of Edelman's argument in the next chapter in the context of his disagreements with Berlant. Here I merely want to note that it is not a coincidence that Edelman's version of queer theory has come to be known as "antirelational": as I mentioned in the last chapter, the subject of the drive—of jouissance—is an intrinsically solipsistic one, cut off from any connection to others, even those who might facilitate its jouissance. I do not think that there is any way around the fact that the subject of the drive, in shunning all objects, risks withdrawing into an insulated universe that rejects not only the logic of consumer capitalism but also the imprint of everything that resides outside the self; that is, such a subject rejects the trace of otherness, the possibility of relationality, that arguably constitutes one of the most enriching components of human experience.

Lacan's ethics of desire

I have never been an unqualified proponent of relationality, which, frankly, often sounds better (or more noble) than it actually is. For example, as we saw in the previous chapter, I am critical of Butler's ethics of precarity which, in a Levinasian vein, elevates relationality to an unquestioned ethical virtue: I believe that relationality can be just as toxic, just as corrupted by power disparities, as any other aspect of human life. At the same time, I fear that Lacanian theories centered on the drive (on jouissance), such as Edelman's—and, perhaps even more notoriously, Žižek's—lose track of relationality to such an extent that they risk giving the impression that Lacan has nothing useful to say about either affective connections or the ethics of intersubjectivity.

It is in order to counter this impression that I will spend the rest of this chapter delineating what I consider to be Lacan's greatest contribution to ethics: the ethics of not ceding one's desire, succinctly captured by Lacan's claim, in *The Ethics of Psychoanalysis*, that "the only thing of which one can be guilty is of having given ground relative to one's desire" (319). "It is because we know better than those who went before how to recognize the nature of desire," Lacan specifies, "that a reconsideration of ethics is possible, that a form of ethical judgment is possible, of a kind that gives this question the force of a Last Judgment: Have you acted in conformity with the desire that is in you?" (314).

It would be easy enough to object to this formulation, for surely there are many other things besides betraying our desire that we could feel guilty about. But the important point in the present context is that Lacan contrasts his ethics of desire with normative morality, which he describes as "the morality of the master, created for the virtues of the master and linked to the order of powers" (1959–1960, 314–15). This morality of the master facilitates what Lacan calls "the service of goods": the principles of efficiency, productivity, and performance that underpin Western capitalism. As Lacan elaborates, "The essential point is 'Carry on working.

Work must go on.' Which, of course, means: 'Let it be clear to everyone that this is on no account the moment to express the least surge of desire.' The morality of power, of the service of goods, is as follows: 'As far as desires are concerned, come back later. Make them wait'" (315).

The morality of the master computes the value of life by purely pragmatic criteria, so that its model citizen is a subject who shows up at work reliably every morning, undertakes its duties with a degree of diligence, does not allow its desires to get the better of its productivity, and seeks satisfaction ("enjoys") in efficiency-augmenting ways. This, Lacan maintains, "is what is known as the postrevolutionary perspective": "Part of the world has resolutely turned in the direction of the service of goods, thereby rejecting everything that has to do with the relationship of man to desire" (1959–1960, 318). That is, the service of goods, in instrumentalizing desire, reflects the mindset of the levelheaded utilitarian subject who has deemed revolutionary change to be unrealistic.

To such levelheaded utilitarianism Lacan juxtaposes the subject of desire who is willing to act in accordance with its desire even when doing so is socially inconvenient or politically disruptive—that is, precisely, a subject who refuses to cede its desire. We have seen that for Lacan, the archetype of such a subject is Antigone, who chooses to die rather than to obey Creon's ban against burying Polyneces, stubbornly insisting on her act of insubordination in the face of Creon's efforts to intimidate her. This may in part explain why critics such as Žižek and Edelman have been so quick to leap from Lacan's ethics of not ceding one's desire to the suicidal act I mentioned above. For these critics, the subject acts "ethically" when it embraces the death drive in an "antisocial" act of rebellion, as Antigone supposedly does.

However, as I pointed out in the previous chapter, what this reading ignores is that even though Antigone's act is antihegemonic in the sense that she refuses to uphold Creon's version of the big Other, it is not easily categorizable as "antisocial" (let alone "antirelational"): Antigone, after all, defies Creon not solely for her own sake but also for the sake of Polyneces, for the sake of making a politico-ethical statement about the importance of staying faithful to intersubjective ties in the face of persecution. If anything, in deeming the worth of Polyneces higher than her own, Antigone exhibits an almost Levinasian respect for the vulnerability of the other. She illustrates that the self-destructive drive can be motivated by a desire centered on an object, so that the distinction between the drive and desire becomes blurry at best.

Perhaps it is this blurriness that has caused Žižek and Edelman to valorize the drive over desire even though, as I have demonstrated, Lacan explicitly characterizes his ethics of psychoanalysis as an ethics of *desire*. Unfortunately, by supplanting desire with the drive, these critics lose track not only of the social dimensions of defiance but also of the potentially defiant character of desire. Their tendency to approach desire from the perspective of ideology critique—which defines desire simply as an extension of dominant ideology—makes it hard for them to appreciate the more resistant frequencies of desire.

Two types of desire

It does not help that Lacan operates with (at least) two different definitions of desire. The first of these is the kind of desire that cannot be detached from the desire of the Other. I have already conceded that this definition accords with the insights of ideology critique. Indeed, one of the strengths of recent Lacanian political theories, such as those of McGowan, Žižek, and Edelman, has been to clarify that even when desire supports the capitalist "service of goods" (which insists that "work must go on"), it should not necessarily be understood in terms of constraint. Quite the opposite, inasmuch as Žižek is correct in his assessment that contemporary society is governed by the injunction to enjoy rather than to limit enjoyment, we must recognize that the disciplining of desire is these days no longer primarily a matter of repression. Rather, it is a matter of *manipulating* desire in ways that feed the relentless performance demanded by the service of goods.

Consider, for example, the common practice of using online pornography to take a break from work so as to recharge one's ability to tackle the next task or to endure the dullness of the day. From this perspective, pornography is an efficient tool of biopolitical conditioning, perhaps even the epitome of neoliberal efficiency: you take your break, you satisfy your desire while neatly sidestepping the (potentially time-consuming) tangles of intersubjectivity, and then you go right back to "producing." The libido, in this scenario, is not repressed but rather drawn into the neoliberal game of keeping up with a multitude of practical, psychic, emotional, and work-related pressures.

It is therefore hardly a coincidence that the contemporary culture industry is saturated by overt forms of sexuality that would have been unthinkable during Adorno's time: more or less any sexual predilection can find instant satisfaction on the Internet; every form of sexual "transgression" has been commodified, advertised through some of the most powerful mechanisms of mass entertainment. In a world where even the most vanilla of straight bedrooms have been infiltrated by various shades of gray, it seems increasingly difficult to think about sexual transgression outside of the capitalist injunction to enjoy.

In addition, the very fact that we are being trained to think that sex is (and should be) available to us at all times with a mere click of the mouse seems part and parcel of the capitalist mentality that presents consumerism as a solution to all of our problems; it explicitly promotes the idea that it is our inalienable right to "enjoy" the offerings of our affluent societies. The sad fact is that at the very moment that we experience ourselves as sexually "free" (better off than earlier generations), we are being instructed to desire in accordance with the desire of the big Other, including its desire to make money off our desire, whether directly through pornography or indirectly through our improved productivity. This is precisely why McGowan argues that "more enjoyment"—the unshackling of "bodies and pleasures" that Foucault advocates—does not represent an effective response to capitalism.

Clearly, then, it is extremely difficult to differentiate our desire from the desire of the Other. This makes it all the more noteworthy that Lacan conceptualizes ethics in terms of the subject's unwillingness to give ground on its desire. This is where Lacan's second definition of desire—desire as a stubborn fixation on objects that might confound the expectations of normative ideology—becomes relevant, for even though Lacan knew perfectly well how challenging it is to shatter the spell of biopolitical conditioning, his ethics of not ceding one's desire demands precisely the capacity to do so. In other words, though Lacan understood that there is no such thing as desire wholly divorced from its social environment, he believed that there are degrees of freedom and unfreedom, that some of our desires are more primary (fundamental to our basic constitution) than the desires driven by the master's morality and the service of goods. Such primary desires reach toward the rebellious drive energies (jouissance) of the real rather than the conformist symbolic, which is why our capacity to animate them is essential for our ability to defy the hegemonic decrees of the latter. In this sense, a kernel of identity-dissolving negativity—a trace of the (death) drive—may be found in more or less any desire that does not coincide with the desire of the Other, which may further explain why critics such as Žižek and Edelman so consistently slide from desire to the drive. However, in so doing they get stuck on the most extreme articulation of Lacanian ethics: the suicidal act as a rupturing of all social ties.

My interest, in contrast, lies in Lacan's suggestion that it is the task of psychoanalysis as a clinical practice—as a practice of ethics—to produce the kind of subject that might be able to attain a degree of critical distance from the desire of the Other (without thereby destroying itself as a subject of symbolic and relational capacity). In other words, I do not believe that one needs to follow Žižek and Edelman to the place of social suicide to appreciate the rebellious spirit of Lacanian ethics, for I think that Lacan implies that any subject who resists normative forms of desire by choosing to pursue the thread of its distinctive desire qualifies as a defiant subject. This is what Lacan is getting at when he states, "If analysis has a meaning, desire is nothing other than that which supports an unconscious theme, the very articulation of that which roots us in a particular destiny, and that destiny demands insistently that the debt be paid, and desire keeps coming back, keeps returning, and situates us once again in a given track, the track of something that is specifically our business" (1959–1960, 319).

Lacan here proposes that analysis enables us to understand something about the eccentric distinctiveness of our most fundamental desire as well as about the track of destiny that this desire carves out for us (and that is therefore "specifically our business"). This process entails, among other things, recognizing that the destiny we owe to our desire can never be definitively overcome, that the debt of desire can never be fully redeemed (for how are we to compensate the signifier for having brought us into being as subjects of desire?). Our destiny—which may sometimes coincide quite seamlessly with our repetition compulsion—consists of recurring efforts to pay off this debt, which is why it keeps ushering us to the same track of desire, the same nexus of psychic and affective conundrums, our unconscious hope being that if we wear out the track of our desire by incessant reiteration, one day we might be able to absolve ourselves of our debt. But since we cannot, the only thing to be done is to "own" our destiny even as we may seek to mitigate its more painful dimensions. In other words, the point of analysis is not to obliterate our psychic and affective destiny but merely to elaborate it in more satisfying directions, away from the incapacitating effects of the repetition compulsion and toward the rewards of subjective autonomy; the point is to peel off some of the layers of social conditioning so as to allow us to access forms of desire that might evade the demands of both conventional morality and economic exigency, that might express something elemental about our singular way of taking up the challenge of living.

The echo of the thing

Let me unpack this insight more carefully. The track of desire that Lacan is referring to must be understood in relation to what he, following Freud, calls the Thing (*das Ding*). Recall that, according to Lacan's theory of subject formation, we give up primordial jouissance for the signifier, unmediated pleasure for the capacity to desire. This dynamic becomes crystallized around the fantasy of having lost the Thing, the original (non)object that (supposedly) offered unmitigated jouissance. Nothing of course was lost in reality; there never was any unmitigated jouissance. But the fantasy of having lost this jouissance brings us into being as subjects of lack who experience ourselves as having been deprived of something unfathomably precious.

The result of this formative loss is that we spend our lives trying to find substitutes for what we imagine having lost: we stuff one object of desire after another into the void left by the signifier in the hope that one day we might be able to heal our wound (undo our alienation). More specifically, we pursue objects that seem to contain the *objet a*—the slice of sublimity or glowing ember—that, according to the logic of our fantasy life, has become sundered from the Thing and that consequently appears to resurrect something of the Thing's magnificence. Yet no object is ultimately able to satisfy us because the lack within our being is constitutive of our subjectivity and, as such, utterly irredeemable. In other words, the gap between the (fantasized) Thing as the (non)object that causes our desire and the objects (objects that appear to contain the all-important yet inscrutable *objet a*) that our desire discovers in the world is why we are never entirely satisfied.

McGowan is surely correct in proposing that capitalism's effectiveness arises from its capacity to exploit this gap between the Thing (as a wholly imaginary site of full satisfaction) and concrete worldly objects (which never fully satisfy): it is because of this gap that we are vulnerable to capitalism's promise that eventually we will chance upon a commodity that will complete our being. Yet if we approach the matter from the opposite direction, it is possible to argue that the gap between the Thing and worldly objects *is the very reason we are able to take any pleasure in objects in the first place.* After all, we are not constitutionally designed to endure unmediated jouissance—jouissance that closes the gap between the Thing and the object—for longer than fleeting moments of orgasmic bliss.

As Lacan notes, the Thing replicates the structure of the Kantian sublime object as what both causes our desire and threatens to engulf us, with the consequence that if we ever actually possessed it, we would instantly be overwhelmed by unmanageable jouissance; we would be extinguished as (sociosymbolically viable) subjects. From this point of view, it is only because we cannot have the Thing that pleasure—the kind of pleasure we are able to experience without destroying ourselves—emerges as an existential reality for us.

On my reading, this is what Lacan has in mind when he argues that the Thing is "found at the most as something missed. One doesn't find it, but only its pleasurable associations" (1959–1960, 52). "If the Thing were not fundamentally veiled," Lacan continues, "we wouldn't be in the kind of relationship to it that obliges us, as the whole of psychic life is obliged, to encircle it or bypass it in order to conceive it" (118). In other words, it is precisely because we feel that we have lost the Thing that we hunt for its "pleasurable associations," that we hunt for crumbs of sublimity that give us a little taste of the jouissance that is forbidden to us. Such crumbs may grant us mere muffled echoes of the original sublime object, yet they still manage to satisfy us because they transmit a muted imprint of this object.

Moreover, some objects satisfy us more than others for the simple reason that they contain a stronger echo of the Thing. Such special objects cause our desire to meet up and commingle with the jouissance of the drive, thereby bringing us within striking distance of the Thing. Yet because of the aforementioned gap between the Thing and all worldly objects, including the most satisfying ones, they do not push us fully into the whirlpool of jouissance. As a consequence, they bring us (some) satisfaction without causing an utter dissolution of subjectivity.

Notably, such special objects also give us a more enduring satisfaction than the ecstasy of undiluted jouissance (a.k.a. good sex). That such satisfaction is always partial at best does not, in my opinion, constitute a good enough reason for its categorical rejection. Surely the fact that objects never fully satisfy us—that they cannot definitively seal the void of our being—does not mean that they grant us no "real" satisfaction, that there is no jouissance to be had from our relationship to them. As Danny Nobus deftly conveys, "Any artificial stuffing of the hole in the Symbolic coincides with the production of jouissance" (31).

It is therefore because we are forced to approach the Thing obliquely, through the various objects of desire that we find in the world, that we are able to experience pleasure in manageable bits. This is how I interpret Lacan's claim that the Thing has the power to usher us onto a singular track of desire. This singularity arises from the fact that even though the loss of the Thing is a universal precondition of subjectivity, each of us relates to this loss in a manner that is wholly peculiar to us. More specifically, every object that we place into the void left by the Thing is, to borrow Lacan's term, "refound" in the sense that it always reflects something about our unique experience of the Thing as a site of melancholy yearning (1959–1960, 118).

This is why there tends to be a degree of consistency to our desire: we regularly find ourselves drawn to particular kinds of objects because these objects appear to resuscitate some of the Thing's aura for us. Such consistency, taken to an extreme, is what the repetition compulsion consists of. But it is also—and here we have reached the gist of my argument—at the core of the kind of stubborn desire that Lacan deems emblematic of the ethics of psychoanalysis, for the distinguishing feature of such desire is, precisely, its (obstinately consistent) singularity. The ethics of psychoanalysis "works" to the degree that it is able to conjure up this singularity, that it is able to revive forms of desire that owe their existence to the loss of the Thing rather than to social conditioning, for only such forms of desire have the power to resist the hegemonic desire of the Other. To state the matter more directly, if social conditioning gives rise to generic desires—desires that concur with the master's morality and the service of goods—the loss of the Thing produces inimitable desires (our specific track of desire), which is why the latter represent an ethical force that we can only betray by betraying something essential about our very being.

Outshining the lures of capitalism

It is true that capitalism generates sparkly objects to lure our desire. But not all objects of desire can be reduced to the economy of consumption. Lacan's analysis of the kind of desire that cathects to the echo of the Thing in worldly objects—that, as he puts it, raises such objects "to the dignity of the Thing" (1959–1960, 112)—explains why our object choices can sometimes be so idiosyncratic and unpredictable that they fall outside the utilitarian logic of neoliberal society. Along related lines, it explains why some things matter to us more than others, why we value some interpersonal relationships more than others, and perhaps even why some personal aspirations and modalities of life appeal to us more than others. It may even clarify why some books, poems, oceans, or skyscrapers please us more than others.

Lacan gives a number of concrete examples—which I here reproduce from my more extensive analysis in *The Singularity of Being*—of how an entirely mundane object can become invested with special meaning. One of the most compelling is his description of a decorative string of match boxes that one of his friends has hung around his mantle piece: "This arrangement demonstrated that a match box isn't simply something that has a certain utility, that it isn't even a type in the Platonic sense, an abstract match box, that the match box all by itself is a thing with all its coherence of being. The wholly gratuitous, proliferating, superfluous, and quasi absurd character of this collection pointed to its thingness as match box. Thus the collector found his motive in this form of apprehension that concerns less the match box than the Thing that subsists in a match box" (1959–1960, 114).

Lacan thus asserts that his friend's collection of match boxes reveals the "thingness"—rather than the utility or even the Platonic "type"—of the match box: it shows "that a box of matches is not simply an object, but that, in the form of an *Erscheinung*, as it appeared in its truly imposing multiplicity, it may be a Thing" (1959–1960, 114). Rather than being merely an assemblage of match boxes, the collection illuminates the trace of the Thing that "subsists" in the match box: it makes the sublime appear in the most commonplace of objects; it induces the Thing to materialize within the weave of everyday life.

Although Lacan goes on to admit that the match box "is a thing that is not, of course, the Thing"—that the ordinary object that his friend has elevated to the nobility of the Thing remains a substitute in the sense that it does not yield the Thing-in-itself—he insists that the example demonstrates "the sudden elevation of the match box to a dignity that it did not possess before" (1959–1960, 117–18). That is, the match box, in this particular instance, grants us a tiny bit of jouissance that connects us to the luster of the Thing.

Lacan maintains that something similar happens when we view an apple painted by Cézanne, for "everyone knows that there is a mystery in the way Cézanne paints apples, for the relationship to the real as it is renewed in art at that moment makes the object appear purified; it involves a renewal of its dignity by means of which these imaginary insertions are, one might say, repetitively restated" (1959–1960, 141). When Cézanne paints an apple, he "renews" its dignity. Inasmuch as his art forges a relationship to the real—to the dwelling place of the Thing—he taps into a mystery that resides beyond his skill at imitating his object. Cézanne's apple is never just a simple depiction of an apple, for the deeper objective of his art is a dimension that exceeds mere imitation: the singularity of his art resides in the fact that it "makes the object appear purified," that it manages to capture something about the enigma (and even the sublimity) of the Thing in its representation of an utterly banal object.

Lacan offers yet another example of how objects can emit the aura of the Thing in the following anecdote: Lacan and his wife are staying in a quaint London guesthouse. One morning, his wife comes back to their room and says that she knows that Professor D—one of Lacan's former mentors—is also in the guesthouse. Baffled, Lacan asks her how she knows this. She responds, "I've seen his shoes." Lacan reports that he remained skeptical, not willing to take a pair of worn clodhoppers outside a door "as sufficiently convincing evidence" (1959–1960, 296). But lo and behold, it turned out that Professor D *was* staying at the guesthouse, as Lacan discovered when he caught the esteemed professor slipping out of his room in his dressing gown, "exposing as he went a pair of long and highly academic drawers" (296).

Lacan segues from this anecdote to Van Gogh's painting of peasant shoes, famously analyzed by Heidegger, concluding that "any object may be the signifier by means of which that reflection, mirage, or more or less unbearable brilliance we call the beautiful starts to vibrate" (1959–1960, 297). A pair of clodhoppers, he asserts, may "in spite of its dumbness" (197) speak—and speak quite eloquently—about the singularity of its owner. Professor D's shoes, in short, were a site where "the universality belonging to the shoes of an academic was intimately joined to whatever it was that was absolutely specific to Professor D" (296–97).

If ordinary objects can "vibrate" on the unique frequency of a given individual—in this case Professor D—the reverse is also the case: we may feel irresistibly summoned by things (match boxes, apples, shoes, and so on) that correspond to the distinctive outlines of our desire. Even though we undoubtedly frequently fall for the lures of capitalism, we do usually know when we have stumbled upon the "real" thing; we know when we have discovered something that is not easily replaceable. This dynamic is perhaps most obvious in relation to people we love, as Lacan conveys when he proposes that when I desire you, it is because I perceive that there is "in you more than you" (Lacan 1964). This "in you more than you" is precisely the echo of the Thing that I have been talking about: it is the "extra" (the *objet a*) that is added to the desired person by the one who desires.

Because this formulation may sound like a recipe for narcissism, and because Lacan does admittedly sometimes read it as such, I want to stress that the "extra" added to the desired other is not a fabulous (narcissistically pleasing) part of the subject that the subject self-servingly deposits in the other in the hope that this other will then meekly reflect it back to the subject like a pristine mirror; it is not expressive of a definable quality that the subject of desire possesses (or could ever possess) but rather of its incapacity to coincide with itself. That is, insofar as desire arises from the subject's constitutive lack, the "extra" that this subject adds to its object is not a function of what it has (or could ever have) but rather of what it does not have, or more precisely, of what it only "has" as a ghostly trace of what it imagines having lost (the Thing). In other words, this "extra" will not bring narcissistic satisfaction in the form of self-completion even when this is what the subject may want.

I will return to relevant arguments about desire and love in Chapter 5. Here I merely want to mention that my reading of the singularity of desire—of desire's link to the inimitable destiny of each subject—is why I part ways with those, such as Edelman, who regard desire purely as a regressive quest for an imaginary wholeness. It may be true that desire on some level always strives to fill the void within the subject's being, but given that it never succeeds in this endeavor, I do not see any need to align it with narcissistic self-closure: the very inability of desire to fully attain the satisfaction it seeks guarantees the subject's continued status as a being of lack (and therefore of openness). In contrast, it is the subject of the drive—the subject who has no need for objects—that closes upon itself, that erases the distinction between solipsism and narcissism.

Let me press the argument a step further by proposing that desire, far from resulting in self-closure, *decenters the subject insofar as it centers on an object*: the more important the object becomes, the more the subject is drained of its ego-bound cohesiveness. Freud (1914) already made this point when he remarked that when we fall in love, we trade our ego cathexis for an object cathexis: we direct our libido away from the self toward the other (the object). What is more, as Roland Barthes (1977) hauntingly conveys through his "lover's discourse," the disappointments of desire can ravage us to the point of paralysis, with the result that even if self-completion is what we seek through our desire, this is frequently the last thing it delivers; the fantasies that desire generates may aim at the stabilization of life but the lived realities of desire tend to push us in the opposite direction of existential turmoil.

There are few psychic or affective events that cause us as much suffering as the loss of a lover who seemed to contain a morsel of the Thing. This alone illustrates why our cathexes cannot always be explained by capitalist brainwashing—why our desire is *not* always the desire of the Other: although it is in the interest of the neoliberal capitalist system to produce specific types of desires, it is surely not in its interest to devastate us to the point that we become incapable to upholding the service of goods—the principle of good performance—upon which the system is predicated.

The same could be said of our "bad" (wounding) attachments. Affect theorists such as Ahmed and Berlant have been able to offer convincing accounts of how we come to desire hegemonic modes of life. And McGowan provides a powerful depiction of how capitalism spawns the kinds of desires that generate surplus value. But attempts to theorize desire as a function of dominant ideology cannot explain the irrational manner in which we sometimes remain devoted to objects that we *know* are likely to make us miserable, sometimes because they are unavailable (already lost), sometimes because they are obviously injurious (such as hurtful lovers), and sometimes because they have been culturally deemed to be the cause of unhappiness (such as same-sex objects of desire). In other words, *while ideology critique explains why we attach ourselves to objects that promise happiness without delivering on this promise, it finds it more difficult to explain why we attach ourselves to objects that do not promise happiness, that are frank about the fact that they will never make us happy*. If our culture's ethos of positive thinking demands cheerfulness, then there is something extremely enigmatic about the kinds of desires that can only prolong our pain. In contrast, Lacan's theory of desire as a residue of the lost Thing sheds some light on such counterproductive attachments by illustrating the psychic mechanisms that render some relational ties virtually unbreakable.

The Thing's code of ethics

This dynamic of painful attachments can obviously lead to problematic levels of masochism. The fact that desire does not always promise us a better future—and that it cannot consequently always be thought of as an instance of cruel optimism—does not mean that it is not traumatizing. In many ways, this type of desire is merely more forthright about the trauma it inflicts. It does not ask us to dig for covert reasons for our misery but clearly shows that clinging to an object or scene of desire that hurts us . . . well, hurts us.

However, what most interests me in the present context is Lacan's claim that our allegiance to the Thing introduces a code of ethics that is drastically different from the master's morality. As he observes, "There is another register of morality that takes its direction from that which is to be found on the level of *das Ding*; it is the register that makes the subject hesitate when he is on the point of bearing false witness against *das Ding*, that is to say, the place of desire" (1959–1960, 109–10). This is an ethics that is not dictated by the practical imperatives of the service of goods but rather assesses the value of objects on the basis of their proximity to the Thing: the object that comes the closest to the Thing is, ethically speaking, more important than one that is merely useful.

Concretely speaking, whenever the Thing's echo reverberates strongly enough in the object we have selected, it overshadows the voices that might be telling us that we have made an imprudent choice. For example, those around us may attempt to convince us that we have fallen in love with a person of the "wrong" age, race, gender, ethnicity, religion, social class, or educational level. The miraculous thing about the Thing's echo is that it gives us the courage to fight the fight, so to speak; it is robust enough to override the warnings and cajolings of the social order, making it possible for us to desire in counterhegemonic ways.

Think of it this way: the vast machinery of our commercial culture works overtime to eclipse the Thing's aura: in a society of commodity fetishism, nothing is easier than losing sight of the singular track of our desire. Against this backdrop, insisting on this track becomes an ethical stance, making it possible for us to appreciate the preciousness of what we may be culturally encouraged to shun, ignore, or trivialize. When we raise a mundane object to the dignity of the Thing, we infuse it with the Thing's incomparable worth, thereby signaling that as far as our desire is concerned, only *this* object will do; we, in short, deem the object in question irreplaceable.

To the extent that we are able to do this, that we are able to insist on the singular track of our desire, we might be said to have inherited some of Antigone's insubordination. And to the extent that we are able to hold our ground in the face of the culture industry—to the extent that we are able to resist being seduced by the shiny decoys that this industry routinely throws at us—we are kept from becoming a mere cog in the commercial machine. This in turn offers some protection against the impression that the world is a lackluster place where nothing can rouse our passions or move us in any meaningful manner; to the degree that the Thing's aura lends mundane objects an exceptional dignity, it fends off the kind of complacency that strips the world of all ideals, all higher aspirations. But this only works if we are able to recognize the highly specific timbre of our desire, which is why Lacan is adamant that psychoanalysis should help us revere the specificity of our desire even when it would be easier to capitulate to the desire of the Other; it is why he asserts that there is nothing that is, ethically speaking, more important than not ceding our desire.

If McGowan (correctly) argues that capitalism exploits the structure of desire, I would add that our desire is also capable of arresting the restless movement of consumption that capitalism relies on: the subject who decides that "only this object will do" forsakes all alternative objects, thereby refusing to participate in the mentality that tells us that every object is disposable, that in fact encourages us to discard our objects almost as soon as we have acquired them. Such a subject of desire obstinately fixates on a specific object in ways that undermine capitalism's demand that we float from one object to the next in a frenzy of consumption. In this sense, our attachment to certain objects of desire can actually *counter* the ethos of the culture industry that the Frankfurt School criticized. The objects we attach to in this manner may fall short of the sublime object yet they still lend meaning to our lives.

Again, it is prudent to admit that this dynamic can have problematic consequences in the sense that it can induce us to injure ourselves for the sake of our object: Antigone is an extreme example of this; the masochistic lover who is unable to reject a beloved who repeatedly devastates him can be found at every street corner. Yet Lacan also suggests that there are times when our object deserves our loyalty, when the fact that some things matter to us more than others causes us to act ethically (as Antigone does in relation to Polyneces, and as any of us might do when we defend the object of our desire against external attempts to denigrate it). Either way, Lacan's ethics of not ceding one's desire explains why some of our object choices are so surprising, why we are capable of the kind of desire that defies the happiness narratives and economic objectives of our society. On an even more basic level, it explains why some objects incite our passion while others leave us cold or easily fall into oblivion; it explains why some things speak to us while others remain mute, why it is that some things transcend their "thingness" and come to signify on such a profound level that our attachment to them feels nonnegotiable.

Why is there so much anxiety?

My account of how Lacan's ethics of desire allows us to discriminate between objects that merit our attachment and others that do not makes it possible for me to speculate about why so many relatively well-off Western subjects—subjects who in principle do not have anything obvious, such as poverty, to worry about—seem these days to experience high levels of anxiety. Neoliberalism's heightened educational and professional (performance-related) demands are obviously a factor. But they do not seem to fully explain the phenomenon of extreme levels of anxiety among individuals who are not subject to systemic inequalities or uncertain about their ability to pay the bills. To borrow Kathleen Stewart's apt wording, we live in a society where "unwanted intensities simmer up at the least provocation" (47). Why?

In *Penis Envy and Other Bad Feelings*, I offer an extensive analysis of anxiety from a Lacanian viewpoint. Here I merely want to briefly discuss the prevalence of anxiety in relation to the injunction to enjoy that I mentioned above in the context of Žižek and Zupančič. My intuition is that this injunction generates a situation in which affluent and middle-class Western subjects are surrounded by so many objects of desire—objects that moreover appear to actually be available (in a way that they are not available to less privileged subjects)—that they lose the capacity to discriminate between these objects. This loss of the ability to cut a path through the ocean of sparkly objects, in turn, manifests itself as the kind of anxiety that seems to have no clear cause.

In his seminar on anxiety—*Seminar X*—Lacan discusses anxiety from two seemingly opposite directions. The first—which

I will only mention in passing—is the account that we might expect on the basis of earlier psychoanalytic models of anxiety, such as those of Freud and Klein: anxiety has to do with the fear of separation, so that the infant's dread of losing primordially significant things such as the penis (Freud's preoccupation) or the breast (Klein's preoccupation) gets translated into an adult dread of losing a part of oneself. This is how we end up at castration anxiety, analyzed by Lacan in *Seminar X* not just (literally) as a man's fear of losing his penis, but more generally (and metaphorically) as the subject's fear of losing mastery, of being found lacking in one way or another.

However, what is more relevant to us in the present context is that, in this seminar, Lacan does not limit his investigation of anxiety to castration anxiety. He pays equal attention to the ways in which anxiety is linked to the overproximity of the other. As he writes:

> I told you that anxiety isn't the signal of a lack, but of something that has to be conceived of at a duplicated level, as the failing of the support that lack provides. . . . Don't you know that it's not longing for the maternal breast that provokes anxiety, but its imminence? What provokes anxiety is everything that announces to us, that lets us glimpse, that we're going to be taken back onto the lap. It is not, contrary to what is said, the rhythm of the mother's alternating presence and absence. The proof of this is that the infant revels in repeating this game of presence and absence. The most anguishing thing for the infant is precisely the moment when the relationship upon which he's established himself, of the lack that turns him into desire, is disrupted, and this relationship is most disturbed when there is no possibility of any lack, when the mother is on his back all the while, and especially when she's wiping his backside. . . . Anxiety isn't about the loss of the object, but its presence. The objects are missing. (1962–1963, 53–54)

Here anxiety arises when the lack-in-being—gap, void, or absence—that sustains the subject's desire disappears: the subject gets terrified when it risks losing the lack that lends support to its subjectivity. The annulment of lack, and therefore of the capacity to desire, would result in the dissolution of the subject. What could be more anxiety producing than this?

Lacan's statement also implies that it is lack—in this case the mother's absence—that fosters creativity. The child revels in the game of fort-da only insofar as the mother is not there: the moment she becomes too present, too available, the creative impulse is extinguished. I have long argued (see Ruti 2009, 2012, 2015b, 2017) that, from a Lacanian point of view, creativity arises from lack, as Lacan clarifies in *Seminar VII* where he gives his famous account of the potter who fashions a vase around a void, his point being that the emptiness of the vase and the possibility of filling it, lack and the signifier, are introduced into the world simultaneously. More generally speaking, as I have emphasized, Lacan teaches us that it is only insofar as the subject lacks that it is compelled to turn outside of itself, exceed its own being, in quest of objects that might satisfy it. And sometimes the best (most satisfying and certainly most reliable) way to attain such objects is to create them.

When the subject loses its lack due to the overproximity of the other, it also loses its capacity for creativity. Lacan's allegory for this type of overproximity is the praying mantis that decapitates its mate after copulation. Even though losing one's head is obviously a form of castration—of (seriously) losing something—I think that what is most evocative about this image is the vision of claustrophobic closeness it offers. From this vision it is possible to jump to the idea that in late capitalist society, consumer goods take on the role of such a devouring praying mantis: they are everywhere, there are too many of them, and there is no way to avoid them unless one moves to some rock of an island accessible only by a row boat and devoid of Internet access.

It may be that walking into a well-stocked department store seems to alleviate the fear of nothingness, of castration: you buy stuff in order to fill the void within your being. Some people describe their experiences with shopping in these terms. However, it may also be that when we walk into the bowels of a huge department store, we walk into the claws of a giant praying mantis that produces anxiety because it throws too many items at us at once. Perhaps shopping lists are an attempt to cope with such anxiety: they delimit in advance the number of items to be acquired. At a grocery store that one frequents, shopping lists—or the mental imprint of a routine shopping list—streamline the process so one can ignore 99 percent of the available options. This explains why shoppers can experience a great deal of frustration when their grocery store reorganizes its stock: suddenly they are forced to search for their items amidst unfamiliar ones that assault their senses with their overproximity.

I recently witnessed this at my store which, due to renovations, shifted items to new positions, with the consequence that the store was suddenly filled with anxious customers whose discomfort about having to navigate their way through previously "invisible" items was palpable, and sometimes even explicitly articulated ("This is terrible; I can't find anything; why is there so much stuff here?; I just want to find the three items I came in for").

Those who have known deprivation can get anxious because they fear that they might once again experience it: an older friend of mine who experienced depression-era scarcity stocks her fridge so full that when you open the door, items—many of them molding or rotting—fall out. When I ask her why she does this, she says that she gets anxious about running out of food. Rational explanations about how she only needs one bag of onions at any given time do not make a dent in her affective response to the idea of not having enough. When I tell her that my fridge on average holds about seven items, her eyes turn into petrified saucers. Weirdly, I also experienced a scarcity of food—not exactly hunger but the constant threat of going hungry—growing up, but my reaction to this legacy is the opposite of hers: I reckon that seven items is more than what I used to have so that it must be plenty. And I get anxious when the fridge gets too full (which only happens when I have visitors I need to feed): twelve items are just too many.

What produces anxiety is thus unpredictable, but Lacan's observation that it arises either in response to the possibility of lack/loss or in response to potentially engulfing excess/overproximity explains at least some of it. My sense is that those neoliberal subjects who have grown up in the lap of luxury (not just in their solicitous mother's lap but in the lap of overstocked stores) might well experience it when there is no escape from this lap. This is where self-sabotage becomes tempting: you scratch your hardwood floors, you drive your Porsche into a lamppost, you dump the lover who seems too loving. You ruin the good things you have so as to reintroduce lack and dissatisfaction into your life. If McGowan is right that it is ultimately our dissatisfaction that satisfies us—that it is the drive's inability to attain its goal that is its ultimate aim—such behavior makes perfect sense. And the death drive is obviously never far from the picture.

The predicament of finding it challenging to cope with excess is unlikely to elicit much sympathy from those who have experienced too much of the kind of context-specific lack, such as poverty or racism, that exceeds the Lacanian lack-in-being (more on this in the next chapter). But a cognizance of the anxiety that excess can cause may be one way to grasp why anxiety is so rampant in today's affluent Western society. This society of the spectacle, as Julia Kristeva (2002) calls it—this society of countless commodities, endless entertainment, and limitless information on the Internet—creates anxiety by virtue of its abundance. Or to state the matter differently, the problem is that this bloated, oversaturated society robs us of the ability to distinguish between objects of desire, goals, ideals, aspirations, and preoccupations that are meaningful and others that perhaps are not. It distracts us from our lack—the support of our subjectivity—so thoroughly that we no longer feel any clear connection to this subjectivity.

Desire as a remedy to anxiety

The steady stream of commodities and stimulations offered by the society of the spectacle augments the overagitation that many subjects might feel even without this added incitement: their attention is so diffuse, so indiscriminately dispersed over various objects and preoccupations, that their desire cannot find a resting place, with the result that this desire gets replaced with anxiety. Interestingly, Nietzsche already diagnosed the restlessness that ensues from the scattering of desire—a theme I discuss in Chapter 6. Here it suffices to note that there appear to be two nonpharmaceutical remedies to this quandary.

The first is implied by Lacan's analysis of creativity as a sublimatory undertaking. For many artistic people, creative activity "burns off" anxiety so that while they create, they do not feel anxious. And sometimes the effect lingers, so that the aftermath of creative spurts is devoid of anxiety. But because the effect of reducing anxiety through creativity never endures indefinitely, individuals who respond to this effect must repeatedly find new ways of entering into creative activity. They write book after book, paint apple after apple, and compose song after song, because this is the only way to keep anxiety at bay.

The person who deploys desire in its more direct (less sublimated) form—the person who moves from one commodity to the next—attempts to attain the same effect, to gain relief from anxiety: hence the afterglow of shopping sprees. But this strategy is always temporary, which is why those addicted to shopping will head back to the store (or online site) almost as soon as they have taken the tags off the items they have just purchased.

The opposite of this scenario—and the second "remedy" I want to reference—is the one I have described in this chapter: the situation where the subject's desire is cathected to a specific object so strongly that it loses interest in all others. This dynamic can apply to inanimate objects so that, for instance, your love of your coat makes you uninterested in buying a new one even when the old one no longer keeps you warm. But it is most obvious in the context of the subject's desire for a beloved person who, as I have said, feels irreplaceable.

In his seminar on transference (*Seminar VIII*), Lacan supports this reading when he connects the truth of the subject's desire, the kind of desire that does not allow itself to be derailed by social demands, to the alleviation of anxiety, arguing that a "slight lifting of anxiety . . . occurs every time the subject's desire is truly at work" (1960–1961, 368). Lacan continues as follows: "If anxiety is what I told you it is, a relationship that props up desire where the object is lacking, then by inverting the terms, we see that desire is a remedy for anxiety. We observe this constantly in psychoanalytic practice. Anyone who is slightly neurotic knows as much about it as you do, if not even more. The support found in desire, as awkward as desire may be given all the guilt that accompanies it, is still much easier to maintain than the position of anxiety" (370).

The fixation of desire—the kind of fixation that those who are "slightly neurotic" (and who isn't?) experience—is here "a remedy for anxiety." If desire that cannot settle anywhere, that roams around without any moorings, causes anxiety, the fixity of desire, though often a sign of neurosis, counters it. Perhaps this is why Freud thought that it is necessary to love in order to not fall seriously ill (rather than remain merely slightly neurotic). In any case, Lacan here suggests that as derailing or awkward as desire can be, it is still easier to bear than anxiety, for which it offers a paradoxical kind of antidote. As Lacan explains, when the subject's desire is "truly at work," anxiety is alleviated. Inversely, when desire is absent, when there is no possibility of genuine desire—perhaps because there is nothing, no object to truly desire, or because there are so many objects that the truth of your desire remains obscure—anxiety is heightened.

I do not think that there is any reason to interpret Lacan's commentary on desire and anxiety as a conservative defense of monogamy. Rather, the idea is merely that those whose desire is "truly at work" may be less prone to anxiety than those whose desire remains so dispersed that they cannot focus on a particular object with any degree of genuine passion. This has nothing to do with the securities of marriage, as our doctors sometimes try to tell us. I can well imagine a situation where desire is "truly at work" in the context of a fleeting connection: it is not the longevity of the encounter but its intensity that matters. If anything, longevity might well destroy the necessary intensity, might well keep desire from being "truly at work" (which is arguably exactly what happens in many marriages), in which case relationality would not offer any antidote to anxiety.

This is an instance in which I reason differently from Badiou: I do not believe that the event of love requires the fidelity of endless labor, as he often suggests. Yet I also do not want to veer too far in the opposite direction of valorizing situations where the restless subject compulsively pursues new objects. As I see it, there is a difference between sitting at a bar chatting with someone while simultaneously eyeing the other prospects in one's vicinity (or checking one's phone) on the one hand, and sitting at a bar chatting with someone in a manner that causes one's surroundings to fall into oblivion on the other. The former is a scene of anxiety; the latter is a scene of concentrated desire. I do not care how long (an hour or a lifetime) it lasts; the important part is the affect (anxiety or desire) it carries.

Again, a comparison to creative activity may clarify the distinction. When I sit at my computer trying to write a book while also keeping an eye on my email, anxiety is what I am likely to feel. But when I write in a space where I have no access to my email, anxiety recedes and the joy of creative labor—the concentration of desire on the task at hand—flows freely. In this context, it is worth considering the extent to which our society renders the latter scenario more or less impossible. Both those who lead privileged lives of intellectual labor and those whose lives are so precarious that they are required to hold multiple jobs in order to make a living are forced to multitask in ways that prevent them from focusing on one object of desire—in this case one task—at a time.

Vassilis Tsianos and Dimitris Papadopoulos offer an excellent description of this state of affairs—one that Berlant reproduces in the context of arguing that the politico-affective situation of contemporary subjects frequently entails messy situations, gestures, and scenes rather than dramatic events. This distinction between dramatic events (which is what Lacanian political theorists tend to focus on) and piecemeal quotidian scenes (which affect theorists such as Berlant tend to focus on) will be the topic of the next chapter. The "archive of exemplary bodily adjustments" that arises in response to anxiety-inducing lives—the "series of nervous-system symptoms" experienced by those who perform mental labor—that Berlant lifts from Tsianos and Papadopoulos provides an apt preface to the discussion to come (Berlant 2011, 196–97).

This series of symptoms is worth quoting in its entirety:

> (a) vulnerability: the steady experience of flexibility without any form of protection; (b) hyperactivity: the imperative to accommodate constant availability; (c) simultaneity: the ability to handle at the same [time] the different tempi and velocities of multiple activities; (d) recombination: the crossings between various networks, social spaces, and available resources; (e) post-sexuality: the other as dildo; (f) fluid intimacies: the bodily production of indeterminate gender relations; (g) restlessness: being exposed to and trying to cope with the overabundance of communication, cooperation and interactivity; (h) unsettledness: the continuous experience of mobility across different spaces and time lines; (i) affective exhaustion: emotional exploitation, or, emotion as an important element for the control of employability and multiple dependencies; (j) cunning: able to be deceitful, persistent, opportunistic, a trickster. (Berlant 2011, 197)

The only item on this list that does not strike a chord with me is the one about indeterminate gender relations. For me, it is determinate (inflexible, predictable, normative) gender relations that cause anxiety. But the rest of the list captures exactly what I mean about desire being too diffuse, too free floating, too detached from meaningful objects. Berlant links the items on Tsianos and Papadopoulos's list to an argument about the retraining of "ordinary affective states" that late capitalist society demands of its subjects. This retraining goes beyond what Berlant, following Adam Phillips, portrays as "psychoanalytic training in contingency management": the ability "to live and flourish under conditions of ongoing disorientation and insecurity" (2011, 197; 194). Such "psychoanalytic training" is what Lacan depicts as the attempt to persuade analysands that there is no cure for the distortions of human subjectivity. In contrast, as Berlant explains, the retraining of "ordinary affective states" demanded by late capitalism entails the psychically and affectively draining necessity of embarking on a ceaseless effort to learn "how to maintain footing, bearings, a way of being, and new modes of composure amid unraveling institutions and social relations of reciprocity" (197).

We have here arrived at two very different levels of distortion—of lack, anxiety, or alienation. While Lacanian political theorists usually remain on the level of the "psychoanalytic training" that aspires to teach subjects to cope with constitutive (existential) disorientation and insecurity, affect theorists are more interested in the debilitating "ordinary affective states" (context-specific terrors) that characterize inegalitarian neoliberal society. The objective of the next chapter is to move between these two levels in a manner that illustrates that Lacanian theory and affect theory do not need to be at odds but can instead enrich each other.

4

Rupture or resignation?

Lacanian political theory versus affect theory

In the preceding chapters, I have outlined some of the revolutionary rhetoric that characterizes Lacanian political theory. We have seen that Lacan's ethics of psychoanalysis as an ethics of the act, of rejecting "the morality of the master" (1959–1960, 315), has given rise to a rich, if at times contested, lineage of theorizing about revolt, defiance, self-pulverization, and event-driven ethics in the work of Alain Badiou, Slavoj Žižek, Lee Edelman, Paul Eisenstein, and Todd McGowan. In this chapter, I return to some aspects of this lineage in order to consider its complex relationship to affect theory, arguably its most powerful contestant within today's progressive critical-theoretical terrain. If back in 2000, the battle lines seemed to be drawn primarily between Žižek's Lacanian and Butler's Foucauldian approaches (see, for instance, Butler, Laclau, and Žižek 2000), the rapid rise of affect theory has changed—or at least recalibrated—the terms of the debate.

I do not mean to say that Butlerian theory and affect theory are at odds, for affect theory owes a great deal to Butler, not only to her early theorization of the relationship between the psychic and the social but also to her more recent theorization of the centrality of grievability and mourning to posthumanist ethics. I also do not mean to say that Lacanian theorists and affect theorists are engaged in an open scuffle, except perhaps in the 2014 exchange between Edelman and Berlant in *Sex, or the Unbearable* (to which I will briefly refer below). Nevertheless, as I demonstrated in *The Ethics of Opting Out*, the differences between Lacanian political theory and affect theory are responsible for some of the major rifts within recent queer theory, which in turn informs a whole host of other theoretical trends.

This is why I believe that it is impossible to understand the underlying reasons for the obstinate conflicts that characterize the contemporary critical-theoretical terrain without understanding the different inflections of Lacanian theory and affect theory. Lacanian theory—particularly Lacanian *political* theory, which will be the focus of this chapter—and affect theory find it difficult to speak to each other in anything but exasperated tones. Yet—as my discussion of Eisenstein and McGowan (Lacanian political theory) and Ahmed (affect theory) in Chapter 1 already illustrated—they both manage to speak to me, frequently for seemingly incompatible reasons, which is why I want to devote this chapter to an examination of some of their idiosyncrasies in the hope that doing so will open a theoretical clearing that allows for communication to flow between them without suffocating what is distinctive about each.

The event, the act

Because I have already discussed Badiou, Žižek, Eisenstein, and McGowan, I have provided the main outlines of the Lacanian approach. We have seen that the event, act, or rupture reconfigures the subject (or a collective "situation") in ways that make its established manner of living (or the established version of the collective arrangement) unfeasible. As Žižek explains the event/act, "An Absolute intervenes which derails the balanced run of our daily affairs: it is not so much that the standard hierarchy of values in inverted—it is much more radical, another dimension enters the scene, a different level of being" (2014, 72). The most succinct definition of "an authentic act," according to Žižek, is the following: "In our ordinary activity, we effectively just follow the (virtual-fantasmatic) co-ordinates of our identity, while an act proper is the paradox of an actual move which (retroactively) changes the very virtual, 'transcendental' co-ordinates of its agent's being" (128). The act, Žižek concludes, is "a contingent decision whose outcome defines the agent's entire life" (128). Caesar only becomes Caesar by crossing the Rubicon. A revolutionary only becomes a revolutionary by engaging in revolutionary action. And a lover only becomes a lover by falling madly in love.

Žižek thus reproduces the main outlines of Badiou's theory of the event: a contingent event retroactively creates its own necessity, so that it comes to seem inevitable, as what was fated to happen all along. The subject who is brought into being in this manner then faces the challenge of staying fateful to the repercussions of the event regardless of how impossible such faithfulness may appear, regardless of how tempting it might be to give up due to self-doubt, exhaustion, obstacles, or external opposition. Although even Badiou admits that an event is frequently replaced by a new event, that the subject always lives "between two events," in "the interval between the past event and the coming event" (2014, 13), he regards fidelity to the life-altering event—be it in the realm of politics, science, art, or love—as essential.

Both Žižek and Badiou furthermore complain that one of the main problems with capitalism is that it denies the possibility of paradigm-shifting events, thereby making it look like neoliberal consumerism (our market-driven economy) is our only option, that no definitive break from this order of things is possible. Badiou notes that we seem to be caught between pornography and mysticism, between rampant commercialism and "the sinister invocation of tradition," exemplified for instance by "the return of the religious" in its most fundamentalist and violent forms (2014, 78). Even though the return of fundamentalist religion might at first glance look like an event, for Badiou it is a mere simulacrum because, like Nazi Germany, it relies on an ideal of a unified tradition that cannot but exclude those who do not belong to its paradigm whereas a genuine event would arise from the place of exclusion, from the place of the "part of no-part" that I have mentioned several times.

On the side of affect theory, there are those who might insist that Islamic extremism—as opposed to Christian extremism—emerges from a place of exclusion, that it represents precisely the "part of no-part." But Žižek and Badiou ban from their theorization of the event anything that aims at unification, anything that rallies people around the ideal of an integrated tradition, culture, or custom. The reason for this is simple: unification and integration by definition demand the elimination of those who do not fit into the reigning template. This is why tradition, culture, and custom, for Žižek and Badiou, are intrinsically conservative formations that impede the advent of authentic events.

The "global process of dis-eventualization" (Žižek 2014, 146) that capitalism (and the invocation of tradition as a response to capitalism) produces erects invisible barriers to genuine transformation: even though we live in a frantic, fast-moving society where change is endemic, where the demand for productivity, performance, and constant self-reinvention can make it virtually impossible to find a moment of rest, nothing ultimately changes in any meaningful manner. In other words, it is part of the current collective status quo to insist that events in the sense that Badiou and Žižek understand them—as radical openings to new possibilities, to new subjective and collective configurations—are inherently impossible. Religious fundamentalism in this vision is no better than global capitalism: both lead to dis-eventualization.

The sublimity of failure

In this context, I want to revisit Eisenstein and McGowan's theory of rupture—the universalist aspects of which I discussed in Chapter 1—because it represents the most convincing, yet largely overlooked, elaboration of the event that I have come across. Eisenstein and McGowan convey what they mean by rupture via vocabulary that echoes that of Badiou and Žižek, but they add an important insight by explicitly linking rupture to the Lacanian subject of lack (the subject of signification), suggesting that the emergence of this subject—the severance from nature that this emergence represents—is the original event (or rupture) that all subsequent events (or ruptures) are modeled after:

> A rupture occurs when the coordinates that organize existence undergo a shift, such as when culture emerges out of the natural order. The emergence of culture out of nature is the fundamental and foundational rupture, but throughout history this same process happens through the introduction of a hitherto impossible idea whose emergence transforms the terrain of the possible. . . . From the perspective prior to their onset, these

> events are impossible, and yet transpire nonetheless. Rupture is the occurrence of the impossible, when the very ground under our feet shifts in order to transform the point from which we see. (4)

Eisenstein and McGowan's characterization of the emergence of culture out of nature as "the fundamental and foundational rupture" gestures toward the basic psychoanalytic, and particularly Lacanian, idea that subjectivity arises through a break from nature (through a break from biology).

As we know, in Lacanian theory, it is the signifier that brings the subject into being. More precisely, it is the lack-in-being introduced by the signifier that brings the subject into being as a subject of discourse, as a socially viable subject with a connection to the big Other. The subject's connection to the Other may be antagonistic, yet in the absence of some sort of a link to the symbolic order, the subject would cease to function as a subject; it would fall into psychosis. This in turn means that human subjectivity is intrinsically alienated from nature: derailed, distorted, contorted, and devoid of the capacity for any unmediated relationship with its bodily experience (except in fleeting moments of jouissance). In Eisenstein and McGowan's words, subjectivity is always "dislocated and damaged in relation to its being" (193).

This way of conceptualizing subjectivity allows Eisenstein and McGowan to offer a compelling explanation for the distinction between humans and other animals. They emphasize that the rupture between the human and the animal does not mean that humans are superior to animals; instead, it means that humans are "maladjusted animals, deformed by the signifier and no longer capable of fulfilling their needs without sustaining the self-destructiveness of their drive" (34). Let me quote them at length:

> Humanity has a value not because of its dignity but because of the sublimity of its failure. It is the being for which failure counts as the only possible success. For the human, the repetition of the drive provides suffering, but it is also the source of the subject's enjoyment. Rather than being the master of the animal kingdom, it is a misfit there. . . . Rather than minimizing the difference between the human and other animals, we see this difference as fundamental—not because the human is endowed with a soul

> that the animal lacks but because, as a speaking subject, the human is no longer simply a living being, in contrast to the rest of the animal world. While other animals are just animals and live out their instincts rather than relating to them, the human animal fails to coincide with itself; it is inhuman. The human is the political animal because of the interruption in its biology; psychoanalysis is the first theory to recognize this interruption that derives from the subject's entrance into the realm of the signifier. (34, 193)

Three insights arise from Eisenstein and McGowan's statement that are worth elaborating. First, note the emphasis on failure, on failure as "the only possible success" that is available to the human subject (a notion that resonates with McGowan's claim, discussed in the previous chapter, that what satisfies us is our dissatisfaction). What Eisenstein and McGowan are referring to is the idea that the subject inevitably fails to realize its desire even when there are no obvious obstacles preventing this realization.

In the last chapter, I proposed that the subject's inability to obtain the ultimate object of its desire, the Thing, does not cancel out its capacity to attain some satisfaction—some glimmer of the Thing—from mundane objects; I focused on the satisfaction that is available to the subject rather than on its impossibility. But this does not mean that I do not appreciate Eisenstein and McGowan's way of expressing the matter, for it is true that failure—the repetition of the failure to attain its object—is built into human desire in the sense that, as I have conceded, no object can bring the complete satisfaction that the subject (fantasmatically) seeks. This is because, as Eisenstein and McGowan state, "the human is a being driven to sabotage itself and to repeat the initial loss that constitutes it as a subject" (34). It is for this reason that the human is defined by "the sublimity of its failure."

Eisenstein and McGowan postulate that the subject is driven to repeat the loss of the Thing, and the experience of being rendered lacking (castrated) that this loss implies, indefinitely; instead of finding satisfaction, the subject repeats the failure of satisfaction. This is the repetition compulsion at its purest—on the most fundamental, fate-defining level that the death drive operates. Yet Eisenstein and McGowan speculate that even though the death drive functions destructively, making it impossible for the subject to coincide with itself, to fulfill its desire, the repetition that the death drive imposes on the subject nevertheless also on some level satisfies it; in the context of the repetition compulsion, suffering and enjoyment cannot easily be disentangled. The failure of satisfaction is what ultimately satisfies the subject precisely because it guarantees the persistence of the object as lost.

Given that it is only insofar as the object is lost that there is a subject—a subject of lack (a human subject of signification rather than an animal driven by its instincts)—to begin with, only the repetition of this loss (of the constitutive lack that brings the subject into being) can offer the subject any satisfaction. Stated differently, given that it is only insofar as the subject exists as a subject of the drive (rather than of animal instinct) that it exists as a human being, only the repetition of the drive (to fail) can offer it any satisfaction. In this sense, it is the inhuman within the human, the human's propensity to mechanically repeat the loss of its object, that distinguishes it from other animals. As Eisenstein and McGowan state, "The drive that subtends this repetition—the death drive—separates the human from its animality" (35).

Second, Eisenstein and McGowan remind us that psychoanalysis was the first theory to recognize the "interruption that derives from the subject's entrance into the realm of the signifier": one of Freud's most significant contributions to the history of thought was to discern that the human and the animal find satisfaction in very different ways, and that for the human, satisfaction (enjoyment) is inevitably linked to loss, failure, repetition, and the death drive. In other words, there is nothing straightforward or straightforwardly biological about human satisfaction, which is why human subjects, unlike other animals, constantly reflect on—and even obsess about—the complexities of their (dis)satisfaction (and other related "existential" matters).

On a basic level, this is why we need psychoanalysis: if humans were able to find satisfaction straightforwardly, without suffering, no one would seek out a psychoanalyst (or a therapist, psychiatrist, psychic, astrologer, meditation guru, or drug dealer). In other words, the level of dissatisfaction—of anxiety, depression, psychosomatic pain, and other "distortions" of being—even among those (say, the wealthy and the "healthy") who in principle have no reason to feel tormented reveals the degree to which humans are "dislocated" in relation to their own satisfaction.

At the end of the last chapter, I linked the excessive levels of anxiety that characterize contemporary Western societies to social factors, particularly to the profusion of commodities and constant overstimulation. And as I will argue below, generally speaking I believe that it is possible to distinguish between constitutive forms of dissatisfaction—forms of dissatisfaction (losses, failures) that are intrinsic to human life—on the one hand and forms of dissatisfaction that are politically, economically, and socially generated (context-specific, circumstantial) on the other. But this does not lessen my appreciation for the fact that one of the most fundamental lessons of Freudian psychoanalysis—the legacies of which Lacan sought to defend against those who insisted that psychoanalysis could render analysands "whole," "balanced," or "adjusted"—is that there is a level of constitutive dissatisfaction (the death drive) that resides beyond any possibility of a cure. As Lacan maintains, for the human subject, there is no Sovereign Good (1959–1960, 300).

In Lacan's opinion, the object relations theorists and ego-psychologists, including Anna Freud, who followed Freud squandered the radical edge of psychoanalysis when they started trying to heal people of their pathologies (or "distortions") so as to allow them to better fit into their social environment. Lacan believed—correctly I think—that one of Freud's most valuable insights was to recognize the extent to which the social environment, the big Other and its systems of signification, is what causes "distortion" (suffering) to begin with, and that once this distortion has been introduced, it cannot be conjured away: it becomes constitutive rather than circumstantial. That is, although many forms of human suffering are caused by context-specific factors that could be eradicated through more egalitarian social arrangements, there is always a part of this suffering that, independently of circumstances, has to do with the simple fact that human subjectivity is born through a painful encounter with the signifier. This part is what cannot be alleviated through improvements in the collective organization. As Eisenstein and McGowan explain, "Patients come to the psychoanalyst because they are suffering when they shouldn't be suffering. . . . It turns out, however, that the damage done by the signifier cannot be so easily repaired" (194).

Once lack has been introduced into human "being" through the signifier—once the subject of the signifier has come into existence—the subject can no longer find satisfaction by directly attaining its object;

it is a "misfit" within the animal kingdom because its satisfaction can only be sought through the structure of the signifier. This is why it cannot experience satisfaction without lack, without failure. In the best scenario, the subject's distortion can merely be transmuted into a different form of distortion. This is what sublimation in the Freudian sense aims to accomplish: the conversion of one form of distortion into another, perhaps more tolerable one.

As I have argued, the loss of the original object, the Thing, is always a retroactive fantasy: the subject has not in reality lost an object but merely (unconsciously, nostalgically) concocts a special object of loss that becomes privileged precisely inasmuch as it remains lost. In analyzing the loss of the Thing, Lacan is emphatically not talking about the loss of an actual object—such as the mother, the breast, or the bottle—but about the fantasmatic conjuring into existence of a sublime object that promises wholeness (the undoing of alienation). This promise is illusory, but it is what motivates the subject to repeat its failure to attain its object as its only mode of satisfaction (which, incidentally, implies that a version of cruel optimism may be built into the very constitution of subjectivity).

Third, although the lengthy quotation from Eisenstein and McGowan that I provided above does not address the matter directly, it reminds—should remind—us of the reasons for which Lacanian psychoanalysis was instrumental to the rise of deconstructive feminism, to feminist theory spanning from the feminist film theory of the 1970s to the feminist/queer theory of the 1990s: precisely because Lacan stressed the manner in which the signifier dissociates human beings from any possibility of biological immediacy, he gave feminist theorists the tools to dismantle the naturalistic gender system that had reigned—and severely constrained the lives of people of all genders, particularly women and the ambiguously gendered—since time immemorial. Despite what Lacan's critics sometimes assume, Lacan is nothing but consistent on this point, insisting on the mediation of the signifier in all "bodily" matters, all the way to his extensive commentary on the phallus.

The phallus as lack

Lacan has often been accused of phallocentrism. Even Judith Butler, who in her early work drew heavily on Lacanian theory, makes this accusation in her 2000 exchange with Laclau and Žižek in *Contingency, Hegemony, Universalism*. Yet a careful reading of Lacan's seminars reveals that nothing could be further from the truth. It shows that the deconstructive feminists who relied on Lacan's insights about the socially constructed nature of every aspect of human experience were right on target: because Lacan believes that even the drives have come into contact with the signifier, there is for him no such thing as a biological human "instinct" of any kind. Likewise, there is no feeding breast that does not contain a social message. There is no penis that can live up to the cultural mythology of phallic power. There is no "lack" in the woman (beyond the constitutive lack that characterizes human subjectivity as such) that is not a heteropatriarchal invention. And there is no penis envy that is not a result of social relations of power.

As Lacan insists with regard to penis envy: "Of course it's symbolic. It is in so far as the woman is in a symbolic order with an androcentric perspective that the penis takes on this value" (1954–1955, 272). In this sense, there is nothing missing in the woman; there is only the heteropatriarchal fantasy that she lacks something that the man has. If anything, if she lacks "it," so does the man, for the phallus "only ever appears as a lack" (1962–1963, 269). The phallus may be "called upon to function as an instrument of might," but "this is an illusory game" (269). The phallus, in other words, is nothing but a signifier of lack, of the (male) subject's failure to coincide with itself: phallic "detumescence" (the inevitable outcome of every erection) demonstrates this in the most concrete manner conceivable. As Lacan humorously puts it, in the (hetero)sexual act, the penis always yields, ducks out of the game, prematurely, becoming "no more than a scrap" that is of no use to the woman "save as a keepsake, a souvenir of tenderness" (264).

This "evanescence" of phallic capacity is why the penis only has power as long as it remains invisible: the minute it is unveiled, it loses its aura of empowerment; the actuality of crinkly flesh can never live up to the cultural hype (1962–1963, 265). Lacan argues that this is why heteropatriarchal society asks women to prop up men's egos by pretending that phallic power possesses the kind of validity that it absolutely does not in reality have: according to heteropatriarchal reasoning, it is the woman's task "to offer man's desire the object behind the phallic claims, the non-detumescent object to sustain his desire, namely, to make her feminine attributes the signs of man's almightiness" (265). That is, women are expected to play down their power in order to buttress men's imaginary phallic power, to translate the detumescent object into an (almighty) tumescent one. In this, Lacan's argument is essentially identical to that of Virginia Woolf.

Eisenstein and McGowan are able to remind us of Lacan's importance to feminist theory more convincingly than Badiou and Žižek in part because—despite their revolutionary rhetoric—their emphasis ultimately lies on failure (precisely, "detumescence") as the quintessential experience of human subjectivity. It also helps that they believe that female thinkers are worth talking about. Besides Lacan, they name Walter Benjamin, Hannah Arendt, Rosa Luxemburg, Jean-Paul Sartre, Simone de Beauvoir, and Frantz Fanon as the twentieth-century critics who understand, and remain faithful to, the traumatic impact of rupture, who do not flee from the antagonism, interruption, and disarray necessary for revolutionary change.

As I noted in Chapter 1, Foucault does not receive an equally welcoming reception from Eisenstein and McGowan. In their dismissal of Foucault, they once again follow Badiou and Žižek, who tend to be similarly skeptical of Foucault. This is one of the main reasons for the split between Lacanian political theory and affect theory that I am working toward, for affect theory, like Butlerian theory, tends to work with a loosely Foucauldian understanding of social power and biopolitics.

In *The Ethics of Opting Out*, I argued that the conceptual divide between Lacan and Foucault is less pronounced than most critics appear to believe. And in Chapter 1, I suggested that Eisenstein and McGowan may underestimate the degree to which Foucault also regards antagonisms (resistances to power) as an intrinsic component of every system of power. Nevertheless, it is true that Foucault advocates an incremental rather than a revolutionary approach to social change whereas Eisenstein and McGowan, arguing from a more Lacanian perspective, place an emphasis on the break from social context that rupture (the event, the act) represents. And as we have seen, they flee the particularism of Foucault to a place of universality.

Different levels of negation

The disagreement between (Foucauldian) particularism and (Lacanian) universalism is worth revisiting because I believe that it is perhaps the most far-reaching rift in contemporary progressive theory—the rift of rifts that generates a great deal of related animosity. As my outline of Ahmed's critique of Žižek and Badiou in Chapter 1 illustrated, this disagreement creates a more or less insurmountable obstacle between affect theory and Lacanian theory. In that context, I argued that while affect theorists (not just Ahmed, but generally speaking) regard the universal as a malicious master signifier—a big U propagated by the big Other—that is brutally imposed on those who cannot, or do not want to, live up to its (white masculinist) ideals, Lacanian political theorists, in pointed contrast, celebrate the universal as what unites those who find themselves *excluded* from our society's constellation of master signifiers: those who feel either destitute or excessive, who grasp their denigrated status as the tainted remainder that has been excised from dominant society. In other words, if affect theorists focus on the manner in which not being included, not belonging, in the universal damages those who are deemed too "particular," Lacanian theory insists that it is precisely not being included—not belonging—that allows a given subject to participate in the universal in the first place.

Recall that for Lacanians universality is inextricable from singularity, that they believe that it is possible for the singular to participate directly in the universal. This is why the contrast that Eisenstein and McGowan set up between Foucault's "historicist" defense of particularity and their own defense of singularity is simultaneously a contrast between Foucault's rejection of universalism and the Lacanian defense of universalism. Affect theorists have for the most part followed Foucault's lead, which is why the particular for them functions as a way to displace the hegemonic universal and to question the potentially individualistic singular. For Lacanians, in turn, the universal is what dislodges the oppressive particular: the particular that holds subjects hostage to tyrannical forms of tradition, culture, and custom.

Besides the distinction between Lacan and Foucault, this antagonism regarding the political valence of the universal can be traced to the (related) fact that, as I just noted, it is possible to think about lack, negation, and distortion on two very different levels:

the subject's constitutive lack-in-being and more context-specific, circumstantial forms of wounding. It is unfortunate that most Lacanians tend to be primarily interested in the former whereas most affect theorists focus on the latter. That is, although affect theorists do not usually deny that human beings are intrinsically (ontologically) lacking, they tend to be more attentive to forms of negation that operate beyond the foundational negation—or rupture—that brings the subject into existence as a subject of signification; they tend to emphasize the ways in which different subjects are differentially negated by political, economic, and social inequalities, with the result that, from their point of view, the Lacanian accent on ontological lack comes across as too generalizing, too universalizing—in short, too neglectful of the particularity of subject positions.

One of the most obvious entry points to this disagreement is the debate that Edelman—one of queer theory's leading Lacanians—and Berlant—one of queer theory's leading affect theorists—stage in *Sex, or the Unbearable*. Because I have discussed this debate in detail earlier (see Ruti 2017), here it suffices to offer the gist of the dispute: although both critics reject "projects of queer optimism that try to repair the subject's negativity into a grounding experiential positivity" (5), Edelman continues to focus on the Lacanian lack-in-being—and the ethos of death-driven queer destructiveness that, in his opinion, arises (or should arise) from this lack—that he developed in *No Future*, whereas Berlant insists on the importance of more sociohistorically specific scenes of negation, undoing, and nonsovereignty, suggesting that Edelman's Lacanian discourse of negativity fails to capture "negativity's multiplicity" (5). In other words, while Edelman adheres to a strictly Lacanian notion of constitutive alienation, Berlant wishes to examine the material, psychic, and affective effects of more concrete forms of alienation; she is interested in understanding the manifold ways in which specific subjects can be negated—rendered lacking—by specific (oppressive, wounding) circumstances. Berlant in fact emphasizes that many subordinated subjects experience negativity (deprivation or dispossession) as an utterly ordinary—even a banal—component of everyday life, which is why she shies away from Edelman's valorization of the extraordinary "event" of subjective destitution (the suicidal plunge into the jouissance of the real that he advocates as the ethical act of queer antinormativity).

For Edelman, trauma—the rupture in the symbolic order generated by the jouissance of the real—is extraordinary, which is why he (according to Berlant) dramatizes it; for Berlant, in contrast, trauma is ordinary, quotidian, predictable, and unsurprising, which is why (again, according to Berlant) she seeks to dedramatize it, to illustrate how very commonplace it really is among the deprivileged and—due to neoliberal capitalism's reliance on the general fragmentation and destabilization of life worlds—perhaps even increasingly among the relatively privileged. As Berlant argued already in *Cruel Optimism*, crisis is not necessarily fast—a sudden rupture—but rather slow, stretched, and sometimes almost catatonic. Indeed, Berlant posits that the attrition of the quality of life under neoliberal capitalism is so endemic that it has become difficult to know what it means to have a life in the first place: "Is it to have health? To love, to have been loved? To have felt sovereign? To achieve a state or a sense of worked-toward enjoyment? Is 'having a life' now the process to which one gets resigned, after dreaming of the good life?" (2011, 117).

We are here quite far from life-altering events, acts, or ruptures. As I will show below, Berlant's rhetoric of resignation—here expressed as the idea that "having a life" is now something that one gets resigned to after one's dreams of the good life have collapsed—is characteristic of affect theory. This is why the title of this chapter contrasts Lacanian revolt with affect theoretical resignation. However, the affect theoretical tone of resignation regarding the pitiful parameters of contemporary subjectivity should not distract us from its robust political investments. It is just that because affect theorists disagree with Lacanian theorists about the level at which negation truly counts—stipulating that it is on the level of the minutia of daily life, rather than on some lofty existential level, that negation ultimately most matters—their political aims remain modest, calibrated to the mundane realities of circumstantially wounded subjects rather than to the ontological realities of the Lacanian subject of lack.

I do not mean to say that Lacanians do not care about social justice. As we saw in the context of Eisenstein and McGowan's analysis of the Haitian Revolution, they do. Even Badiou and Žižek constantly refer to economic disparities: as I have argued, the problem with their argument is not that inequality does not interest them but merely that class inequality is the only inequality that they appear to recognize as worth analyzing. But it is nonetheless the case that the affect theoretical focus on circumstantial forms of material, psychic, and affective wounding is more pronounced than what one finds in much of Lacanian theory.

Conversely, affect theorists do not *oppose* revolutionary change; they usually just do not view it as a feasible option for those who already lead precarious lives (more on this below). For this reason, Lacanians might accuse them of the same type of dis-eventualization as capitalism generates. At the same time, there is a great deal to be said for the affect theoretical wish to comprehend how circumstantially wounded subjects manage to bear their damaged lives, how they manage to navigate complex social contexts that do not have their best interests in mind and that frequently even actively seek to undermine them. In addition, there is surely much to learn from the affect theoretical interest in the role that psychic and affective attachments to normativity—cruel optimism—play in enabling such subjects to survive their eroding, exhausting, and decomposing lives.

This difference in viewpoints regarding the level on which negation most matters explains a further theoretical divergence between Edelman and Berlant: while Edelman rejects all attempts to find a foothold in the world—to recenter the self—as a fantasmatic quest for mastery, as a refusal to face nonsovereignty (lack-in-being), Berlant exhibits a measure of appreciation for the desire of subordinated individuals for security, coherence, and belonging. Even though Berlant is just as suspicious of the idealism of (false) hope as Edelman is, she retains some empathy for those who cling to it in their ambivalent efforts to attain a life that feels, if not worth living, then at the very least minimally livable.

With regard to this issue, Edelman's position somewhat unexpectedly converges with that of Butler in the sense that, as we learned in Chapter 2, Butler deems all attempts to recenter the self as intrinsically unethical (and perhaps even evil). Berlant, in contrast, insists on the nuances of the matter, maintaining that there are situations where the ability to recenter the self is essential for the subject's continued viability. Although Berlant is critical of the kinds of fantasies of future flourishing that allow the subject to overlook the cruelty of the present, she does not wish to pathologize those who adhere to such fantasies because she recognizes that they can be the only way to make life bearable for those subjected to extreme forms of deprivation and dispossession. In other words, psychic and affective attachments to normativity, for Berlant, are not invariably reactionary (as they seem to be for both Edelman and Butler); sometimes they are, quite simply, necessary for survival.

Who can afford rupture?

It is easy enough to map the distinction between universalism and particularism onto this debate between Edelman and Berlant, for Edelman's vision is universalist in the sense that he interprets lack as a universal (intrinsic) constituent of subjectivity whereas Berlant—without denying this constitutive lack—wishes to investigate the context-specific forms of negation (lack) that impact particular subjects in particular ways. Likewise, Edelman, like the other Lacanians I have discussed in this book, advocates a politics of rupture whereas Berlant, like Ahmed and many other affect theorists, questions robust displays of agency, including radical ruptures from context. This is because, as Eisenstein and McGowan themselves readily admit, rupture demands the ability to tolerate the loss of one's moorings, including one's sense of belonging to a social milieu; it demands the ability to bear the trauma of dislocation.

Lacanians valorize this ability because—despite their talk about the Haitian Revolution and class inequality—they tend to privilege the subject's constitutive lack-in-being. However, one can see why the affect theoretical accent on "negativity's multiplicity" leads to a different conclusion: affect theorists are less likely than Lacanians to sing the praises of the event, act, or rupture because they focus on subjects who have already been so thoroughly destabilized by circumstantial factors that they might find it impossible to embrace further instability.

For Eisenstein and McGowan, rupture destabilizes the social status quo in order to create an opening for values such as freedom, equality, and solidarity. In addition, because rupture is always connected to the original cut of the signifier that brings the subject into being as a subject, it repeats something about this cut, perforating the subject's being in ways that unsettle its relationship to its environment. This is difficult enough for anyone who has already been unsettled due to political, economic, or social inequalities. But even more difficult (to live) may be Eisenstein and

McGowan's conviction that it is only possible to sustain the values that emerge from rupture by sustaining this rupture—by dwelling within, and defending, the traumatizing disorder that it represents.

For instance, speaking of the values of freedom and equality specifically, Eisenstein and McGowan explain: "Freedom . . . must remain a freedom that violently tears the subject from its external determinants, and equality must constantly uproot the subject from its place in the social order. To champion a value, one must also champion the interruption within being that makes the value possible. No one is naturally free, and no one is equal while retaining a proper place. Value requires an embrace of the trauma of the rupture" (35).

As long as we stay on the level of the Lacanian lack-in-being, the constitutive "deformation" of the subject, this reasoning makes perfect sense. The ideal of embracing the trauma of rupture is fundamentally Lacanian even if it is also in many ways existentialist, the idea being that it is only when we admit that there is no cure for the subject's constitutive lack (castration) that freedom emerges as a possibility. And it is only when there is freedom that there is any chance of equality. From a Lacanian perspective, if psychoanalysis has an aim, it is to allow the subject to welcome the rupture from nature that the signifier introduces and that brings it into existence as a subject; in this sense, the goal of psychoanalysis is to enable the subject to withstand insecurity, ambiguity, disorientation, and deformation (what, as we learned at the end of the last chapter, Adam Phillips portrays as "psychoanalytic training in contingency management"). Inasmuch as the subject, for Lacan, is "essentially the want-to-be that has arisen out of a certain relationship to discourse—that has arisen from a kind of poetry," it has to be able to cope with a lack of security, a lack of guarantees (1960–1961, 368).

When Eisenstein and McGowan translate the Lacanian leap from nature to discourse (the cut of the signifier) into a more general theory of rupture as the foundation of political (revolutionary) change, they adopt the idea that being orphaned—being traumatically "cut adrift" from the securities of social belonging (36)—is a desirable state of affairs. Even though they admit that in the long run it may be "impossible to remain wholly within the rupture"—that despite rupture's transformative potential, "the trauma of it may be unsustainable"—they nonetheless believe that "what is not impossible is making the traumatic rupture the organizing principle of the political order that we constitute" (36). Consequently, as attentive as Eisenstein and McGowan are to social inequalities such as heteropatriarchy, racism, colonialism, and economic exploitation, their understanding of lack—of negation—remains on the level of constitutive deprivation and dispossession in ways that are difficult to reconcile with affect theory's attention to context-specific forms of deprivation and dispossession. This is why they speak a language of rebellion whereas affect theorists—who possess an acute understanding of why it might be impossible for deprivileged subjects to dwell within the rupture in the manner that Eisenstein and McGowan idealize—tend to speak a language of resignation, a language that, as I have emphasized, focuses on quotidian (often mundane) struggles of survival rather than on life-altering ruptures. Simply put, from the affect theoretical viewpoint, rupture is not something that most people can afford.

Negotiating with power

The divide between Lacanian political theorists and affect theorists thus culminates in the question of whether the event, act, or rupture is a concrete possibility for most people. As I have argued, one of the most fundamental distinctions between Lacanian political theorists and affect theorists is that while Lacanians believe that it is possible (precisely through the event, act, or rupture) to break the material, psychic, and affective hold of disciplinary power, most affect theorists, like Butler, seem doubtful about this possibility. I have specified that this distinction can be traced not just to the two different levels of deprivation and dispossession that I have foregrounded but also to the fact that affect theorists, again like Butler, usually function with a loosely Foucauldian understanding of disciplinary power, with the result that resistance for them becomes a process of negotiating with power rather than of the kinds of radical events, acts, and ruptures favored by Lacanian thinkers.

Butler's early theory of gender performativity already assumed that resistance is a matter of working with power rather than of trying to step outside its reach. And a decade after *Gender Trouble* Butler openly acknowledged that for her negotiating, even collaborating, with power is "the condition of agency rather than its destruction" (2000, 277). Likewise, affect theorists usually favor a gradual, reiterative approach premised on working with, rather than directly against, power. This is the logical outcome of the Foucauldian line of reasoning: inasmuch as this reasoning does not allow for the possibility of breaking with one's sociohistorical context, it must conceptualize resistance in relation to this context (power) rather than in rebellious opposition to it.

According to the Foucauldian view, biopolitical conditioning cannot be transcended, with the consequence that even subjects who most suffer from this conditioning are materially, psychically, and affectively beholden to it. The best they can do is to concoct (usually fragile) everyday strategies for enduring its wounding effects. From this perspective, agency consists of diffuse efforts to negotiate a slightly better life for oneself, to survive the challenges of one's context (of what Badiou calls "the situation").

Berlant expresses the matter succinctly when she states that cruel optimism "is a scene of *negotiated* sustenance that makes life bearable as it presents itself ambivalently, unevenly, incoherently" (2011, 14; emphasis added). She adds that under challenging personal or collective conditions, the quest for normativity can be "a form of bargaining with what is overwhelming about the present, a bargaining against the fall between the cracks, the living death of repetition that's just one step above the fall into death by drowning or by hitting the concrete at full speed" (180).

In my earlier work, I have voted for Lacanian rebellion over Foucauldian acquiescence (see Ruti 2015b, 2017). Nevertheless, I understand why affect theorists avoid the revolutionary rhetoric of Lacanians: for deprivileged subjects whose relationship to the dominant social order is tenuous at best, radical acts of resistance are not an option unless they are willing to destroy themselves completely. Such acts do not usually feel like a tenable option even for me even though I am these days—in contrast to how things used to be—unquestionably a highly privileged subject. I know that if I defiantly slam my fist on the counter when an American Homeland Security officer questions my right to enter the United States—or denies my work visa application because I am not carrying an original copy of my Ph.D. diploma (this happened recently)—I risk worse than a few hours of waiting, panicking, and responding to offensive interrogation in the backroom. This is why when one Homeland Security officer asked me—presumably in an effort to justify denying my visa application—whether I am "one of those feminists who hate men," I smiled rather than screamed (even though I wanted to strangle him—so I guess I might be on my way to becoming one of those feminists who actually *do* hate at least some men). My larger point is that I comprehend why Berlant argues that under the current regime, agency is rarely a matter of refuting the social establishment but merely of bargaining with it.

Berlant specifies that the hyperexploited—those without stable income, shelter, or social ties—usually do not fantasize about opposing normativity but rather about being able to one day enter into its folds; they are not dreaming of a revolution but of making it to the next day. As Berlant explains, when you are "stuck in what we might call survival time, the time of struggling, drowning, holding onto the ledge, treading water"—"the time of *not-stopping*"—you seek the kind of normativity that promises to provide just a tiny bit of rest without anxiety (2011, 169). In this scenario, Berlant adds, you do not worry about getting exploited: you feel lucky if "you *get* to be exploited"; you feel lucky if "you can avoid one more day being the focus of a scene that hails and ejects you when it is time to again become worthless" (171).

Under these conditions, exploitation—say, boring, taxing, soul-slaying, and low-paying jobs—is not seen as an antagonist but as a privilege of sorts: it gives you what those who are even more marginalized do not have, namely a place to be and a way to eat. As Berlant puts it, individuals who find themselves in this predicament "want to be exploited, to enter the proletarian economy in the crummy service-sector jobs it is all too easy to disdain as the proof of someone's loserdom or tragedy. The risk would be opting out of the game" (2011, 171).

Having watched my parents work at such jobs—jobs that were not even in the service sector but consisted of factory work and (sporadic, seasonal) physical labor—I would not go as far as to say that the marginalized necessarily "want to be exploited." Rather, it seems to me that they tolerate their exploitation reluctantly and resentfully because they recognize—like I do at the US border—that they have no choice, that the cost of opting out of the game would indeed be too high. Nonetheless, on a broader level, I appreciate Berlant's insight about how individuals—deprivileged and privileged alike—can become affectively attached to scenes of normativity because such scenes "might be what remains to animate living on" (2011, 167).

Berlant essentially suggests that affective investments in various scenes of hope are what bond people to dominant ideological formations. Sianne Ngai makes a parallel point by arguing—in this instance drawing from Lawrence Grossberg—that it is "affective investment which enables ideological relations to be internalized and, consequently, naturalized"; affect is what "makes things matter" to people (46, 54). From this viewpoint, affective investments generate psychological commitments: they enchant people with ideals or—when they are negative—cause them to become disenchanted with ideals. As a result, they structure collective behavior. This in many ways is exactly Berlant's argument regarding cruel optimism, namely that it is a means of suturing people to scenes of hopefulness that cause them to invest in forms of dominant sociality, in what she calls "aspirational normativity" (2011, 164), that undermine or otherwise damage them.

As I just noted, I am more skeptical than Berlant (and I suppose that the same skepticism applies to Ngai's argument) about the causal relationship between affect and ideology, for I believe that most deprivileged individuals are perfectly capable of seeing through the ideological structures that oppress them even if they, out of necessity, obey the dictates of those structures; obedience, in other words, does not imply an affective investment of any kind: the same people who display meek compliance at work might rail against every aspect of their jobs after work. They may not agitate for a revolution but this does not mean that they are dupes of dominant ideology either. However, I am more convinced by Berlant's argument regarding how the hope that things might eventually get better—cruel optimism—might induct individuals into dominant ideologies. I may hate my job in ways that make me resistant to the false appeal of such ideologies; but the hope that I might one day be able to find a better job might well seduce me, unless I have lived long enough, and been disappointed frequently enough, to recognize that my hope is unwarranted.

When the normative good life feels like it might one day be within reach, dominant ideologies encounter little affective resistance. Optimistic projects of self-making and life-building, of social mobility and belonging, are powerful palliatives to, and distractions from, the hardships of living. But this dynamic ends when hope ends. And for many of us it does eventually end. In addition, for some, the pessimists among us, it ends sooner than for others. As far as I can tell from listening to my mother talk about her past, for her hope ended at the age of twenty, which is why she never thought that her job at a factory was anything besides a tedious but necessary means of buying food; there was no affective investment in any ideal of a better future.

Berlant tells "a story about the conditions under which fantasy takes the most conservative shape on the bottom of so many class structures," one where "adults want to pass the promise of the promise to their children" (2011, 174). The American dream of eventually making it is obviously one such conservative fantasy, a pure instance of cruel optimism. Yet I am once again not sure that those on the bottom of the class structure are likely to naïvely buy this dream. Berlant herself in fact comes close to admitting that this dream—the promise of the promise—often fails when she draws on Lillian Rubin's work to argue that the children of low-income families sense their parents' helplessness, vulnerability, and frustration, and that they consequently learn both to take up as little space as possible and to protect their parents even when the latter act brutally; they understand where this brutality arises from. Such children know that there is not much that their parents can do to change their circumstances. They do not like their parents' powerlessness, nor do their idealize their parents. Rather, they become "depressed realists" who strive to shield their parents from "the ordinariness of their social humiliation" (187).

Such a situation can lead to a transgenerational "inheritance of an impossible life" (2011, 187), which Berlant reads as a recipe for cruel optimism, for the fantasy of getting out, of transcending the present. I am more inclined to read such an inheritance as the end of all optimism, cruel or otherwise. I would hypothesize that it is the slightly better off who might be more prone to respect the fantasy of the American dream because, for them, there is at least a small possibility of this fantasy becoming a reality. In contrast, those who have inherited an impossible life may see right through this fantasy. Still, I agree with Berlant that the comfort many individuals take in scenes, ideals, or objects that promise relief from life's instabilities—that promise continuity, dependability, or lack of conflict—are not *merely* hegemonic pleasures but also, and sometimes even instead, ways of keepings precarious lives afloat.

What is agency?

Lacanian theory has a stark reputation. Yet at the background of Lacan's idea that there is no cure for one's lack-in-being, for one's existential malaise, hovers the deeply utopian notion that accepting one's lack, learning to live with one's deformation, releases resources for agency, creativity, and even flourishing. In contrast, in affect theory, there is no possibility of turning negativity into something affirmative; there is no potter capable of fashioning a vase out of a void. Negativity, in affect theory, usually leads to debilitating despair rather than to innovative transformation, let alone to revolutionary events, acts, or ruptures.

One might summarize the distinction as follows: On the Lacanian side we have Antigone's heroic defiance; Badiou's Maoists, scientists, artists, and passionate lovers who persist in their fidelity to their cause regardless of what this fidelity costs them; Žižek's "crazy" but laudable subjects who are willing to destroy their social viability through a suicidal plunge into the jouissance of the real; Edelman's death-driven queers; and the Haitian Revolution. On the side of affect theory, we have subjects who are just trying to get through the day.

This does not mean that affect theorists are not interested in agency. It is just that if Lacanians link agency to radical action, affect theorists view it as almost invariably damaged: brittle, friable, and tenuous. To be sure, there are times when the affect theoretical conception of agency converges with that of Lacanians, as I noted in Chapter 1 in the context of Ahmed's feminist who snaps. At first glance, the same could be said about Berlant's argument regarding the subject who chooses to detach "from a desire for the political as such" (2011, 231). In this scenario, the subject finds mainstream politics so vexing that it withdraws from the political scene altogether. Such a disengagement is arguably one form that a rupture from one's sociohistorical context can take.

Disengagement may be a gentler form of rejecting the terms of the political than the Lacanian *No!* to the big Other but its result can be the same: the utter refusal to participate. Nevertheless, because affect theory focuses on the painful material, psychic, and affective realities of the deprivileged—as well as on the price (such as overstimulated and hyperactive lives) that neoliberalism extorts even from the relatively privileged—it tends to conceptualize agency as always already compromised. From this perspective, even the detachment from the desire for the political that Berlant describes cannot be envisioned as a potent genre of agency; instead, it is the limping agency of those who find that the promise of a better future constantly eludes them.

Affect theory is deeply suspicious of agency as a synonym for active resistance. Kathleen Stewart—who was among the first to develop the affect theoretical line of reasoning about the importance of the quotidian—expresses the matter as follows: where grand theories of social change dream "of a return to a pristine past and the redemption of human agency," the type of agency that can be found in the empirical flow of ordinary life, in the flow of everyday struggles, "can be strange, twisted, caught up in things, passive, or exhausted" (88, 86).

I have demonstrated that McGowan is also wary of political visions that promise the end of alienation, repression, or restriction, as much of twentieth-century progressive theory (including Marxism, psychoanalysis, Derrida, and even Foucault in his own way) does. This is presumably one reason that Eisenstein and McGowan advocate dwelling within the rupture rather than the ideal of building a new (more liberated) social system in the aftermath of this rupture (as Badiou does). Nevertheless, when it comes to envisioning agency, the tone of affect theory is very different from that of Lacanian political theory: cautious, tentative, depressed, and . . . resigned.

Consider the manner in which Stewart describes the subject's messy, profoundly compromised agency:

> Out there on its own, [the subject] seeks out scenes and little worlds to nudge it into being. It wants to be somebody. It tries to lighten up, to free itself, to learn to be itself, to lose itself. None of this is easy. Straight talk about willpower and positive thinking claims that agency is just a matter of getting on track, as if all the messy business of real selves could be left behind like a bad habit or a hangover. But things are always backfiring. Self-making projects proliferate at exactly the same rate as the epidemics of addictions and the self-help shelves at the bookstore. The figure of beefed-up agency becomes a breeding ground for all kinds of strategies of complaint, self-destruction, flight, reinvention, redemption, and experimentation. As if everything rests on agency's shoulders. (59)

The subject Stewart describes is not the Lacanian subject of the event, act, or rupture but rather a forlorn subject who strives to keep up with the neoliberal game of productivity, performance, and positive thinking, only to find itself slipping, losing ground, and falling behind. This subject attempts to "nudge" itself into being, into being "somebody," at the same time as it seeks to lighten up, to free itself, to learn to be itself, and to lose itself by fleeing the burdens of responsibility. But this is an impossible endeavor because the neoliberal ideal of being carefree (and free)—loose limbed—clashes with the (equally) neoliberal ideal of getting back on track through willpower and positive thinking. Agency thus takes contradictory forms, which means that too much rests on its shoulders. The self tries to remake itself, to reinvent itself, to redeem itself, to experiment with itself, but the weight of "beefed-up agency" frequently proves to be too much to bear, with the result that the subject finds various ways, including addictions and self-destructive behavior, to undermine itself.

One is here reminded of Eisenstein and McGowan's argument, discussed at the beginning of this chapter, regarding the sublimity of failure. The difference, once again, is that if failure for Eisenstein and McGowan is constitutive of subjectivity—so that there can be no subject without failure, without distortion, without a lack of adaptation—for Stewart it results from the subject's entanglement in compromising social arrangements. For Stewart, like for many other affect theorists, agency functions reactively rather than proactively. As she explains, "Things happen. The self moves to react, often pulling itself someplace it didn't exactly intend to go" (79). Agency, she continues, "takes unpredictable and counterintuitive forms": "It's lived through a series of dilemmas: that action is always a reaction; that the potential to act always includes the potential to be acted on, or to submit; that the move to gather a self to act is also a move to lose the self; that one choice precludes others; that actions can have unintended and disastrous consequences; and that all agency is frustrated and unstable" (86).

In such circumstances, life is not punctuated by life-altering ruptures but drifts by, runs in place, or "treads water," to return to Berlant's wording. It is characterized primarily by a fantasy of escaping, of somehow finally pulling one's life together so that one will not be quite so exhausted, quite so fearful, anxious, or stressed out. Stewart portrays such a fantasy concretely as a dream of a "perfect getaway cottage" (43), a "dream of a finished life" (48), a dream of "giving capture the slip" (49), a dream of "the well-tended suburban lawn" (58), and a dream of a "simple life that winks at us from someone else's beautiful flowerbeds" (10). This is a dream of disappearance, of fading away, rather than of bold appearance: agency as a function of flight rather than of fight. As Stewart sums up the matter, people "dream of getting by, getting on track, getting away from it all, getting real, having an edge, beating the system, being ourselves, checking out" at the same time as they "bottom out watching daytime television" (10).

Ngai analyzes similar forms of compromised agency—what she describes as "suspended agency" (1), "restricted agency" (2), "obstructed agency" (3), and "blocked or thwarted action" (27)—that lock individuals into "situations of passivity" (3) with no clearly defined goals, ideals, values, or passions. Berlant in turn labels this type of agency "lateral agency": coasting along, getting distracted, spacing out, not giving a damn, devouring mass entertainment, and eating more than one needs to. Berlant proposes that such scenes of quotidian disobedience—scenes that counter our society's performance principle—are a way of "inhabiting agency differently," of interrupting the demands of the production cycle: they offer a fleeting pleasure, a diversion from the pressures of keeping up with the ever-accelerating pace of everyday life (2011, 116–17). In other words, they function as techniques of "self-suspension," as "small vacations of the will" from the relentless demands of self-responsibility, thereby offering an antidote to wearing out (116). They provide an "intermission from personality, the burden of whose reproduction is part of . . . the obligation to be reliable" (116). They, in sum, represent "reliable pleasures" in the "diffuse, sensual space between pleasure and numbness" (117).

Berlant therefore argues that people, especially deprivileged ones, devise all kinds of ways of sidestepping the pressures of quotidian instability. Her analysis of the "slow death" of overeating—of the American obesity epidemic—is among her most arresting examples of what it might mean the conceptualize agency anew, in a manner that discards the heroism of grand actions and focuses instead on the myriad ways in which deprivileged subjects manage to bear social contexts that feel unbearable. Berlant maintains that for many American workers and other marginalized subjects, eating constitutes one of the few remaining pleasures. Eating not only creates potentially supportive communities—as happens when people gather around a table during a holiday, a celebration, or a gathering of friends—but also enables individuals to take precisely the kinds of "small vacations of the will" that I referred to above: it, for instance, allows them to take a break from their hectic or tedious jobs.

Berlant proposes that eating "can produce an experience of self-abeyance," with the result that it serves as a way to bypass "the vampirism of profit extraction" that characterizes contemporary life (2011, 116, 119). Eating is not productive—not a form of tactical agency—but it can still be "directed toward making a less-bad experience. It's a relief, a reprieve, not a repair" (117). The desire for such "a less-bad experience" moreover explains other "pointless activities," such as dwelling in depression, relishing alienation, retreating from social life, or deliberately slowing down one's pace of work. Even acquiescing to the general will so as to avoid standing out can function as a ritual of lateral agency.

Anne Cheng reasons along related lines when she reminds us that in the context of those facing discrimination, agency is not invariably generative but can also consist of ongoing, convoluted, and at times contradictory negotiations with pain. "The internalization of dominant oppression," Cheng asserts, "may not signal pure conformity or defeat but rather point to new ways of thinking about what agency means for one stripped of it" (21). Ahmed in turn states, "A desire for a more normal life does not necessarily mean identification with norms, but can be simply this: a desire to escape the exhaustion of having to insist just to exist" (2014, 149).

As much as I wish to problematize the Foucauldian-Butlerian idea that complicity with power is a precondition of agency, that resistance can only emerge from within power (even if power simultaneously generates resistance), I understand why affect theorists maintain that the sheer act of surviving yet another day can be a form of defiance for those whose lives are so precarious, so severely negated by unfair social circumstances (or by idiosyncratic instances of personal abjection), that the simple process of putting one foot in front of the other is draining. In such situations, the distinction between normativity and rebellion blurs. I suppose that this was my point above when I insisted that the marginalized do not necessarily "want" to be exploited but are merely trying to make the best of conditions that leave them few choices.

Refusing to answer to *comrade*

Lacanian political theorists bristle at the charge of "masculinism" that I referred to in the context of Badiou and Žižek in Chapter 1, and that affect theorists routinely level against Lacanian revolutionary ideals. But even as a sometime Lacanian, I comprehend this charge: I recognize that it is hardly a coincidence that one finds it repeated from one (female-authored) affect theoretical text to the next. For instance, Ngai juxtaposes affect theory's interest in the compromised agency of the deprivileged to "the language of conspiracy theory" that, in her view, seems "intimately tied to the hermeneutic quest of male agent-intellectuals, in contexts ranging from *Critical Inquiry* to Fox Television" (300). Ngai's comparison between *Critical Inquiry* and Fox Television may appear extreme, but her point is that paranoid theorizing about ideology and conspiracy—the search for "a holistic and all-encompassing system" that would explain all the wrongs of the world—appears to have become the model for theorizing as such, "a viable synecdoche for 'theory' itself" (299).

In Chapter 1, I mentioned that in my opinion Eisenstein and McGowan manage to avoid the white masculinist inflection of much of grand theorizing. But, then again, they are not the Lacanians and other male theorists of the revolution whom affect theorists find so troubling, for it the Badious, Žižeks, Edelmans, and maybe even the Hardt and Negris of the theoretical universe who elicit the frustrated rejoinder of affect theoretical feminists. This rejoinder is perhaps most succinctly conveyed by Nelson who declares that she has "never been able to answer to *comrade*" (27).

Berlant posits that the belief in the possibility of change on the grand historical scale "requires the drama of inflated sovereignty, or politics" (2011, 258). According to affect theorists, this drama is what many deprivileged people are too tired to entertain, with the consequence that they embrace nonsovereignty and political complacency instead. Berlant admits that the affect theoretical archive "might look minor because it is not situated in gestures of heroic action we associate with the political; because it turns rather toward deflation, distraction, and aleatory wavering in unusual arcs of attentiveness; and because some of [its] cases do not counter hegemonic ideologies with philosophies of refusal" (259–60). At the same time, if there seems to be something "quietist" about these "depressive aversions to the political sans gestures of repair," they may also represent a "departure from the circuit of reseduction and despair that so often absorbs genuine energy for social change": that is, perhaps depressive aversions to the political are "doing some of the delicate work" of allowing us to detach ourselves "from the cruel optimism of a political fetish" (259). In this sense, it is hard to tell the difference between a political (or ethical) failure and a much-needed respite that keeps us from being reseduced by overly optimistic fantasies of overarching social change.

It is not that affect theorists oppose ideology critique. As I mentioned in the last chapter, Berlant for example sees affect theory as the most recent genre of ideology critique. Rather, affect theorists object to the ways in which the revolutionary models of Marxists such as Badiou and Žižek, and the language-centered models of thinkers such as Lacan and Derrida, drown out the seemingly trivial movements of affect, including the manner in which negative feelings travel from one person to another in intangible yet palpable ways; they object to the ways in which revolutionary and language-centered models ignore ordinary experiences of traumatization that, as Ngai points out, are just as politically, economically, and socially important as "the institutions and collective practices that have been the more traditional objects of historicist criticism . . . and as 'material' as the linguistic signs and significations that have been the more traditional objects of literary formalism" (25). "Although feeling is not reducible to these institutions, collective practices, or discursive significations," Ngai adds, "it is nonetheless as socially real and 'infrastructural' in its effects 'as a factory'" (25).

What's good about feeling bad?

As I have argued all along, as an alternative to the grand conceptual schemes of paranoid theorizing, affect theorists offer an analysis of the minutia of everyday life, of how deprivileged subjects manage to navigate their experiences of quotidian trauma. This is why the examination of bad feelings—such as sadness, despair, depression, abjection, anxiety, bitterness, listlessness, disappointment, disenchantment, embarrassment, resentment, and remorse—has been prevalent within, and perhaps even emblematic of, the field. Such "ugly feelings" (Ngai) may seem politically useless. But the affect theoretical wager is that in reality they function as a stealthy form of resistance that may not enjoy the noble reputation of events, acts, and ruptures but that may nevertheless represent a defiant response to neoliberal society's demand for productivity, performance, and positive thinking.

Importantly, affect theoretical accounts of bad feelings do not suggest that there is something productive—say, a therapeutic gain or a deepening of character—that might emerge from feeling bad; rather, the idea is that there is something about feeling bad that is *in itself* potentially valuable, that bad feelings function as a valuable means of opposing the dictates of normative sociality. Simply put, not getting out of bed in the morning because one is feeling too depressed, indulging addictions to the point of being unable to work, and the kind of agoraphobic withdrawal from the collective world that keeps one from participating in the "normal" current of daily experience are ways of rejecting dominant definitions of the good life. They may not carry the flamboyant rebelliousness of the Lacanian *No!* but they nevertheless represent an attempt to resist oppressive political, economic, and social circumstances.

Jack Halberstam clarifies the matter through his argument about failure—here not understood as the type of "existential" (or ontological) failure that Eisenstein and McGowan analyze but rather as a mundane experiential reality of those who keep failing at their attempts to attain the (normatively) good life—and the bad feelings that failure engenders: "While failure certainly comes accompanied by a host of negative affects, such as disappointment, disillusionment, and despair, it also provides the opportunity to use these negative affects to poke holes in the toxic positivity of contemporary life" (3). In this manner, Halberstam joins a chorus of queer and affect theorists who have determined that bad feelings provide an antidote to the ethos of positivity that underpins American neoliberal culture. Halberstam, in short, strives to defeat the "idealism of hope," the attitude that tells us that success depends "upon trying and trying again," which is why he urges us to leave success "to the Republicans, to the corporate managers of the world, to the winners of reality TV shows, to married couples, to SUV drivers" (3, 120). In other words, bad feelings are politically subversive because they weaken the normatively agentic subject as well as the social order that asks high productivity, good performance, and relentless cheerfulness from this subject.

On the one hand, I have a great deal of appreciation for this way of reasoning. On the other, I understand why, when my graduate seminar on Lacanian political theory and affect theory reached this point in the semester, one of my students asked with evident despair, "Is this all we have left—a politics of failure?" A good question indeed. In this context, it is also relevant to recognize the degree to which bad feelings can be coopted by the very neoliberal system that they seemingly destabilize: if it is true that bad feelings can dampen a person's productivity, our economy has found a way to profit from them anyway through the marketing of antidepressants, tranquilizers, and self-help books.

The inadequacies of grieving

I admit that I also wonder about the real-life viability of the advocacy of all manner of misery that characterizes much of affect theory. Here a contrast with Lacanian theory is once again instructive. I have already noted that, despite its hard-nosed reputation, Lacanian theory is frequently remarkably utopian. With the exception of Edelman's hardline take on negativity, Lacanian negativity—as I have emphasized—usually gestures toward some form of creativity or vitality. For instance, even if Eisenstein and McGowan promote dwelling within the rupture, their point is not that we should resign ourselves to despondency; rather, their proposal is that coming to terms with subjective deformation and instability allows for less defensive modes of living in the world.

Consider Eisenstein and McGowan's conceptualization of freedom: on the one hand, as we have learned, rupture is the means through which "we assert our freedom from the context out of which we emerge"; on the other, "the rupturing loss that creates our subjectivity also deprives us of any sense of mastery over ourselves or others" (148). In other words, freedom is not a matter of seamless sovereignty or self-mastery; and it is emphatically not linked to any attempt to dominate the world. Instead, it is an opening to self-creation, to the kind of liberation from the dictates of the big Other that facilitates the emergence of the subject's singularity of being. This singularity, in turn, becomes the foundation for a universalist ethics where each singularity, ideally at least, relates to other singularities from a platform of equality and solidarity. In contrast, affect theorists sometimes seem to celebrate despondency for the sake of despondency.

Although much of affect theory's analysis of bad feelings is obviously diagnostic, designed to capture something about the lived realities of present-day subjectivity, its rhetoric of bad feelings sometimes veers toward the prescriptive, implying that the only way to remain a politically or ethically tolerable subject is to adopt bad feelings as a way of life. Given that (active) agency is the last thing that most progressive critics (besides Lacanians and Marxists) want to claim for themselves, feeling dreadful seems to supply a viable alternative ("at least I'm not asserting agency!"). Insofar as (active) agency has been thoroughly demonized (see Chapter 2), feeling wretched may appear commendable for the simple reason that it represents the antithesis of such agency. Yet my hunch is that deprivileged subjects outside the academy have no wish to feel even more wretched than they already do: telling them that feeling bad makes them politically defiant or ethically laudable would likely not be well received.

I may take some solace in my depression due to my intellectual understanding of the manner in which it can function as a counterhegemonic force (even if it is also produced by the very hegemony it counters). But telling my mother that her depression is a political or ethical statement would be met with utter bewilderment (and most likely extreme annoyance). In this sense, ironically enough, even though affect theory is acutely attuned to the experiential realities of marginalized subjects, its politicization of bad feelings can turn bad feelings into a politico-ethical goal that has no practical traction with the very population that it aims to understand.

In the same way that Butler implies that every attempt to recenter the self is an ethical disaster, affect theory sometimes implies that every attempt to feel good is a politico-ethical disaster. This is why I have reservations about the sweeping scope of the rhetoric of affliction within affect theory, about the fact that bad feelings appear to have become the field's good—virtuous—feelings. This trend is of course not unique to affect theory but can also be found, for example, in Butler's Levinasian attempt to ground ethics in the precariousness and vulnerability of human life. As a result, the discourse of traumatization, suffering, dejection, and grieving has become endemic in progressive critical theory.

This discourse is seductive. Furthermore, it is true that a shared platform of grief can become an impetus for ethical indignation and political agitation. We have recently seen powerful examples of the capacity of grief to galvanize communities in the context of black men being murdered by police officers who are subsequently absolved of any responsibility. Along related lines, I appreciate queer theory's analysis of how the refusal to forget historical wrongdoings—the insistence on grieving the past rather than ignoring it in the name of a homonormative embrace of mainstream respectability—aids in the forging of political coalitions not only among queers but also between queers and other marginalized individuals. There is no doubt that there are plenty of situations in which grief functions as a potent political motive.

For these reasons, it is difficult to object to Butler's claim that, politically and ethically, there is "something to be gained from grieving, from tarrying with grief, from remaining exposed to its unbearability and not endeavoring to seek a resolution for grief through violence" (2004, 30). Yet it is also possible that the politicized discourse of grief and other bad feelings, paradoxically enough, serves as a distraction from concrete solutions to social problems: to the degree that it allows us to experience ourselves as benevolent politico-ethical subjects, subjects who recognize their own bad feelings, and who are capable of proper empathy for the bad feelings of others, it can thwart more tangible forms of political action; when feeling bad becomes a political intervention in its own right, no further intervention is deemed necessary. In this sense, the rhetoric of bad feelings can be a way for intellectuals to feel like they are doing something politically and ethically useful when in reality absolutely nothing is changing in the world.

From this point of view, there is something to be said for the Lacanian emphasis on revolutionary events, acts, and ruptures. Still, I do not see the need to choose between Lacan and Foucault, between radical ruptures and everyday strategies of survival. Although I have always been more Lacanian than Foucauldian, I appreciate the reasons for which so many progressive critics have chosen to follow Foucault's lead in investigating the difficulties of breaking with one's sociohistorical context. And I know from firsthand experience that there is an enormous difference between constitutive and circumstantial forms of negation. I do not think that admitting this fact cancels out the importance of either level of negation. Instead, I believe that it is vital for us to hold these two levels in tension, to consider the ways in which both are (differently) essential for teasing out the complexities of human life.

Sometimes the constitutive and the circumstantial are related, so that a quotidian negation deepens one's constitutive negation or one's constitutive negation causes a quotidian negation to sting all the more acutely. Other times they diverge. Either way, I think that it is because both Lacanian political theorists and affect theorists for the most part keep to their own corners—Lacanians focusing on the subject's foundational lack-in-being and affect theorists focusing on context-specific varieties of wounding—that their discourses can sometimes seem so incompatible. In my view, this split is theoretically (and ideologically) unnecessary, for I believe that it is possible, indeed necessary, to understand how subjects are rendered lacking both ontologically and contextually, and how these two forms of lack can sometimes converge in the life of a specific subject in ways that can only be described as devastating.

5

Socrates's mistake: Lacanians on love, Lacan on *Agálmata*

I ended the last chapter by noting that for all of their robust revolutionary talk about events, acts, and ruptures, Lacanian political theorists—and in this chapter I draw on Badiou, Žižek, and McGowan specifically, leaving Edelman and Eisenstein behind—are utopian in their outlook, not in the sense of (cruelly) optimistically expecting a rosy future to arise from the upheaval of the event but in the sense that they view negativity as the foundation of subjective and collective transformation. I have moreover explained that Badiou is the most affirmative of these three Lacanians because he regards the event as an opening to a new (and potentially improved) subjective and collective organization. Žižek and McGowan, for their part, focus on the antagonisms that underpin both subjectivity and collectivity, asking the subject to embrace the negativity of the act (or rupture).

These same affective modulations carry into the recent commentaries on romantic love offered by these thinkers, although what is perhaps most striking about these commentaries is that they, in contrast to the acidic attitude toward love that characterizes the rest of progressive theory, suggest that there is such a thing as a life-altering, fate-defining love. The sentimental approach of Lacanians counters the cynicism of affect theory about the cruelly optimistic lures of emotional and sexual intimacies; queer theory's rejection of relational longevity in favor of promiscuous sexual landscapes; feminist condemnations of love as a heteropatriarchal trap that reproduces normative gender configurations; Foucauldian dismissals of love as a form of biopolitical control designed to form stable families, productive citizens, and individuals willing to trade passion for security; and progressive theory's general suspicion of the emotional appeal of love as a tactic that creates privatized subjects turned toward the couple form rather than toward collective political action.

It is not that Lacanian political theorists are unaware of such critiques. Rather, they see these critiques as applying to love's commercialized nemesis, romance, rather than to love "in the real": love as an event that demolishes the subject's ordinary cadence of life, forcing it into a path that it may not have anticipated but that it, in the aftermath of the amorous event, feels bound to follow. Like the other kinds of events I have mentioned in this book, love, according to Lacanian political theorists, derails the subject in ways that are both traumatizing and exhilarating.

Romance versus love

Although Badiou, Žižek, and McGowan do not use the vocabulary of desire that I resorted to in Chapter 3, preferring to speak about the drive instead, by the end of this chapter it should be clear that their analyses have a great deal in common with what I have argued about the ethical potential of desire. Importantly, all three thinkers get around the problems that arise from the fact that Lacan operates with two different conceptions of desire—one leaning toward social complacency, the other leaning toward expressions of singularity (and even rebellion)—by drawing a sharp distinction between romance and love, suggesting that romance activates desire in its socially conformist register whereas love activates desire in the jouissance-filled register that I associate with its ethical edge. Once again, one can see why the latter kind of desire, for these Lacanians, usually gets translated into the drive. I merely differ from their interpretation in the sense that I do not want to automatically undertake this translation, not the least because I take seriously the fact that Lacan associated his ethics of psychoanalysis with not ceding one's desire. I trust that if he had thought that desire was intrinsically antithetical to ethics (or simply unimportant), he would have asked us to forget about desire and to replace it with the drive (which, essentially, is what the Lacanians I have named in varying degrees do).

However, what is significant in the present context is the following. I have argued that socially complacent desires lend the subject's identity symbolic and imaginary support whereas the kind of desire that meets the jouissance of the drive functions on the derailing level of the real. Lacanian political theorists make a similar distinction when they propose that romance as a commercial construct provides symbolic and imaginary support to the subject's coherence of being whereas the love event shatters this coherence. This is why these theorists deem romance to be fully compatible with capitalism's demand for performance, productivity, and social conformity whereas love, in their view, wars against the demands of capitalism by yanking the subject out of the circuits of both performance and consumption. If in the heteronormative order of things, the masculine subject in the thrall of romance works hard to afford expensive dinners, flowers, chocolates, and engagement rings, and the feminine subject works hard to afford expensive clothes, shoes, diets, highlights, and bikini waxes, the subject of love could not care less about fitting into such predictable roles.

A slightly different way to express the matter is to say that while romance obfuscates the subject's lack, love in its untamed form reveals and even intensifies this lack. In romance the beloved may temporarily expose my lack but ultimately he or she seeks to heal it, which is why romance makes me feel good: it makes me feel whole. Love, on the other hand, does not allow me to close my lack any more than it allows me to ignore the lack of the one I love, but rather forces me to face both. Or to state the matter in yet another way, if romance bestows the beloved object with nameable traits that seem to justify my desire for it, love steers me to what is unnameable, unknowable, and inscrutable about the other; love, in short, compels me to confront the opacity of the other's jouissance.

Badiou's amorous event

Badiou's conceptualization of the amorous event is perhaps the best known of the three Lacanian visions I will refer to in this chapter. Badiou (2001, 2012, 2013) regards the amorous event as an electrifying bolt of lightning that changes the subject's life forever (and for the better). The love encounter—the fortuitous meeting that surprises even as it captivates (or captivates because it surprises)—locks "chance into the framework of eternity" (2012, 47); it transforms something that seems to appear accidentally into a necessity, a new destiny that cannot be resisted because, like Badiou's other events, it carries the force of truth; it throws the subject's life out of joint by revealing something that has hitherto remained concealed.

Like Badiou's other truth events, the amorous event is what brings the subject into existence as a subject to begin with. However, this is a very particular kind of subject, a subject composed of the Two, in the sense that the amorous event gives rise to an experimentation in difference that allows both parties to exceed their usual parameters. Such love does not seek to fuse two individuals into one unit but respects the singularity of both, striving to create a life from the perspective of the two. If romance fetishizes the other by transforming it into an object—one that appears to contain the *objet a* that promises to complete the (narcissistic) subject's being—love reaches toward the totality of the other's being.

In this sense, love is not merely an imaginary construct that elevates desire into something that is socially palatable; it is not a polite cloak for the unseemly aspects of sex. Instead, as Badiou explains, it "produces the effects of desire" (2012, 36): the subject of the amorous event does not love because it desires; rather, it desires because it loves. And because such love slices diagonally through oppositions, because it forges a new world that is forced to accommodate the uniqueness of those it draws into its circle, it irrevocably alters the lives of both parties, asking them to step into a new destiny that emerges from the gap between them.

This is why Badiou believes that there is no such thing as a safe, risk-free love. Badiou is in fact immensely critical of the tendency of our pragmatic, levelheaded society to reject the unsettling aspects of love by forcing it to conform to the ideals of romance—crystallized in the streamlined attempts of dating services to match partners based on desirable characteristics and shared interests—and (eventually) marital harmony. Such an instrumentalization of love serves as a force of biopolitical conditioning that extracts out of love everything that renders it inspiring, making it instead serve the needs of cultural stability, political expediency, and the market economy.

Simply put, the less messy, the more rationally organized, our relationships are, the better we perform, produce, and serve the collective social order. This is why our culture sells us a syrupy image of romance as a means of taming the amorous event. It may allow us to briefly court the risky aspects of love under the auspices of a heady romance, but ultimately romance is supposed to result in a secure relationship that comforts because it is reliable; in intimate relationships, as in everything else, our society looks for efficiency above everything else.

Badiou's scathing critique of the pragmatism of our society's romantic culture does not keep him from advocating relational longevity. On this issue, he often sounds so quaintly (or suspiciously, depending on one's perspective) traditionalist that even I, who otherwise find his discourse on love compelling, find it difficult to agree with him, in part because the accent on longevity comes too close to old-style heteronormativity. I understand that, generally speaking, his theory of the event as an experience that demands the undying fidelity of those who commit themselves to living out its consequences automatically implies permanence: one is supposed to defend the truth unveiled by the event—in this case by the initial love encounter—against all doubts, barriers, complexities, and losses of courage. Moreover, Badiou explicitly states that the amorous event does not need to be heterosexual. Nevertheless, because he, like some other Lacanians, relies on an (in my opinion archaic) notion of sexual difference as the fundamental difference (or antagonism) upon which all other differences (antagonisms) are in some ways modeled, heteronormativity seeps into his analysis like rain water into a damp basement.

The Lacanian point about sexual difference may be that it is among the main collective fantasies that (violently) order heteronormative society. This is how I read the matter. But it is not necessarily always how Badiou and Žižek read it, for they imply that there is a biological kernel to it. Beyond this problem, it is possible to read Badiou either critically or generously. A critical reading would focus on the fact that, due to his conviction that there is nothing worse than betraying the amorous event, he characterizes the aftermath of this event as a "tenacious adventure" that demands hard, and sometimes even painful, labor (2012, 32). As I have argued elsewhere (see Ruti 2015a, 2017, 2018), this idea that love requires incessant labor all too easily slides into the very instrumentalization of intimacy that Badiou otherwise criticizes: after all, what could be more pragmatic than the idea that you need to work at love even after it has lost its spark because nothing is more important than its permanence? In this model, love becomes yet another form of work (performance and productivity).

A generous reading of Badiou, however, would admit that relational longevity in this pragmatic sense is not what he advocates. Instead, his insistence on the importance of staying faithful to the amorous event has to do with the idea that even when complications arise, even when it might be tempting to betray the event, there is always something truthful ("real") about it. In other words, Badiou's account of fidelity aspires to rescue the spark (truth) of the amorous event rather than merely to mechanically work at preserving the relationship after this spark has died. Indeed, for all his emphasis on fidelity, Badiou does not in the final analysis see love as being *necessarily* synonymous with an enduring relationship: love can be "true" even when a separation cannot be avoided; on the flipside, a marriage can be "false" (tedious, corrupt, or oppressive) even when it survives. In addition, the amorous event remains true even when it is replaced by a new love: in the same way as the "truth" of communism is not (for Badiou) erased by its failure, the truth of the amorous event is not erased by the failure of love, even by the advent of a new love.

Although Badiou stresses that the amorous event drastically alters the course of the subject's life, he focuses almost exclusively on the inspiring rather than the dislocating aspects of love. And somewhat surprisingly, in *Event: A Philosophical Journey Through a Concept*, Žižek—usually the more cynical of the two thinkers—follows Badiou remarkably far, writing like a man in love. "Falling in love," Žižek explains (summarizing Badiou's position), "is a contingent encounter, but once it occurs, it appears as necessary, as something toward which my entire life was moving. . . . It imposes on a lover the work of love, the continuous effort to inscribe into his/her being all the consequences of love, to structure his/her love around the fidelity to the event of love" (129). This is why "to say 'I love you because you have a nice nose/attractive legs,' etc., is *a priori* false. With love it is the same as with religious belief: I do not love you because I find your positive features attractive, but, on the contrary, I find your positive features attractive because I love you and therefore observe you with a loving gaze"; "the 'miracle' of love is that you learn what you need only when you find it" (117;

118). And finally, "Love implies absolute trust: in loving another, I give him or her the power to destroy me, hoping/trusting s/he will not use this power" (171).

Did Žižek stumble and hit his head on his Hitchcockian staircase?

Žižek's final statement at least acknowledges the potentially devastating dimensions of love. And in the end, Žižek does foreground these dimensions more than Badiou. Taking his lead from Plato's account of Socrates standing frozen in one spot for hours, Žižek proposes that Plato is describing "an event par excellence, a sudden traumatic encounter with another, suprasensible dimension which strikes us like lightning and shatters our entire life" (2014, 71). The vocabulary of being struck by lightning is the same as Badiou uses, but Žižek's accent falls more heavily on the traumatic, cataclysmic aspects of the event, including the event of love. This is why he reminds us that Plato, in the *Phaedrus*, likens love to madness, to being possessed by an alien force, depicting the lover as a person who is willing to prostrate himself before his beloved and commit other humiliating acts in public as a testimony of his love.

Love in this mortifying sense is, as Žižek puts it, a "permanent state of exception" (2014, 71): all balance is lost, everything is disturbed, and we cannot think of anything except the person we love. In other words, if the love event is transformative, it is also decentering, for it gets under our armor, renders us defenseless, and sometimes even leaves us crying in the dark (as Neil Gaiman, quoted by Žižek, describes it). For this reason, Žižek, like Badiou, ridicules our society's attempts to rationalize love, particularly the self-commodification demanded by online dating agencies that encourage individuals to present themselves as a list of attractive characteristics. "Within this model," Žižek writes, "if we marry today, it is more and more in order to re-normalize the violence of falling in love, the violence nicely indicated by the Basque term for falling in love—*maitemindu*—which, literally translated, means 'to be injured by love'" (73).

Love's traumatic dimensions

For Badiou love is enlivening even as it is a little dangerous. For Žižek it is both exhilarating and potentially injuring. However, it is

McGowan who, without ignoring love's animating potential, fully brings out its traumatic dimensions. In this context, trauma should once again be understood as a disturbance in the subject's ontology rather than, say, as the wounds inflicted by the cruelly optimistic bonds of intimacy that Berlant analyzes. Even though I do not wish to rehash all the distinctions between Lacanian political theory and affect theory that I outlined in the previous chapter, it is useful to recall that while Lacanians are primarily interested in the subject's constitutive "deformations," affect theorists are more interested in the politically, economically, and socially inflicted deformations that impact subjects unevenly due to collective structures of inequality. This distinction extends to the theme of love, which is why affect theory's commentary on love remains largely incompatible with the Lacanian perspective.

As a shortcut to grasping the reasons for this incompatibility, let us consider Berlant's depiction of love in terms of affective scenes of intimacy that undermine the subject's well-being even as they appear to render its life coherent, consistent, and dependable. Like the rest of cruel optimism, such scenes allow the subject to survive its suffering (the "cruelty of the now") even as they frequently cause even more suffering. As Berlant maintains, the fantasy of "the potentially good enough love enables crisis to feel ordinary" (2011, 174); the fantasy of intimacy allows one to feel normal, like one belongs somewhere, with someone who cares.

Berlant specifies that particularly in situations of extreme social precarity where individuals are unable to control other aspects of their lives, such as earning a living, the fantasy of a nourishing love can offer a much-needed palliative. This fantasy conveniently ignores the fact that in today's neoliberal world—a world that demands constant flexibility and adaptability—love, as Berlant expresses the matter, "is only slightly less contingent than work": "in love as at work, one might well be only a temporary employee" (2011, 185). The fantasy of enduring intimacy counters this state of affairs by providing a reassuring vision of the kind of sanctuary that the subject may never have experienced (and may never in fact experience). Yet as we have learned, the fantasmatic nature of this desire for a refuge cannot be interpreted merely as a conservative attachment to normativity, even if this is what it might also be; it must also be understood as what allows the subject to cope with otherwise dispiriting conditions.

Why does such a subject not revolt rather than pursue survival in the folds of a system that obviously injures it? The answer is simple enough: as I have argued, the already injured, the already precarious, cannot easily risk added injury or precarity. The revolutionary gesture takes more energy than the work-weary and emotionally exhausted have at their disposal. There are of course exceptions: times when the deprivileged rise up in rebellion. But this is less common than one might expect. The problem is not that the deprivileged are hoodwinked—that they do not see that they are being exploited—but rather that the utter instability of their lives makes it impossible for them to court the instability of insurgency. As I have stressed, this is why affect theorists are less interested in revolutionary gestures than in analyzing how marginalized subjects manage to withstand turmoil as an ordinary component of their lives.

Against a backdrop of desolation, the fantasy of lasting love is enticing. Yet Berlant also reminds us that it is not only the deprivileged who cultivate such a fantasy. The socially privileged may resort to it for different reasons than the deprivileged, but it is equally alive among them, as Habermas illustrates through his analysis of the bourgeois subject who uses the ideal of love, located in the private sphere, to counter the utilitarian tenor of its public life. As Berlant, drawing on Habermas, explains, such a subject "shifts between his identity as a calculating man of the market and his identity as an *homme* who locates this true self in the performance of intimacy in the theater of the domestic space" (2011, 181). If the fantasy of love among the deprivileged serves the needs of survival, the bourgeois scenario allows the privileged subject to disavow its aggressive tendencies by relegating them outside its "true," ethical self.

Neither of these portraitures of intimacy is compatible with the account of love offered by Lacanian political theorists. But they are deeply compatible with what Badiou, Žižek, and McGowan have to say about the commodification of love under the auspices of romance. And it is McGowan who, of these three thinkers, takes the critique of the transformation of love into romance the furthest.

As I have already specified, McGowan does not focus on the context-specific negations of subjectivity that constitute Berlant's main concern but rather on the constitutive negativity of the Lacanian subject of lack. Beginning from the elementary Lacanian insight that this subject is driven to fill its lack, McGowan postulates—and here I briefly dip back into some of the concerns of Chapter 3—that consumer capitalism exploits the structure of desire by offering an enticing array of objects that promise self-completion (the undoing of lack). This fantasy of fulfillment accompanies every commodity, which is precisely why commodities are so difficult to resist. Still, as McGowan acknowledges, with most commodities we see through the illusion; we understand that they are unlikely to bring us lasting satisfaction. Even though we purchase chocolate bars, tubes of toothpaste, and organic tomatoes, we do not *really* believe that these items will definitively solve our existential dilemmas. With cars, boats, houses, and computers, things can get more complicated because they feed the soothing notion that there are some things in our lives that will sustain us for longer than a month. But even such items are not expected to neutralize our desire once and for all: no matter how fabulous our car is there is going to be another car on the streets that seems even more fabulous.

McGowan proposes that things are very different with the object of romantic desire, for this object, more than any other, promises everlasting satisfaction. This is why McGowan believes that romance, particularly the romance sold by dating agencies, is the quintessential commodity—one that is essential to capitalism because it convinces consumers that somewhere out there in the world there exists a perfect, and perfectly satisfying, commodity. Even if every act of consumption entails the attempt to undo the loss of the Thing, to find an object that will make up for this loss, the romantic object is a privileged one in the sense that it enables us to fully invest ourselves in the promise of such an object: the soul mate.

McGowan hypothesizes that as much as mainstream ideology of romance tries to convince us that the soul mate resides outside the capitalist system of exchange, the notion of the soul mate is in fact the key to the functioning of this system because when we believe that a perfect commodity exists in the guise of the soul mate, we automatically (and unconsciously) take a step closer to believing that other commodities might also satisfy us. As McGowan humorously explains, "Though a hammer at the hardware store most likely cannot function as my soul mate, I will find more pleasure in purchasing it with the idea of an ideal commodity informing the purchase, and this is what the soul mate provides. That is to say, the idea of the soul mate underwrites all consumption within the capitalist universe" (2016, 191–92).

Because there is no commodity that can definitively heal the subject's lack, capitalism needs an ideological fantasy of such an object: this is what the soul mate provides. This is why the dating agency is so central to late capitalist society: it promises a solution to the problem of desire in the ideal of a soul mate. As McGowan asserts, "The dating service is a synecdoche for capitalist society as such: When I go to the dating service, I seek love as an object available for purchase" (2016, 179). But of course, even under the best circumstances, what we usually get is romance rather than love.

In this context, McGowan draws the same distinction between love and romance as Badiou and Žižek do: where the event of love derails the subject, romance reassures it. In addition, McGowan stresses that the derailing aspects of love are traumatizing, heightening the constitutive deformation of the subject and forcing it to confront its complete lack of control over the affective scenario that has taken hold of its being. This does not mean that the romance that the dating service sells completely domesticates love. McGowan proposes that capitalism needs its subjects to feel a hint of love's trauma because this trauma—when experienced in moderation—animates these subjects, making them feel like their lives are worth living; courting the disruptiveness of love enlivens those under the thrall of romance, thereby generating the necessary energy for them to endure the banality of the rest of their lives (here there is an obvious conceptual link with Berlant's analysis of intimacy as a palliative against unbearable conditions). At the same time, capitalism must contain this disruptiveness, place limits on it so as to ensure that its subjects do not lose their ability to handle other (pragmatic) aspects of their lives. This is why, according to McGowan, even if "love isn't a capitalist plot, romance is," for romance "enables us to touch love's disruptiveness while avoiding its full traumatic ramifications" (2016, 180).

In neutralizing (or at least mitigating) the traumatic dimensions of love, romance robs it of its character as an event. McGowan stipulates that the list of desirable qualities that the subject provides to the dating service is vital for the service's ideological viability because it erases love's "ability to attack the subject at the most inconvenient time and in the most unanticipated form" (2016, 178). If the subject in the throes of the love event experiences the trauma of every separation, every disappointment, every "unrequited phone call" (191)—if the love event constantly reminds the subject that the beloved other cannot be controlled—the dating service turns the other into an object that can be securely possessed.

More generally speaking, our society's ideology of romance, instead of rupturing the subject's identity in the way that the love event does, offers the subject a new symbolic identity in the guise of a husband, wife, or partner. That is, romance stabilizes the subject's relationship to the potentially derailing object. As a result, romance allows the subject to feel confident in its social status; it allows the subject to feel like its object is authorized by the social order.

In contrast, the subject in love could not care less about social authorization. This subject does not want recognition from the big Other. Rather, it is the beloved other who, as McGowan states, "takes the place of social authority itself": "When I love the other, I want to count for this other more than any recognition that might come from society at large. I want to matter more than everyone else put together. . . . Love demands that the little other take over the function of the big Other" (2016, 189–90). This is why, as Plato already understood, lovers do not care a whole lot about how they appear in public, about the kinds of awkward gestures they undertake; the only thing that matters to them is the recognition granted by the beloved.

This dynamic obviously gives the beloved a great deal of power and can lead to immense suffering on the part of the loving subject (more on this in the next chapter). But it is effective in loosening the ideological hold of the social establishment on the subject, which is exactly why capitalism wants to translate love into romance, why it seeks to deactivate love's disruptiveness. If Bruce Fink—whose commentary on Lacan's take on love I will touch on below—sees love as the bond between people that rescues them from the fragmentation that capitalism brings, McGowan sees it as what destroys capitalism's ability to control the subject. As I argued in Chapter 3, it is precisely this insubordination that love introduces into the subject that accounts for love's ethical potential: the subject in love is willing to sacrifice its social viability for the sake of its love object.

As I have emphasized, because of McGowan's suspicion of desire as a pure (narcissistic) fantasy, he uses the vocabulary of love rather than of desire to describe the phenomenon of the subject being able to dissociate itself from the dictates of the big Other. In contrast, I grant the possibility that there exists the kind of jouissance-filled desire that results in love in exactly the sense that McGowan (like Badiou and Žižek) understands the word. I hope to have already explained my reasoning. Here I merely want to add that in his seminar on transference (*Seminar VIII*), Lacan explicitly aligns the subject who is "disturbed" by the signifier with the dangers of desire: "If psychoanalysis has not succeeded in getting men to understand that their desires, first, are not the same thing as their needs and, second, are in themselves of a dangerous nature, threatening to the individual—this is shed light on by the fact that their desires are obviously threatening to the herd—then I wonder what purpose psychoanalysis has ever served" (1950–1961, 368).

Lacan thus suggests that psychoanalysis reveals—should reveal—that desire threatens the individual in part because it threatens the herd, the collective, which might consequently be driven to exact vengeance on the "straying" individual. From this it follows that desire might make it possible for the subject to counter the herd, as happens when it stands its ground in relation to its desire instead of capitulating to the herd's aggressive demands that it fall in line with the general will of the social order. This is what, in my view, gives desire its ethical valence.

Why love is not a good investment

Whether one uses the vocabulary of love or desire—and it feels to me that McGowan and I are talking about more or less the same phenomenon—the subject under the spell of this type of love or desire feels that it cannot survive without its beloved. This is why McGowan posits that even though love seems like an anomaly in Badiou's grid of truth events, it may in fact be "the paradigmatic truth procedure" because its disruption of our daily existence is much more palpable than the disruption generated by political, scientific, or artistic events: "It is much easier to imagine subjects dying for the sake of love than for the sake of the twelve-tone system of modern music" (2016, 189). This is why, unlike romance, love, McGowan specifies, "is never a good investment" (180). Even if it does not lead to the subject's death, it can cost it its symbolic and imaginary equilibrium. As I argued in Chapter 3, by introducing a sliver of eternity into the flow of time—a sliver of the real into the symbolic and imaginary aspects of life—love both elevates and destabilizes.

Echoing Badiou and Žižek, McGowan maintains that love "forces the subject to change its life entirely without any clear guidance as to how it should do so. . . . Life no longer just goes on" (2016, 187–88). But it is precisely for this reason—that love does not allow life to just go on—that it brings "real" satisfaction. As I already noted, partly this is because, as opposed to romance, love accepts the lack in both the self and the other. In *Seminar VIII*, Lacan in fact repeatedly tells us that to love is to declare our lack. After all, there is no desire without lack, so that when we desire, we inevitably reveal ourselves as lacking. As Lacan states, "Love is giving what you don't have" (1960–1961, 34).

Lacan here suggests that whenever the subject utters an "I love you," it cannot but affirm its constitutive lack, its castration. This is one reason that love is so traumatizing: instead of curing the subject's lack, it augments its awareness of this lack. As Fink glosses Lacan's idea, when we admit "that we love, we admit that we lack"; "to declare that one loves is to declare that one lacks" (38; 201). In love, Fink specifies, "we give the gift of what we don't have" (39). What is more, love allows us to enjoy our not having, our self-division, in ways that few other experiences do. In some ways, this is the very point of love: it allows us to abandon ourselves, to lose ourselves, or—as McGowan puts it, to "escape the constraints of our symbolic identity and to enjoy our nonidentity" (2016, 180).

Love leaves the loving subject with a sense of incompleteness, yet this is what makes love "real." I will return to this insight below. At this juncture, the important point is that if to love is to declare one's lack, it is also—and here I add specificity to what I said above—to cherish the lack in the other. McGowan expresses the matter beautifully when, in defending love against its commodification in romance, he writes: "In love the subject confronts the incompletion of the beloved object, how this object is fundamentally at odds with itself. When one falls in love, it is precisely this noncoincidence of the beloved object with itself that triggers the fall. The apparently self-identical object, like a contact lens or a blow-up doll, is not an adequate object for love because it lacks the explicit self-division that makes love possible" (2016, 185). "The self-division of the beloved," in short, "is the cause of love" (185). This in turn means that to love is never to possess the other for the simple reason that the other is not a rounded subject that could become an object of possession (like a contact lens or a blow-up doll) but instead also a subject of lack—an entity whose very ontology prevents it from being possessed "in its entirety."

Behind this formulation one can hear the existentialist notion—which is also a Lacanian notion—that it is only to the extent that the subject is a creature of nothingness that it is not an object. Unlike a rock, which lacks nothing, the subject is split and alienated from its own being, and it is this self-estrangement that makes it conscious of its own existence, self-reflexive, and ultimately resistant to being possessed: we cannot pick up a subject and put it in our pocket in the way that we can pocket a rock, sometimes even forgetting for months that we have done so. To be sure, people have throughout the atrocities of human history tried to treat human subjects like rocks: slavery attempts to turn the slave into an object; rape attempts to turn the raped person into an object; torture attempts to turn the tortured person into an object. Such violence can even to some degree succeed, at least when its target dies and becomes inert matter. But in principle it can never completely accomplish its goal, which is why, despite what some object-oriented ontologists imply, there is a difference between a human subject and a rock.

McGowan believes that loving the other in its lack and self-division removes it "from the terrain of the commodity with its initial promise of plenitude and subsequent disappointing lack" (2016, 185). In other words, if romance disappoints the moment the other is found lacking and self-divided, love "in the real" thrives on this discovery because it does not ask for plenitude, with the consequence that the (incomplete) object of love satisfies in a way that the (seemingly complete) object of romance never can. In a related vein, if romance enables the subject to keep the object at a safe distance, love does not: love besieges the subject with the object's disorienting satisfaction (distinctive mode of jouissance). In romance we recoil from this besiegement—from what is "too much," uncanny, or disturbing about the other—but in love we accept it.

This is why what might under normal circumstances alienate or repulse us about the other becomes indispensable to the experience of love. As McGowan asserts, when we love, the other's obnoxious eating habits or slovenly attitude suddenly seem like "appealing quirks rather than reasons for keeping a distance" (2016, 188). If smelly strangers in the subway cause us to wince, our lover's refusal to shower, McGowan quips, signifies his or her bohemian contempt for the sanitized daily rituals of the bourgeoisie: "The lover embraces the unflattering characteristics of the beloved and treats them as sublime indexes of the beloved's worth. . . . In contrast to desire, love depends on the embrace of what is undesirable in the object" (188).

McGowan here again draws a distinction between love and desire in a way that I do not. But the significant insight for our present purposes is that the acceptance of the other's repellent qualities does not mean that the other is fully available. McGowan explains that if to love is to declare our lack, it is—again, due to the other's lack and self-division—also to love "what the other doesn't itself have" (2016, 183). This implies that the other always "remains outside our control" (183). For McGowan, this inability to attain our object is not a tragedy but what allows love to endure. Romance may promise lasting fulfillment but it disappoints the moment this promise collapses; in contrast, love understands that non-fulfillment is intrinsic to its character. This is why McGowan argues that although we are used to judging monogamy as a conservative response to the repressiveness of our social order, "one is almost tempted to call monogamy an anticapitalist practice" (186).

Many queer theorists would disagree, as would many other progressive critics. But McGowan's reasoning makes sense in the context of his overall analysis of how capitalism seduces its subjects by exploiting the structure of their (normative) desire: the subject who moves from one object to the next acquiesces to the logic of accumulation. Such a subject (of romance) believes that by obtaining a large array of objects of desire, it will find complete satisfaction. Love, in contrast, deprives the subject of everything, even its access to its privileged love object. This is why it can never be a good investment.

Socrates's *Agálmata*

Lacan's *Seminar VIII*—which, in addition to being a commentary on transference, is a close reading of Plato's *Symposium*—allows me to shed light on why Lacanians tend to speak about love in such (seemingly anachronistic) enthusiastic terms. And it also allows me to deepen the analysis of desire's capacity to raise a mundane object to the dignity of the Thing that I began in Chapter 3, for *Seminar VIII* centers on how Alcibiades—who is madly in love with Socrates—does exactly this to Socrates. While Lacan's reading of the *Symposium* contains a detailed account of the speeches of all the characters who accept Socrates's invitation to stay sober in order to pay proper tributes to love, Lacan grants particular importance to the drunken, belated, and disruptive arrival of Alcibiades at the gathering. This is because the unruly entrance of Alcibiades, and the ridiculous confession of love he aims at Socrates (and which stands as the text's rousing finale), metaphorizes both the sublime and derailing (and stubborn) aspects of desire that I have highlighted. It is also Alcibiades's speech that allows Lacan to develop his notion of the *objet a* through the Greek word *ágalma*, for in his speech Alcibiades insists that he finds this *ágalma*, or *agálmata* in the plural, within Socrates.

Lacan explains that, for Alcibiades, Socrates is like a silenus, a container, such as a jewelry box, in which the Ancient Greeks offered gifts—that, for Alcibiades, Socrates holds untold treasures: "What is important is what is inside" (1960–1961, 137). Lacan notes that the word *ágalma* may mean "ornament" or "jewelry," but this is just the beginning of his analysis, for as he pointedly asks, "Why bejewel oneself?" (135). To lure others—why else?

Lacan goes on to argue that, in the context of Alcibiades's desire for Socrates, *ágalma* means "above all a gem or precious object" (1960–1961, 137–38). Lacan paraphrases Alcibiades's "discourse of passion at its peak of trembling"—the discourse that Alcibiades utters in an attempt to explain why his love for Socrates is nonnegotiable and why he consequently has no choice but to meet all of Socrates's demands—as follows (I am leaving out the ancient Greek inserted into these sentences): "No one has ever seen what is in question as I managed to. I saw it. I saw them, the *agálmata* that are already divine—they're wonderful, they're golden—totally beautiful, so utterly amazing that there was only one thing to do, and right away, as directly as possible: to do everything Socrates ordered" (138–39). The *agálmata* within Socrates are thus magnificent: "It is enough to indicate that *ágalma* has to do with the meanings *brilliant* [sheen] and *galant* [gallant], the latter coming from *gal*, meaning *éclat* [sparkle or gleam] in Old French. In a word, what is at stake here if not the function we analysts have discovered that is designated by the term 'partial object'" (143)?

We know that Socrates rejects Alcibiades's advances, implying that Alcibiades's desire is so fantasy driven, so illusory, that it could as well be aimed at Agathon (who, at the symposium, is lounging next to Socrates, and who consequently bears the brunt of Alcibiades's jealousy). Lacan's commentary on this potential interchangeability of the object of desire—the idea that Alcibiades could easily shift his desire from Socrates to Agathon without losing anything essential—accords well with his analysis of the imaginary, narcissistic character of desire, and it would be easy to leave things at that: according to this reading, Socrates does not respond to Alcibiades's desire because he understands the structure of desire; he understands that desire pursues a fantasy object and that, ultimately, he does not possess the treasure that Alcibiades finds in him.

However, I want to focus on why Lacan claims that if Alcibiades is mistaken in believing that Socrates contains a treasure, Socrates is also mistaken in rejecting Alcibiades. Here it is worth quoting Lacan at length:

> But we must not misrecognize here that Socrates, precisely because he knows, replaces one thing with something else. It is neither beauty, nor ascesis, nor identification with God that Alcibiades desires, but rather this unique object, this special something he saw in Socrates and which Socrates turns him away from, because Socrates knows that he does not have it. But Alcibiades still desires the same thing. What he is looking for in Agathon, make no mistake about it, is the same supreme point at which the subject is abolished in fantasy: his *agálmata.* Socrates substitutes here his lure [*leurre*] for what I will call the lure of the gods. He does so quite authentically, insofar as he knows what love is. *And it is precisely because he knows this that he is doomed to be mistaken—namely to misrecognize the essential function of the targeted object constituted by ágalma.* (1960–1961, 159; emphasis added)

And a few pages later:

> Alcibiades demonstrates the presence of love, but only insofar as Socrates, who knows, can be *mistaken about its presence*, and only accompanies him in being mistaken. The deception [*leurre*] is mutual. Socrates is just as caught up in the deception—if it is a deception and if it is true that he is deceived [*leurré*]—as Alcibiades is. But which of them is the most authentically deceived, if not he

> who follows closely, and without allowing himself to drift, what is traced out for him by a love that I will call horrible? . . . recall that Dante [in the *Inferno*] explicitly places the words "eternal love" on the doors of Hell. (163; emphasis added)

Alcibiades is mistaken because he cannot see through the deception—the fantasmatic lure of desire—with the result that he is destined to chase an unattainable, devastating, and horrible love; he idiotically believes that his love is eternal even though it has no basis in the person he loves. But what is even more interesting is that Lacan insists that Socrates is *also* mistaken. Indeed, I will argue that he may be even more tragically mistaken than Alcibiades because he *can* see through the deception, and stupidly believes that this is enough, that this is the whole story. I, for my part, do not think that it is the whole story. I think that, according to Lacan, Socrates is so excessively focused on the lures of love that he is "mistaken about its presence." Simply put, for Socrates, the fantasy aspects of desire hide the real of love. And this is a grave mistake indeed.

Why is Socrates mistaken?

If one follows the early Lacan's commentary on the mirror stage, narcissism, and the function of the *objet a* as an imaginary lure, it is easy to grasp why Alcibiades is mistaken: he is caught up in an illusion that will lead him straight to the gates of hell. The story is familiar to all of those who know the fundamentals of the early structuralist Lacan, for this story has long functioned as the standard narrative of Lacanian theory within the Anglo-American academy: the mirror stage alienates the subject from itself by causing it to misrecognize itself in its image, a grandiose image that becomes the basis of its narcissism; the encounter with the signifier in turn wounds the subject, bringing into existence the Lacanian subject of lack, who will henceforth cathect to objects, particularly beloved people, in the hope that these objects will fill the void within its being; but this quest for wholeness is deceptive, doomed to fail, for no object can definitively satisfy, can in the final analysis undo the subject's lack; the *objet a* functions as the imaginary "in you more than you" (Lacan 1964) that the subject fantasmatically installs in the other in an effort to turn the other into a fully satisfying object, into a perfect narcissistic mirror; but in the end, the other who appears to contain the *objet a* will always disappoint for the simple reason that it does not in reality possess the *objet a* (which is merely a figment of the subject's imagination).

This story about the fundamentally narcissistic structure of desire is the basis for McGowan's portrayal of desire as an illusory quest for satisfaction that capitalism harnesses by feeding the subject's faith in the existence of a perfect object, a commodity that—like a contact lens that undoes the distortions of vision—will put an end to its alienation. And it explains why Alcibiades is mistaken: the *agálmata* he locates in Socrates represent the illusory *objet a* that can only mislead him. However, if I am interested in why Lacan believes that Socrates—who clearly comprehends that the structure of desire is premised on a narcissistic fantasy—is also mistaken when he rejects Alcibiades's desire, it is in part because I would like to emphasize that the Lacanian story does not end with its early structuralist formulation.

One reason that many non-specialists misrepresent Lacan—for instance, as being overly focused on the signifier, as glorifying the phallus, as denigrating the body, as ignoring affect, and so on—is that they do not move beyond the standard structuralist narrative: they do not read Lacan beyond the obligatory set of essays from the *Écrits*, with the result that they do not recognize the extent to which Lacan over the years shifted his emphasis from the signifier to the bodily real. Along closely related lines, they do not recognize that Lacan's understanding of the *objet a* changes over time, gradually losing its moorings in the imaginary and becoming increasingly associated with the real, with the kind of desire that is not merely a fantasy formation but that carries something about the truthfulness that Lacan associates with jouissance. At least by Lacan's 1962–1963 seminar on anxiety (*Seminar X*), which he delivered only two years after his seminar on transference, the *objet a* was no longer just an imaginary lure but had become a little morsel, or remainder, of the real that had been severed from the subject's being as a result of its subjection to the symbolic order.

As I have argued at various points in this book, a distinction needs to be made between desire as a manifestation of narcissistic fantasy and desire as a force that converges with the drive to such a degree that it arrives within striking distance of the Thing. The latter is the kind of desire that bites "into bits of the real," to borrow a felicitous phrase from Roberto Harari (141). What I want to suggest here—as an extension of my argument in Chapter 3—is that this kind of desire comes as close to "real" love as it is possible for human beings to experience, and that it is to the extent that Socrates rejects it that he makes a huge mistake.

Fink correctly remarks that the status of the *objet a* in *Seminar VIII* is ambiguous in the sense that Lacan continues to associate it with the imaginary and fantasy at the same time as he is already gesturing toward the real and jouissance. Fink proposes that this ambiguity is due to the fact that in *Seminar VIII* Lacan is not yet fully aware that his conception of the *objet a* is moving from the imaginary register to the register of the real. In the latter register, the subject's encounter with the *objet a* is either uncanny or transcendent, terrifying or miraculous, depending on which face of jouissance this encounter activates. I agree with Fink that the ambiguity regarding the *objet a* persists until *Seminar X*, but I would date its inception earlier, at least to *Seminar VII* (1959–1960), where Lacan already characterizes the *objet a* as the little piece of the Thing—which by definition belongs in the register of the real—that the subject discovers in its object.

However, the question of when the transformation in Lacan's thinking takes place seems less important than the fact that it does take place, and that it is true that *Seminar VIII* vacillates between the imaginary and real valences of the *objet a*. Furthermore, I want to argue that the seemingly confusing amalgamation of the imaginary and the real in this seminar accounts for one of its most original contributions, namely the idea that the imaginary and the real are not necessarily always mutually incompatible. I would in fact go as far as to claim that by the end of the seminar—for reasons that I will elucidate below—Lacan suggests that on some level it does not matter that the shimmering *objet a* that the lover locates in the beloved object is imaginary (illusory), for its effects can be "real."

In the long passages that I quoted above, Lacan emphasizes that Socrates does not enter the game of love because he is fully aware of the imaginary function of the *objet a*. In other words, proper Lacanian that he is, Socrates understands the dissymmetry intrinsic to love. Lacan describes this dissymmetry as follows:

> Note that the two terms that, in their essence, constitute the lover and the beloved in no way coincide. What the one is missing is

> not what is hidden in the other. This is the whole problem of love. Whether one knows it or not is of no consequence. In the phenomenon of love, at every step of the way one encounters the wrenching and discordance associated it. No one needs, for all that, to dialogue or dialectize, about love to be involved in this gap or discord—it suffices to be in the thick of it, to be in love. (1960–1961, 39–40)

The loving subject, in this scenario, is lacking and, in the romantic haze of its fantasy life, believes that the other contains what it does not have—the *objet a*—even though this is not in the least bit the case. Socrates knows this: he knows that "what is missing in the one is not hidden in the other," that it is Alcibiades himself who has turned him into a jewelry box that seems to contain a treasure. And unlike the average lover—or even the supposedly informed one, such as a Lacanian theorist (because, as Lacan admits, when one is "in the thick of it," whether "one knows it or not is of no consequence")—who falls into the trap of desire even when she knows full well that the other does not have what she lacks, Socrates meticulously avoids this trap.

Lacan postulates that Socrates refuses to participate in the game of love because he "knows the score in matters of love—that is even, as he says, the only thing he knows" (1960–1961, 153). More specifically, Lacan believes that Socrates knows that "there is nothing in him that is lovable. His essence is emptiness or hollowness" (155). According to Lacan, it is as if Socrates said to Alcibiades, "Pay attention—where you see something, I am nothing" (154). It is for this reason that Socrates asserts that Alcibiades might as well desire Agathon rather than him (Socrates), his point being that if the *ágalma* as the cause of Alcibiades's desire originates within Alcibiades, any object of desire can in principle fulfill the role of becoming a container for it.

Socrates is wiser about love than most of us. Yet in the passages that I quoted above, Lacan arguably suggests that Socrates is misguided in thinking that Agathon could serve as a substitute for himself because he misrecognizes "the essential function of the targeted object constituted by *ágalma*," namely that this targeted object is not any old object but the point of fixation to which the truth of the subject's desire—desire as an index of jouissance—is fastened. To express the matter differently, Lacan suggests that

Socrates is misguided in thinking that what Alcibiades ultimately desires is beauty, ascesis, or God rather than the all-important *ágalma*. As Lacan writes:

> If one brings out the love relationship while holding in abeyance its anchor, pivotal point, center of gravity, or hook, it is impossible to say anything that is not simply a crock. We must emphasize the correlative object of desire, for it is this—and not the object that is involved in equivalence, the transitivism of good things, or the transaction of covetous desires—that is the psychoanalytic object. The psychoanalytic object is the something that is the aim of desire as such, *the something that emphasizes one object among all the others as incommensurate with the others*. . . . This is what makes it weighty; this is why it is important to know where this fabulous object is, what its function is, and where it operates in inter- and intrasubjectivity. This privileged object of desire culminates for each of us at the border or liminal point I have taught you to view as the metonymy of unconscious discourse. This object plays a role there that I tried to formalize in fantasy . . . [However], everything revolves around the privileged or unique point constituted somewhere by something we find in a being *only when we truly love*. But what is it? *Ágalma*—the object we have learned to discern in analytic practice. (1960–1961, 146–48)

Although Lacan acknowledges that the *objet a* is a concept that he has attempted to "formalize in fantasy," his main point here, on my reading at least, is that this object—"the psychoanalytic object"—is the anchor, pivotal point, center of gravity, or hook that links the subject to the truth of its desire, which means that when we ignore this object, when we speak about a reciprocal (symmetrical) relationship between two people, when we stay on the level of equivalences, on the level of an always somewhat utilitarian "transaction" (or exchange) of covetous desires, we do not understand the first thing about love: we fail "to say anything that is not simply a crock."

In contrast, the *objet a* gestures toward what is nonequivalent, what is incommensurate with other objects. In other words, the fantasmatic nature of the *objet a* does not in any way lessen but in fact enormously augments its value. As I argued in Chapter 3, this "fabulous object" is precisely what renders the beloved other irreplaceable, so that this other cannot easily be discarded for the sake of another (despite the reassurances of dating services). This magnificent object is the aim of desire "as such": "the privileged or unique point constituted somewhere by something we find in a being only when we truly love."

Ergo: Socrates cannot be replaced by Agathon as Alcibiades's object of desire. Nor can beauty, ascesis, or God displace the *objet a*. On the one hand, the inaccessibility of the Thing, the fact that the Thing, in Lacan's words, "can only ever be refound—in other words, never truly refound" (1960–1961, 242), means that we are forced to dwell among objects that are exchangeable, that exist in the world of other objects. On the other, the *objet a* "creates the gap between the constitution of the extraordinary object that arises in fantasy and every kind of object in the so-called social world—that is, the world of conformity" (242). That is, it is exactly insofar as the *objet a* is a fantasy object (or more precisely, a partial object shrouded in fantasy) that it cannot ever entirely fit into the universe of mundane objects, that it cannot enter into the same economy of exchange as concrete (less fantasy-infused) objects. Instead, the *objet a* is what illuminates the sublime aspects of a mundane object, raising it to the dignity of the Thing. This illumination is what we brush against when "we truly love."

If Socrates is mistaken, it is because he believes that the fact that Alcibiades's desire for him is premised on fantasy means that Alcibiades does not "truly love" him; he is mistaken because he believes that the fact that he does not possess the treasure that Alcibiades discovers in him reveals that Alcibiades's desire is inauthentic when in reality it is precisely Alcibiades's capacity to see this treasure, to fantasize this treasure into existence, that proves the authenticity (or "truthfulness") of his desire.

The psychoanalytic partial object

Let us backtrack a little by returning to Lacan's claim that the privileged object that we find when "we truly love"—the *ágalma*—is the psychoanalytic object par excellence: "the object we have learned to discern in analytic practice" (1960–1961, 148). In making this statement, Lacan is referring to his conviction that one of Freud's greatest discoveries was to understand the immense significance of the partial object, the *objet a*, as opposed to the whole object. Lacan in fact admonishes post-Freudian analysts for having been too obtuse to recognize this significance, for having tried to efface the originality of Freud's discovery of the partial object, to turn this object "into a flat, round, total object . . . the other as a whole person" (143). "We had a real find there," Lacan asserts, namely "that of the fundamentally partial nature of the object insofar as it is the pivotal point, crux, or key of human desire" (143). But because it is disturbing to think that our desire might not have much to do with the other as a whole person, analysis—like the rest of society—engages in a process of totalization that erases the partial object, the *objet a*, in favor of the idea of the beloved other as a full subject in its own right.

The idea that recognizing the other as a full subject in its own right—equal to oneself, equivalent with oneself—is the ethically appropriate attitude is intuitively compelling, and in fact underlies theories, such as Butler's Levinasian theory, that are predicated on the notion that ethics is a matter of recognizing the full humanity of the other. However, Lacan suggests that, in the context of love at least, the attempt to conjure away the *objet a* by putting in its place a whole person is a mistake because, as I have just argued, it is the *objet a* within the other that renders the other incomparable ("incommensurate") and irreplaceable.

In Chapter 3, I argued that the kind of desire that discerns the sublime echo of the Thing in a mundane object has something "real" about it. I now want to add that inasmuch as this kind of desire cannot be dissociated from the *objet a*, we must entertain the possibility that there is something about the *objet a* that exceeds the purely imaginary (fantasy-based) structure of desire. Indeed, Lacan's reading of Alcibiades and Socrates suggests that it is only to the degree that the *objet a* gives rise to fantasy that the subject is able to find the sublime echo of the Thing in a mundane object. This is what I meant above when I claimed that in *Seminar VIII* fantasy and the real are no longer mutually incompatible. Rather, it is through fantasy, through stepping into the fiction of *objet a*, that the subject discovers the real.

Perhaps one could say that the *objet a* manages to satisfy because it translates fantasy into the real of jouissance. The *agálmata* that

Alcibiades deposits in Socrates elevate Socrates to the nobility of the Thing, which explains why his desire for Socrates is unassailable, impervious even to an embarrassing public rejection. As Lacan posits, when it comes to Socrates, to the sign of Socrates's desire that Alcibiades covets, Alcibiades says something like, "I want it because I want it, whether it's for my own good or not"; that is, Alcibiades wants Socrates regardless of consequences, regardless of how dearly he might have to pay for his desire (1960–1961, 157). "And it is precisely for this reason," Lacan concludes, "that Alcibiades reveals the central function of *ágalma* in the articulation of love relations" (157).

Alcibiades may complain. But there is "real" satisfaction in his desire despite his complaints, despite his frustration. As we learned from McGowan earlier, love is never a good investment. But this does not mean that it does not gratify. Indeed, as we also learned from McGowan, there is something uniquely gratifying about the object of love (as opposed to the object of romance) in part because, due to its own self-division, it remains beyond the subject's capacity to possess it. For Alcibiades, Socrates is not "a flat, round, total object" (like a contact lens) but a hollow one (a being of lack). But his hollowness (lack) is what allows him to serve as a container for the partial object, the *ágalma*, as the cause of Alcibiades's fascination. This is what Socrates does not understand. He is mistaken in thinking that his emptiness—the fact that he does not have the treasure that Alcibiades sees in him—renders him unworthy of love when it is exactly his lack, his hollowness, that allows Alcibiades to place this treasure in him.

The event of love: Where two dignities meet

We have established that the object of love does not have what the lover wants. Moreover, the beloved other does not know what it is about its being that arouses the lover's affection. In other words, if the loving subject does not know what it is lacking—does not know the precise nature of *objet a*—the other does not know what it has, what hidden treasure there is within its being that awakens the subject's desire. This is why, as I noted earlier, there may be no relation whatsoever between what the subject is lacking and what the beloved has, which is why the subject never finds what it is looking for.

Yet Lacan asserts that "from the conjunction of desire with its object qua inadequate, the signification called love must arise" (1960–1961, 34). The object may always be hollow, may always lack the treasure, yet from this lack arises what we call love. As Lacan writes: "The gods of Antiquity don't beat around the bush. They knew they could reveal themselves to men only in the guise of something that would cause a ruckus, in the *ágalma* of something that breaks all the rules, as a pure manifestation of an essence that remained completely hidden, whose enigma was entirely below the surface" (162). The *ágalma*—the essence of which remains enigmatic—breaks all the rules, causing a ruckus: what Badiou calls the event of love.

Lacan specifies that the reason the *ágalma* possesses this life-altering power is that it arrests the incessant sliding of the signifiers that constitutes the usual reality of the subject, fixing it to a spot. Under normal conditions, the subject's desire as a function of the signifying chain moves metonymically from object to object (which is why McGowan is able to link it to the functioning of commodity capitalism). In Lacan's words, "Due to the fact that the subject undergoes the mark of the signifying chain, something is fundamentally instituted in him that we call metonymy, which is nothing other than the possibility of the infinite sliding of signifiers owing to the continuity of the signifying chain" (1960–1961, 169). Moreover, everything that at any given time becomes associated with this chain—any circumstantial object—"can be taken as equivalent to each other under suitable conditions" (169). This would be the scenario in which Agathon could be substituted for Socrates as the object of Alcibiades's desire. However, when the *objet a*, the *ágalma*, enters the scene, it halts the sliding of the signifiers; it halts this substitutability, or equivalence, of circumstantial objects.

Lacan explains the matter as follows:

> Now it is precisely inasmuch as something presents itself as enhancing [*revalorisant*] this infinite sliding—this dissolving element that brings signifying fragmentation into the subject—that it takes on the value of the privileged object that puts a stop to the infinite sliding. *An object can thus assume, in relation to*

> *the subject, the essential value that constitutes the fundamental fantasy.* The subject himself realizes that he is arrested therein, or, to remind you of a more familiar notion, fixated. We call the object that serves this privileged function *a*. . . . This object is overvalued. *And it is insofar as it is overvalued that it serves the function of saving our dignity as subjects—that is, of making us something other than subjects subjected to the infinite sliding of the signifier. It makes of us something other than subjects of speech, turning us into something unique, inestimable, and irreplaceable in the final analysis, which is the true point at which we can designate what I have called the dignity of the subject. . . . Individuality consists entirely in the privileged relationship in which we culminate as subjects of desire.* (1960–1961, 170–71; emphasis added)

Lacan expresses a great deal in this remarkable passage. Our individuality is not a matter of some essential trait that we are born with, of the specificity of our body, identity, or character, but instead arises from the way in which we salvage our dignity as subjects through a love object that seems to contain the *objet a*. On the one hand, this privileged, even overvalued, object enhances, revalorizes, the signifying chain: its brilliance accelerates the sliding of the signifier to the point that we spin out of control, fragment, and dissolve, which is why Lacan notes that this object is one "before which we falter, vacillate, and disappear as subjects" (1960–1961, 170). On the other, because this object fixes us to a spot, it saves our "dignity" as subjects by turning us into something other than subjects subjected to the infinite sliding of the signifier.

The privileged object of love—insofar as it contains the *objet a*—ushers the echo of the Thing into our existence, allowing us to touch the real, to experience something of the jouissance of the real; it connects us to our fundamental fantasy. As a result, we—for a moment at least—cease to function as wholly symbolic creatures, creatures enslaved to the signifier (the big Other). We individuate ourselves through the specificity of our desire. Lacan in fact implies that this kind of desire renders not only the object but also the subject "unique, inestimable, irreplaceable." No wonder, then, that Badiou, Žižek, and McGowan all describe the love event as one where the eternal (the immortal) enters the flow of time, stopping the subject on its tracks and transporting it into a transcendent realm.

This type of transcendent experience—the love event—is what Socrates does not allow himself to experience. Furthermore, he ridicules Alcibiades for not being able to resist it. This is why, of the two, he is arguably the one who is more mistaken, or at least more tragically mistaken. Alcibiades may not comprehend the fantasmatic dimensions of desire but at least he is willing to surrender himself to the love event. Socrates, in contrast, commits the cardinal sin (as Badiou might argue) of rejecting the event, thereby depriving himself of the "dignity" that such an event imparts to the subject. He may have other ways of stopping the sliding of the signifier: philosophy fixes him to a spot—so that he stands frozen, deep in thought, for hours—in the same way that the love event fixes the lover to a spot. But when it comes to the love event, Socrates misses the point entirely.

As I have stressed, Socrates does not enter the game of love because he believes that he grasps the structure of desire, and in some ways he of course does: he grasps the fantasmatic nature of the *agálmata* that Alcibiades finds within him; he knows that he does not possess what Alcibiades desires, that he is lacking, devoid of the riches that Alcibiades seeks. However, as I have tried to illustrate, what Socrates does not see is that ultimately it does not matter that he is empty because it is through fantasy, through raising its mundane object to the dignity of the Thing that the loving subject—in this case Alcibiades—both "truly" loves *and* endows itself with the dignity of a subject who is no longer subjected to the endless sliding of the signifier but, instead, has reached a more transcendent domain. Love, in this sense, is where two different "dignities" meet each other: the dignity of the object as what contains an echo of the sublime Thing and the dignity of the subject who, through its love for the object, has also obtained a foothold in sublimity.

Loving the lack in the other

We know—and Lacan mentions this—that Socrates can desire urgently, and that Alcibiades is in fact Socrates's "first love" (1960–1961, 154). Why, then, can Socrates not allow himself to return Alcibiades's desire? Fink hypothesizes that it is because Socrates is unwilling to admit his lack. Yes, he is too wise to step into the fantasmatic structure of desire. But he is also too arrogant, too cocky, to concede his lack, his self-division; he "refuses to fall from grace" (193), as Fink puts it. This in turn renders him incapable of love because, as we learned above, to love is to acknowledge one's lack.

Along somewhat related lines, McGowan speculates that Socrates is unable to love Alcibiades because he does not want to be derailed by love's dislocating dimensions. Recall that McGowan believes that to love is to cherish not only the other's lack but also the distortions of (the other's) subjectivity that result from this lack, including its idiosyncratic ways of enjoying itself. "When one falls in love," McGowan explains, "one falls for the other's way of enjoying itself, for the other's satisfaction with its own form of failure . . . . Love targets the point at which the subject exceeds itself and is not self-identical" (2016, 180). Against this backdrop, McGowan proposes that Socrates is unable to love because he is a figure of purity who cannot withstand the other's jouissance, who avoids "succumbing to the disruptiveness of the other" (182). In other words, if Fink believes that Socrates is unwilling to admit his lack, McGowan believes that Socrates is unwilling to confront Alcibiades's jouissance, Alcibiades's satisfaction with his own failure (with his own lack).

I appreciate both perspectives. But I am inclined to read Socrates a little more generously, as someone who fails to understand that what the subject in love—in this case Alcibiades—loves in the object is not its plenitude but rather, as McGowan himself argues, its failure to achieve self-identity, that is, its lack. Approaching the matter from the opposite perspective, the perspective of the beloved, Fink is getting at something similar when he proposes that we want to be loved for our flaws, for what is undesirable in us, our "warts and all" (41). Based on these viewpoints, I want to restate that I believe that Socrates's problem is that he does not recognize that being lovable, being full of treasures, is not a precondition of being "truly" loved.

Lacan constantly stresses that Socrates does not enter the game of love because he knows that he is empty. So it is definitely not the case that Socrates is too arrogant to admit his lack. The very opposite seems to be the case: Socrates cannot love Alcibiades because he is all too aware of his lack, because he is afraid to be found wanting—devoid of any *agálmata*—and therefore believes that were he to enter the game of love, he would immediately disappoint Alcibiades. It is almost as if Socrates rejects Alcibiades's desire because he deems his lack to be so vast that he does not deserve this desire.

To state the matter in terms that I have developed throughout this chapter, Socrates does not realize that he does not "in reality" need to be full of gleaming gems to be worthy of Alcibiades's desire. As I emphasized above, if anything, it is precisely because Socrates is hollow that Alcibiades is able to place the *agálmata* in him, is able to raise him to the dignity of the Thing, in the first place. From this point of view, Socrates's mistake is to question the very fantasmatic structure of desire that renders him irreplaceable to Alcibiades, that transforms him from an exchangeable object to an inexchangeble one. That is, I think that Socrates is mistaken because he fails to discern that even if love is an imaginary (fantasmatic) construct, its effects—sometimes at least—are real, of the order of what McGowan calls "a secular miracle" (2016, 187).

It may also be that a part of Socrates's mistake is to fail to see that being a *lover*—allowing *himself* to love Alcibiades—would not require that he himself be desirable. If I have this far argued that the object does not need to be desirable (full of riches) to be desired, I am now adding, following Lacan's lead, that the loving subject does not need to be desirable in order to be able to love. As a matter of fact, for Lacan, the analyst is someone—if he or she is a good analyst—who understands this last point: the analyst is able "to conceptualize how a subject can occupy the place of pure desirousness—in other words, abstract or subtract himself, in the relationship to the other, from any supposition of being desirable" (1960–1961, 369).

Here it is worth noting that Lacan would like the analyst to occupy this place of pure desirousness—to recognize the difference between being able to desire and being desirable—so as to keep herself from dumping her anxiety on the analysand. As I argued at the end of Chapter 3, where there is desire, there is less anxiety, the logical conclusion being that when the analyst is able to embody pure desirousness, she does not impart anxiety to the analysand. This is why Lacan argues that, for the analyst, "it is good to always have within reach a little well-polished desire so as not to be prone to bringing into play in the analysis a quantum of anxiety that would be neither opportune nor welcome" (1960–1961, 371).

In this context, Lacan once again brings up Socrates's unwillingness to either desire or be desired by Alcibiades: "If something is incarnated in and signified by the episode with Alcibiades, it is clearly the following: on the one hand, Socrates asserts that he knows nothing except about matters of love, and everything we are told about him is that he is desirous through and through and inexhaustibly so; yet, on the other hand, when it comes time for him to take up the position of he who is desired when faced with Alcibiades' public, scandalous, out-of-control and drunk aggression, he is literally not up to it" (1960–1961, 369).

This statement is ambiguous. On the one hand, one could read Lacan as saying that Socrates is a better analyst than lover. He occupies the place of "pure desirousness" by refusing to act on his desire (even though "he is desirous through and through and inexhaustibly so"). On the other hand, one could read Lacan as saying, "What the fuck is the matter with Socrates? He is *not* an analyst, so why is he acting like one, keeping his hands off the beautiful boy who is begging to see his erection? Being a teacher should not have stopped him in the context of Ancient Greece, where he himself notoriously argued that the beautiful boy is the first rung on the ladder to the Ideal Form of Beauty." I hope to have illustrated why I think that the latter interpretation captures at least some of Lacan's argument.

That said, for all of his talk about the *ágalma* as an opening to being able to "truly love," Lacan does not end his seminar on a transcendent note, for he emphasizes that what Socrates knows, and what the analyst "must at least glimpse," is that on the level of the *objet a*, "the question is entirely different from the question of access to some ideal" (1960–1961, 397). The ideal—the Thing—may be what the lover is after but Socrates knows, and the analyst should know, that love "can only surround this island, this field of being" (397). This is why I have argued that the object of desire can only offer partial satisfaction, that the encounter with the Thing would result in the annihilation of the subject. As Lacan states at the very end of his seminar, "This means that, regarding anyone, you can raise the question of whether desire is totally destructive. With anyone, you can try to determine how far you will dare to go in the questioning of being—at the risk to yourself of disappearing" (398).

Moreover, Lacan stresses that, for the analyst, analysis always entails a degree of mourning because the analyst, much like Socrates, cannot help but believe that any object whatsoever can come to contain the *objet a*, can become a placeholder for transference. This is what Socrates expresses when he chooses "to praise the idiot of idiots, the most idiotic of them, and even the only thoroughgoing idiot [*con*] in the place": Agathon (1960–1961, 397). That is, when Socrates tells Alcibiades that he could as well desire this idiot, Agathon, he reveals what every analyst knows, namely that on a certain level the identity of the object of desire does not matter. Yet according to Lacan's own reasoning about raising a mundane object to the dignity of the Thing, to the rank of the irreplaceable object, this is not the only (psychoanalytic) story or even the most important one.

The overvaluation of love

One reason that Lacan's commentary on love in *Seminar VIII* is so hard to parse, and at times even appears to contradict itself, may be that, from one paragraph to the next, he keeps switching between the symbolic, imaginary, and real registers of love. In other words, not only is the status of the *objet a* ambiguous, sometimes aligned with the imaginary, and other times with the real, but it is also not always clear whether Lacan is talking about the symbolic, imaginary, or real aspects of love (or of some combination of these aspects). In this regard, Fink's commentary on *Seminar VIII* is helpful, for he distinguishes between these registers while at the same time arguing that love, as we usually experience it, is a combination of all three.

More specifically, Fink proposes that it is on the symbolic level that we find the idea that when we speak our love, we reveal our lack; we indicate that something in the other addresses our lack. As Fink puts it, "You bring out the lack in me" (39). This is also the level on which we love what is lacking in the other, privileging the imperfect object over the perfect one; we love what is inadequate, vulnerable, and woundable in the other. Conversely, as I already noted, Fink hypothesizes that we want to be loved for what is unlovable in us. McGowan might say that we want to be loved for our lack, our self-division. One might characterize this as the human—the intersubjective—dimension of love, the dimension that is facilitated by our membership in the symbolic order.

On the imaginary level, we find the narcissistic structure of love that Lacan links to the mirror stage and that I have described in terms of the cruelly optimistic hope that the other will heal our lack, plug the hole in our being, or at the very least distract us from our mortification. Although Lacan shunned this facet of love—the situation where Agathon could easily replace Socrates as Alcibiades's object of desire—I think that it is important to recognize the considerable suffering that it can bring, for when we lose an object who promises to undo our alienation, we in many ways, momentarily at least, lose the foundations of our coherence; this is why losing a beloved who has been an object of narcissistic investment hurts so much.

Finally, on the level of the real we find the experience of hitting jouissance in a way that temporarily causes us to lose our lack, our self-division: suddenly we are no longer aware of ourselves as alienated creatures; our void ceases to exist; we have been lifted to a transcendent plane where self-consciousness is erased. Fink remains somewhat skeptical regarding the transformative power of this type of love "in the real," of the coup de foudre of love, noting that there is something "compulsive" about it (96). In contrast, as we have seen, Badiou, Žižek, and McGowan all deem this level of love to be the most important, as the level on which we "truly love."

On this matter, I find myself in agreement with Badiou & Co. because I believe—indeed know from personal experience—that even when the love event is fleeting, it can have lasting repercussions: the event may be a brief chance encounter but it can lead to a decade, or even a lifetime, of elaborating its implications. Love "in the real" brings "real" satisfaction not because the other completes our being but because it (momentarily) renders our void inactive; as I argued above, it frees us from the sliding of the signifier.

At the same time, as I have emphasized both in this chapter and Chapter 3, the main difference between my interpretation of Lacan and the interpretations of Badiou & Co. is that I believe that it is not a coincidence that Lacan links the ethics of psychoanalysis to the notion of not ceding the truth of one's desire. Badiou & Co. demonize desire—aligning it with the commercial translation of love into romance—because they, like Socrates, see through its imaginary character. This is why they consistently privilege the destructiveness of the drive over the fantasmatic and always necessarily partial satisfactions of desire. In contrast, I prefer the partial satisfactions of desire, the little morsels of the Thing that we discover in mundane objects, to the annihilating cadence of the death drive. I cannot avoid the latter, of course. But along the way, I would like to gather as many of the little morsels of the sublime object—"bits of the real"—as I possibly can.

It may be the lot of the human subject to come to terms with the realization that the object of desire can only ever offer partial satisfaction. Yet partial satisfaction is better than no satisfaction at all. I of course do not deny what McGowan so persuasively illustrates, namely that the exhilarating components of love cannot be dissociated from trauma, that love "in the real" is nothing if not derailing and disruptive. The jouissance of the amorous event can be difficult to withstand for the simple reason that (physical or psychic) overagitation is anxiety inducing even when it arises in relation to positive experiences. Still, as traumatic as the love event may be, it is for Badiou, Žižek, McGowan, and myself also obviously an opening to flourishing, understood here, among other things, as the capacity for an inspired way of dwelling in the midst of life.

This alignment of the love event with flourishing is not without its problems, for it runs the risk of positing love as a privileged route to flourishing, thereby underplaying other equally valuable ways of stepping into the midst of life in meaningful (and even inspiring) ways. To be sure, Badiou presents all of his events as transcendent. But because the amorous event is the one that is available to all of us, it is perhaps too easy to overestimate its gravity.

Badiou proposes that love is "such an intense feeling" because—and we are already familiar with this vocabulary—it is "a declaration of eternity within time: eternity descending into time" (2012, 47). "In the end," he continues, "the sceptics even make us laugh, because, if one tried to give up love, to stop believing in it, it would be a genuine, subjective disaster and everybody knows this. Life, one must say, would become very grey" (47–48). I am not sure that this is invariably the case. Would letting go of love really always be a genuine disaster? Does the lack of love automatically render life gray? Or is it rather that our culture's hype about love makes us believe such things? Might Badiou here be a little too close to the very mainstream ideology of romance that he seeks to discredit?

I worry that the valorization of love as the underpinning of flourishing—as the most important event of our lives—can cause us to overlook other potentially satisfying possibilities; it can cause us to neglect the fact that there are myriad ways of leading a life that feels worth living, and that one of these ways might be to relish every moment of solitude, of separation, that we are able to garner in a world oversaturated by activities, exertions, purposes, and, yes, intimate relationships. Despite my respect for the partial satisfactions of desire—for the bits of the real that I am able to access—I admit that when I look at the lives of those who could be argued to be faithfully (and sometimes belaboredly) unfurling the consequences of an amorous event, I am not sure that I would want to trade places with them. Perhaps in this regard I share some of Socrates's reticence. I certainly like to admire the *agálmata* I deposit in you; I like to see what is "in you more than you." But I am not sure that you are the only worthy container of my treasures. From this perspective, perhaps Socrates's mistake was not a mistake after all.

6

Is suffering an event?

Badiou between Nietzsche and Freud

In *The Gay Science*, Nietzsche writes: "I love brief habits and consider them an inestimable means for getting to know *many* things and states, down to the bottom of their sweetness and bitterness. . . . *Enduring* habits I hate. I feel as if a tyrant had come near me and as if the air I breathe had thickened when events take such a turn that it appears that they will inevitably give rise to enduring habits" (236–37). Nietzsche thus distinguishes between brief habits—which are a means of getting to know many things and states—and enduring ones, which arise whenever the air thickens to produce stagnant (tyrannical) conditions. Although Nietzsche does not use the term *event* in quite the sense that Alain Badiou has given it, the distinction that he draws between enduring habits and brief ones is conceptually similar to the one that Badiou draws between the status quo of life—the enduring habits of any given "situation"—and the event that ruptures this status quo.

Unquestionably, both Nietzsche and Badiou find the status quo boring, complacent, and hegemonic, which is why they deem whatever is capable of derailing it (brief habits, the event) electrifying. At the same time, Nietzsche's wording—"when events take such a turn that it appears that they will inevitably give rise to enduring habits"—subtly erodes the sublime valence that Badiou bestows upon the event by suggesting that events can over time generate deadening habits. Badiou of course also grants that an event can produce a new set of habits: a new status quo. Indeed, his emphasis on the importance of the subject's fidelity to the event—on the necessity of patiently elaborating the consequences of the event after its initial spark has subsided—implies that the event is in some sense "designed," in due course, to create "enduring habits." However, the "enduring habits"—the foundations of the new status quo—brought into being by a (genuine) event are, for Badiou, always worthwhile. In other words, Badiou's paradigm does not allow for the possibility of a genuine event producing enduring habits in the negative sense that Nietzsche gives the notion; for Badiou, there is no such thing as an authentic event resulting in dreadful habits.

This is not to say that things cannot go wrong in Badiou's world of life-altering events. As I have noted, Badiou acknowledges the possibility of simulacra, which exhibit the outward characteristics of an event while compromising its progressive thrust, as was the case with Nazi Germany. Badiou also concedes that events can be betrayed in various ways—say, out of cowardice, laziness, exhaustion, greediness, or opportunism—which is how the Russian Revolution spawned Stalinism (and how the latest musical innovation can end up in the elevators of Macy's). But Nietzsche seems to be referring to something more basic: the way in which events tend, quite simply, to "take such a turn" that questionable habits, rather than inspiring new ways of life, come into being.

Moreover, as I will show in this chapter, Nietzsche recognizes what Freud also stresses but what Badiou sidesteps, namely that traumatizing events can give rise to enduring habits of suffering that are more or less intractable. Freud devised the clinical practice of psychoanalysis as an antidote to this state of affairs (which he called the repetition compulsion). I will illustrate shortly that Nietzsche does not have Freud's patience in relation to suffering, that, like Badiou, he tends to align suffering with a lack of nobility and ethical capacity. But the fact that Nietzsche pays so much attention to the figure of *ressentiment*—a figure of prolonged suffering and of spitefulness arising from suffering—demonstrates that he understands how easy it is for traumatizing events to solidify into habits of suffering that in elemental ways shape a person's entire mode of life. That is, like Freud, Nietzsche is interested in the distortions of life that can result from enduring habits of suffering. This is why the main question of this chapter is why Badiou does not consider suffering as an event: if a political revolution, a scientific discovery, an artistic innovation, and the act of falling in love count as events, why does suffering—the kind of acute, traumatizing suffering that gives rise to enduring habits, to a new personal or collective destiny—not have the same status?

On a basic level, the answer to this question is obvious: if Badiou does not consider suffering an event, if his characterization of the event is so relentlessly optimistic, it is because the event, for him, is by definition a site of devotion. For Badiou, the worst we can do in relation to the event is to betray it. As a result, a traumatizing event cannot be a genuine event in Badiou's sense for the simple reason that it is one that we would usually like to betray as quickly as possible: few of us want to turn suffering into a site of devotion. But here is where Badiou perhaps takes a misstep by ignoring the fact that even though a traumatizing event is one that we may be desperate to betray, *we often cannot accomplish this goal*: our fidelity to our trauma can be so strong that, despite our best efforts, we cannot manage to betray it; one of the tragedies of human life is precisely that we tend to turn suffering into a site of intense and enduring devotion.

This is what both Nietzsche and Freud understand. They recognize that trauma often gives rise to paralyzing habits of suffering in part precisely because we cannot bear to betray it. From this perspective, one could argue that a traumatic event does in reality fulfill at least two of Badiou's requirements for an authentic event: first, it derails the status quo of our lives so dramatically that we cannot continue living as we always have (so that, say, depression becomes the new status quo of our lives); and second, it elicits the kind of fidelity that makes it virtually impossible to betray. This is why I wonder why Badiou believes that falling in love is an event whereas the loss of love is not. Why is it that stumbling upon a person who feels irreplaceable qualifies as a life-defining event but losing this person does not? These are questions I will return to at the end of this chapter, after having considered the insights of Nietzsche and Freud regarding the habits of suffering that all too often determine the basic contours of our lives.

Nietzschean forgetting

Nietzsche's response to suffering is notoriously arrogant: nip the problem in the bud by neutralizing your pain before it gets a chance to harden into an enduring habit; when disaster strikes, dust yourself off, pull yourself together, and step into the future unscathed. More specifically, Nietzsche's distinction between the noble and the herd, the strong and the weak, hinges on the noble's ability to cast off suffering like one might brush off a raindrop that has landed on one's hand. The noble, in short, knows how to forget its woes. As Nietzsche explains, being "incapable of taking one's enemies, one's accidents, even one's misdeeds seriously for very long—that is the sign of strong, full natures in whom there is an excess of the power to form, to mold, to recuperate and to forget" (1989, 39). In this context, Nietzsche offers the example of the French revolutionary statesman Comte de Mirabeau, who, according to Nietzsche, merits our admiration because he was able to shake off "with a *single* shrug many vermin that eat deep into others" (139). Mirabeau, Nietzsche notes, "had no memory for insults and vile actions done him and was unable to forgive simply because he—forgot" (39).

The noble has no need to forgive its wrongdoers because it is able to forget: it does not ponder the potential merits of forgiveness for the simple reason that it does not give its enemies a second thought. Nor does it dwell on life's accidents or its own misdeeds. Nietzsche specifies that whenever the noble needs to, it is perfectly capable of making "a sudden decision for ignorance, for arbitrary shutting out, a closing of the windows, and inner denial of this or that thing, a refusal to let it approach, a kind of defensive posture against much that can be known, a contentment with the dark, with the closed horizon, an acceptance and approval of ignorance: all this being necessary according to the degree of its power to appropriate, its 'digestive power,' to speak in a metaphor—and indeed 'the spirit' is more like a stomach than anything else" (1973, 161).

The noble digests its hardships. It has an excellent stomach, meaning that it is able to forget, to make "a sudden decision for ignorance" in order to close the shutters against the disagreeable. It refuses to allow suffering to approach, to infiltrate its being (more on this below). In contrast, the man of *ressentiment* is like a dyspeptic who "cannot 'have done' with anything" (1989, 38). He turns his weakness into a virtue, into the kind of moral attitude that authorizes the regurgitation of victimization. Overtaken by bitterness, this man's soul "*squints*" (38). No wonder that Nietzsche confidently declares that "I do not want to wage war against what is ugly. I do not want to accuse; I do not even want to accuse those who accuse. *Looking away* shall be my only negation. And all in all and on the whole: some day I wish to be only a Yes-sayer" (1974, 223). Insofar as Nietzsche does not want to become a man of *ressentiment*, he strives to respond to insults by simply looking away, that is, by forgetting.

It is easy to see why many have found Nietzsche's outlook unconvincing, not to mention politically questionable. We know that the Nazis put some of his reasoning to deadly use by constructing an image of invulnerable and magnificent German masculinity that was to defeat the "vermin" of weak and resentful—resentful because weak—Jews. In addition, that Nietzsche ended his life in madness gives ammunition to any Freudians who might want to point out that the attempt to muffle suffering only guarantees that it will leap out in indirect, pathological forms. After all, Freud was convinced that his hysterical patients suffered from "reminiscences" in the sense that the traumatic memories they had suppressed—had "forgotten" on the conscious level—persisted in their unconscious, causing all the more havoc for being unconscious ("forgotten"). Such patients remembered unconsciously what they had "forgotten" consciously, with the consequence that they were unable to free themselves from the past and for its sake neglected "what is real and immediate" (1910, 13). Describing the same predicament seven years later, Freud added: "It is as though these patients had not finished with the traumatic situation, as though they were still faced by it as an immediate task which had not been dealt with" (1917, 340).

The parallels between Freud's description of the hysteric and the Nietzschean dyspeptic are obvious: both find it difficult to "be done" with things; both are stuck in traumatic memory as if it were "an immediate task which has not been dealt with"; both, in sum, are burdened by too much memory (too many reminiscences). The difference between the two descriptions is that Freud is talking about unconscious memory whereas Nietzsche is referring to a conscious rehearsal of resentment. This explains why Freud wants hysterics to recollect what they cannot remember whereas Nietzsche wants emotional dyspeptics to forget what they remember all too vividly;

it explains why Freud sees memory as a tool of liberation whereas Nietzsche sees it primarily as an impediment.

Releasing strangulated affects

I will return to the potential merits of Nietzsche's vision below. But first, let us take a closer look at Freud's approach. Freud believed that traumatic experiences that cannot be remembered on the conscious level, that get pushed to the unconscious, dictate our lives much more strongly than what becomes conscious, often shaping our destiny in ways that we would like to avoid. This, essentially, is what the repetition compulsion does: it is because we are not fully aware of how the pain of the past motivates our actions in the present that we are prone to repeat debilitating, symptomatic patterns of behavior; to the extent that we are not "done" with our formative traumas, we experience them as part of our present, as our current preoccupation. This is why the Freudian "cure" to pathologies—including everyday neuroses—was to induce analysands to become cognizant of the unconscious ghosts that populate their inner world so that they could liberate themselves of their influence; it is why Freud wanted to make the unconscious conscious by removing his patients' amnesias.

Freud explains that whenever "there is a symptom there is also an amnesia, a gap in the memory, and filling up this gap implies the removal of the conditions which led to the production of the symptom" (1910, 17). Freud's assumption is that the active recollection of painful experiences over time dissolves their legacies, thereby enabling traumatized individuals to break their entrenched habits of pain and to focus on other—hopefully more rewarding—aspects of their lives. Moreover, Freud specifies that acts of recollection are only effective when they are accompanied by a release of affect—when affects that have become "strangulated" in psychic fixations find open expression (15). Susan Brison expresses this idea perfectly when she proposes that "piecing together a dismembered self seems to require a process of remembering in which speech and affect converge" (56).

This insight about the curative power of remembering—and narrativizing—repressed memories so as to be able to step into the future without being encumbered by the past remains one of the cornerstones of our therapeutic culture. It has even seeped into mainstream society in the sense that many people believe that unloading their private burdens publicly—even in extremely visible venues such as television talk shows—will free them of these burdens. Freud's intuition also lives on in the notion that the commemoration of collective traumas through public acts of grieving, official apologies, political acts of restoration, museums, monuments, and so on, is not only ethically necessary but also socially salutary. Such acts of remembrance counter the impulse to let sociopolitical atrocities, such as slavery, apartheid, and genocide fall into oblivion; they are a means of honoring those who have suffered, of transmitting traumatic memory from one generation to the next, of building community, and of making political statements about history, power, and oppression. In such contexts, forgetting would be ethically compromising, even indecent.

This is one reason that Nietzsche's valorization of forgetting runs into ethical problems. Is the call to forget not merely a convenient way to brush atrocities under the rug, to let victimizers off the hook? Is not the image of the sufferer as a pathetic dyspeptic who "cannot 'have done' with anything" an insult to those who have been so severely brutalized that they cannot *not* remember? Is not the idea that victims should shrug off their pain akin to saying that rape survivors should make light of their violation or that those who have been damaged by collective structures of oppression, such as poverty, racism, sexism, or homophobia should learn to look the other way?

The legitimacy of resentment

According to Sara Ahmed, this is precisely the message that our individualistic neoliberal society imparts to those who dare to complain about social injustices. Because good feelings are read as conducive to social progress whereas bad feelings—such as anger, sadness, resentment, or unhappiness—are read as what keeps us from overcoming obstacles, those who express their bad feelings are seen as social irritants, as regressive elements whose stubborn rehearsal of bad feelings holds everyone back. As Ahmed states, "The desire to move beyond suffering in reconciliation, the very will to 'be over it' by asking others to 'get over it,' means that those who persist in their unhappiness become causes of the unhappiness of many. Their suffering becomes transformed into our collective disappointment that we cannot simply put such histories behind us. Ethics cannot be about moving beyond pain toward happiness and joy without imposing new forms of suffering on those who do not or cannot move in this way" (2010, 216).

Ahmed correctly asserts that the demand that those who have been traumatized "get over" their suffering merely retraumatizes—imposes new forms of suffering on—those who cannot or do not want to forgot; asking traumatized individuals to understate, or even stay completely silent about, their suffering for the sake of augmenting the comfort of the collectivity is surely a form of ethical violence. For this reason, I do not see any way around the verdict that Nietzsche's call for forgetting, not to mention his disparagement of *ressentiment*, is unreasonably dismissive of the bad feelings of those who have been victimized: not only does he seem to repudiate the legitimacy of suffering but he seems, on a fundamental level, to deny the psychic and affective realities of acute traumatization—the sheer impossibility of simply being "done with" it. His insistence on the rewards of forgetting is also politically problematic in that it denies the fact that unequal social circumstances generate situations where large segments of the population have excellent reasons to feel resentful; it runs the risk of privatizing social problems so that political opposition to such problems becomes recoded as individual resentfulness.

Sianne Ngai argues eloquently that bad feelings such as resentment, anger, or envy are frequently disparaged even when they represent entirely justifiable reactions to social disparities. Regarding penis envy, for instance, Ngai makes the same argument as I do in *Penis Envy and Other Bad Feelings*—and I admit to not having read Ngai's text before mine went to press—namely that instead of signifying some sort of a female deficiency, it is a protest against exasperatingly unequal gender relations. I have mentioned that Lacan already understood this: penis envy, in Lacan's view, is not something that arises from female anatomy but rather from women's recognition that their anatomy is culturally devalued in relation to the socially valorized penis. It is just that our society prefers to interpret penis envy as a passive form of resentment rather than as an active political statement about the unfair privileges that heteronormativity bestows upon men.

Similar arguments can be made about other bad feelings, such as the animosity felt by the poor toward the rich: such animosity is not a passive longing for what the rich possess but rather an active opposition to an unequal distribution of resources. This is why Ngai correctly asks, "Why is a subject's enviousness automatically assumed to be unwarranted or petty? Or dismissed as an overreaction, as delusional or even hysterical—a reflection of the ego's inner workings rather than a polemical mode of engagement with the world?" (128).

Ngai moreover postulates that different subjects are judged differently for their bad feelings: for instance, while the anger of some white men might be recognized as a reasonable response to social disparities, as a justified political stance, the anger of women and racialized subjects is easily ridiculed as an instance of blowing things out of proportion. In other words, the kinds of emotional expressions that are acceptable for some subjects are not for others, are—as Ngai puts it—rendered "merely a reflection of deficient and possibly histrionic selfhood" (129).

Speaking of this predicament in the context of envy specifically, Ngai adds: "Moralized and uglified to such an extent that it becomes shameful to the subject who experiences it, envy also becomes stripped of its potential critical agency—as an ability to recognize, and antagonistically respond to, potentially real and institutionalized forms of inequality" (129). And because it is women specifically who are deemed to be "naturally" envious, prone to a "diseased" selfhood that is incapable of making rational arguments about politics or other serious matters, the feminization of envy has suppressed its potential for becoming a tool of political commentary. This, Ngai argues, "should alert us to the fact that forms of negative affect are more likely to be stripped of their critical implications when the impassioned subject is female": "Envy's concomitant feminization and moral devaluation thus points to a larger cultural anxiety over antagonistic responses to inequality that are made specifically by women" (130).

Nietzsche rarely talks about women in anything but disparaging terms. And it is evident that he feminizes those (the weaklings) he deems excessively resentful, so that Ngai's commentary is directly applicable to his assessment of the distinction between the noble and the herd. In addition, read against the backdrop of our utilitarian society, Nietzsche's argument about the virtues of forgetting has implications that he himself might have found awkward insofar as he advocated a poetic rather than a pragmatic approach to life.

In this context, it may be useful to reiterate what I have claimed about our culture's dominant definition of the good life as one that valorizes performance, productivity, efficiency, positive thinking, and constant self-improvement (preferably undertaken with the props made available by conspicuous consumption). Within this mentality, bad feelings—our inability to shrug off pain—are a problem primarily because they erode our (pragmatic) capacity to perform. This is why, as I have noted, the typical American response to both personal and collective catastrophes is to encourage us to mourn our losses as quickly as possible, to get back on our feet, and to give ourselves a good shake so that we can keep performing. A little bit of mourning shows that we are decent people; but when it turns into long-term despondency, it is judged to be pathological—something that we should strive to overcome as expediently as possible, with medication if necessary.

Although I have cautioned progressive theory against the indiscriminate valorization of bad feelings as an antidote to mainstream optimism, I recognize that our society's aversion toward such feelings is perhaps even more problematic, for it implies that it is our duty to find a way to translate them into something positive; it implies that it is our duty to locate the silver lining in every difficult situation. The American dream, for instance, dictates that we transform obstacles into opportunities. It is almost as if living up to the expectations of this dream does not fully count unless our triumph is preceded by some challenges, unless we are first forced to clear some hurdles. And as I have emphasized, the insidious underside of this mentality is the idea that if we do not succeed, it must be because we are not trying hard enough. Systemic inequalities, such as racism, that keep some people from succeeding no matter how hard they try, have no place in this picture. Perhaps such people are simply just not robust enough for the realities of life? Maybe they have somehow fallen off the positivity wagon?

Clearing the slate

Nietzsche's commentary on the noble's ability to cast off wounding experiences could obviously be accused of feeding this mentality. It is hardly a coincidence that Nietzsche can sometimes sound like an ardent supporter of the American dream: suffering is a sign of weakness; victims are contemptible; stop whining; no one wants to hear about your troubles so find a solution; don't bring everyone else down by your incessant complaining; pick yourself up by your bootstraps and keep marching. However, what ultimately interests me are the deeper ramifications of Nietzsche's assertion that a person who is unable to forget his suffering resembles a dyspeptic who cannot be "done with" anything. That is, I do not think that Nietzsche's fondness for forgetting is simply a matter of celebrating the noble and the strong, the ones with good stomachs. Rather, I believe that he is getting at the preconditions of creativity: the process of clearing the slate so that new shoots of vitality can take root.

Let us recall that, for Nietzsche, creativity always demands a limit of some kind, a degree of constraint, which is why he claims that "every living thing can become healthy, strong and fruitful only within a defined horizon; if it is incapable of drawing a horizon around itself . . . then it will feebly waste away or hasten to its timely end" (1973, 120). In other words, only those will flourish who are able to establish "a defined horizon" within which they can function without being crushed by an excess of stimulation. Forgetting is one way of instituting such a horizon: it functions as a means of forging a void, a clearing of sorts, that facilitates the appearance of new things—that, in short, makes creativity possible. Simply put, when we are pulled in too many directions at once, when we are too filled with recollections, too attuned to the grievances of the past, we cannot relax enough to create anything. Against this backdrop, forgetting becomes the foundation of life's renewal.

Nietzsche explains that when we are crowded by too many memories, we are like insomniacs who are too agitated to sleep but too enervated—too exhausted by our agitation—to accomplish anything useful; we are frenetic in a futile way. In this sense, a surplus of memory overanimates us at the same time as it mortifies our imagination and paralyzes our creativity. When there is too much memory—particularly when there are too many painful memories—there is no space for action, no way to externalize the currents of energy running through our being; our efforts become too scattered, too diffuse, to crystallize in a product of any kind, or even in an activity that might satisfy us.

It is for this reason that Nietzsche proposes that forgetting "is no mere *vis inertiae*," that it is rather "an active and in the strictest sense positive faculty of repression" (1989, 57). Such an active kind of forgetting operates "like a doorkeeper, a preserver of psychic order, repose, and etiquette," so that it is "immediately obvious how there could be no happiness, no cheerfulness, no hope, no pride, no *present*, without forgetfulness" (58). From this viewpoint, forgetting makes the present—the present as a space of creative activity—bearable for us; it is the bouncer at the door that imposes order on our psychic and affective life so that we can rest and consequently, ideally, fashion forms of life for the sake of which it might be worth living.

It would be possible to argue that this vision of creativity—of the kind of activity that *gets things done*—is merely an early articulation of the neoliberal dogma of efficiency that I have criticized, that it merely anticipates the "performance principle" that Herbert Marcuse diagnosed as one of the foundations of Western capitalism. But as I already started to suggest above when I alluded to Nietzsche's preference for a poetic rather than a pragmatic life, I do not think that Nietzsche's notion of creativity can be reduced to the activity of producing what is socially practical or beneficial, for he is much more interested in the idiosyncratic, even eccentric, frequencies of life than in advancing utilitarian collective goals. When he argues that "we want to be the poets of our life—first of all in the smallest, most everyday matters" (1974, 240), he is articulating an art of living, of self-fashioning, that tries to express something about the distinctiveness of the spirit without thereby fixing identity into a stable definition; he seeks to hold in balance uniqueness and becoming, recognizing that we can be singular without being immutable.

Moreover, in the same way that Nietzsche stresses that creativity, generally speaking, demands a defined horizon, he believes that self-stylization is predicated on self-constraint; he believes that those willing to undertake the process of becoming the poets of their own lives must be able to "survey all the strengths and weaknesses of their nature and then fit them into an artistic plan until every one of them appears as art and reason and even weaknesses delight the eye" (1974, 232). In other words, self-crafting demands the ability to conceal, accentuate, reinterpret, and transform aspects of one's being until they form an internally consistent whole. For Nietzsche, the quality of the particular attributes—whether they are appealing or not, gracious or not—is less significant than the overall pattern they compose. What *is* significant in the end, he notes, is that "the constraint of a single taste" has formed everything (232).

Remembering as a way to forget

Nietzsche's portrait of overcoming the agitation of insomnia so as to be able to act—to accomplish something—seems quite different from the neoliberal busybody who is intent on breaking the latest performance record. Nor would it be reasonable to equate Nietzsche's understanding of happiness and cheerfulness with the creed of positive thinking that governs contemporary society, for—more than perhaps any other Western thinker—Nietzsche analyzes the manner in which happiness and cheerfulness presuppose a familiarity with unhappiness and seriousness; lightness and gravity, the ability to skid the surface of life and the willingness to peer into its depths are, for Nietzsche, always two sides of the same coin. As a matter of fact, in a roundabout way we may be back at the notion of constraint, for Nietzsche routinely aligns happiness and cheerfulness with an ascetic sensibility, stressing that a constant state of hedonistic enjoyment would neutralize our capacity to experience genuine pleasure.

From this viewpoint, contemporary society's emphasis on constant satisfaction—what, as we saw in Chapter 3, Žižek characterizes as capitalism's "superego injunction" to enjoy ourselves (2005, 152)—seems more or less antithetical to Nietzsche's art of living. In other words, getting things done in the Nietzschean sense would entail the ability to cast aside the enticements of consumer culture; it would demand the capacity to place constraints on oneself so as to foster the defined horizon—a horizon free of distractions—within which creativity becomes possible. Forgetting serves a similar housekeeping function: it clears out some of the clutter of our lives so as to enable us to imagine rewarding modes of being in the world. In a way, when we forget old grievances, we make room for new passions, which is why Nietzsche believes that forgetting is a precondition of living in the present.

This link between cleaning the slate, as it were, and creating something new is undoubtedly familiar to those who engage in intellectual or artistic activities. It can be a struggle to "forget" about the rest of the world in order to proceed with one's pursuit. This is why intrusions are so frustrating: they recall to memory what one is trying to forget. In the same way that traumatic memories counter one's wish to forget the event of suffering, more banal memories—even just memories of the phone call one made ten minutes ago or reminders of what one is supposed to do an hour from now—counter one's wish to work unencumbered by external disturbances.

Furthermore, even though memories of suffering are particularly immobilizing, exuberant memories can also be distracting, which is why people who fall in love are often no more creative than people who get their hearts broken. They may in fact be less so because those who get their hearts broken may over time be able to harness their pain for the purposes of creative activity, which is why there is, in Western history, a persistent link between the failures of love and the successes of creativity. Being happily in love does not elicit quite the same impulse to find an alternative outlet for one's passion. The sublimation of pain, in contrast, is one of the most surefire routes to images on canvas, rhythms to a song, and words on a page.

Julia Kristeva (1989) proposes that such a release of creativity cannot take place as long as melancholia as a stubborn faithfulness to suffering—usually to the memory of loss—impedes the process of mourning. On this view, melancholia is merely another name for the excess of memory Nietzsche is referring to. As long as melancholia dominates, creativity remains thwarted; but when mourning begins to displace the fixations of melancholia, some room opens for the awakening of creativity. One might say that, on the one hand, creative activity consumes one's attention to the extent that it tends to exclude everything else, including what is painful (more on this below). But on the other, it is a means of freeing up energy that would otherwise be bound up in overagitating memories of past pain.

Speaking personally for a moment, I know that I have often chosen productivity—writing books, staying busy, keeping up with work pressures—as a lesser evil than being defeated by the pain of the past. From the neoliberal perspective that valorizes performance and productivity, this is obviously a questionable solution. There is surely something fundamentally wrong with a cultural system that asks us to work around the clock, that asks us to remain ever-vigilant in relation to constant demands on our time, and that judges us to be losing the thread when we fail to respond to emails within a minute. Likewise, from a psychoanalytic point of view, working too much can be a pathological response to suffering, a defense formation: I should be able to work through the past rather than push it aside by repeated spurts of working for a living (productivity). But from a Nietzschean perspective—which, despite my psychoanalytic predilections, I have always had some appreciation for—this particular strategy for survival is a way to feel alive in a life that might otherwise feel dead (or deadening).

I have already mentioned that the Nietzschean dyspeptic who is unable to digest his suffering is not very different from the Freudian hysteric who is weighted down by (unconscious) reminiscences. Both figures are crowded by too many memories to be able to live in fulfilling ways. Both fail to distinguish between past trauma and the task of living in the here and now, with the result that the latter becomes challenging. It may, then, be that when Freud defines his therapeutic goal to be to fill the gaps in the patient's memory, he is talking less about remembering for its own sake than about remembering *as a way to forget*, as a way to get to a place where forgetting becomes possible. What is unconscious cannot by definition be forgotten. But what is conscious sometimes can. This means that making unconscious content conscious also means making it amenable to forgetting. The analysand lies on the couch trying to remember what has been pushed into the unconscious so that, one day, she does not have to endure the heaviness of remembering it.

In this sense, Freud's aim may ultimately be the same as Nietzsche's, namely, to allow the individual to achieve the kind of respite from memories that frees the present from the demons of the past, that, ideally at least, breaks the habits of pain that have become life-defining. In other words, although it may at first glance seem like the strategies of Nietzsche and Freud are incompatible, Nietzsche valorizing the act of forgetting, and Freud valorizing the act of recollection, they may in the final analysis arise from a similar insight about the part that forgetting plays in the continuation of life: while memory is the precondition of a semicoherent sense of psychic and affective life, too much of it can impede the revitalization of this life. As anyone who has striven to move on after a shattering trauma knows, a surplus of memory weighs one down, which is why both Nietzsche and Freud deem this surplus pathological. The difference between the two thinkers is that while Nietzsche idealizes the act of letting go of the surplus, Freud believes that a process of working through—working through so as to be able to let go—is needed.

Keeping suffering at a distance

There may be a further correspondence between the approaches of Nietzsche and Freud, for even Nietzsche may not ultimately be quite as smug about the ease of forgetting as his portraiture of Mirabeau suggests. It seems to me that when he advocates forgetting, he does not mean that we will, literally, not remember what has happened. Rather, he appears to be talking about developing a relationship to traumatic memory that allows us to distance ourselves from this memory. As Alenka Zupančič explains, Nietzsche's ideal of forgetting past traumas is not a matter of denying suffering but merely of not letting this suffering define our being.

This is the idea I anticipated above when I paraphrased Nietzsche's argument regarding forgetting by stating that the noble refuses to allow suffering to approach, to infiltrate its being. Zupančič in turn glosses Nietzsche's attitude as follows: "It is the capacity not to be injured, and not to suffer because of an injustice, that constitutes the *measure* of one's richness and power—not the capacity to *endure* suffering and injury, to bear pain, but the capacity not to let this suffering as suffering enter the constitution of one's subjectivity (which also means the capacity not to let oneself be subjectivized in the figure of the 'subject of injury,' the figure of the victim). Those who can manage this are 'rich' and 'powerful' *because* they can manage it, not the other way around" (56).

In Zupančič's view, Nietzschean forgetting keeps suffering at a distance. It is a way for the traumatized subject to reject the mantle of the victim, to refuse to become a figure of injury, defined for the rest of its life by this injury. In Chapter 1, I argued that I find Badiou's critique of "victim mentality" problematic because it implies that those who break down due to their traumatization are somehow less noble than those who do not. Zupančič's rejection of "the figure of the victim" is less objectionable because she places the emphasis on the life-enhancing (even therapeutic) benefits of not allowing oneself to be reduced to one's suffering. If pain is the means by which the subject internalizes a traumatic experience as its "own bitter treasure," as Zupančič puts it, Nietzschean forgetting implies "the capacity not to make pain the determining ground of our actions and choices" (57). Forgetting, in this sense, "refers above all to the capacity not to nurture pain": "Nietzschean oblivion is not so much an effacement of the traumatic encounter as a preservation of its external character, of its foreignness, of its otherness" (57).

Forgetting, then, allows the subject to dissociate its suffering from its basic self-understanding. It renders trauma external to the subject, something that may have happened *to* it but that is not synonymous *with* it, with who it is; it is a way of distancing injury from the self. This manner of expressing the matter once again reveals the convergences in the visions of Nietzsche and Freud, for the subject's ability to take some distance from its trauma is arguably also the aim of analytic practice. The talking cure gradually weaves a veil of words (narratives, fragments of a story) between the patient and his or her trauma so as to make this trauma less immediately felt, less identical with the patient's sense of self.

This similarity of goals, however, should not obscure the fact that, as I have attempted to illustrate, the obvious difference between the Freudian and Nietzschean paradigms is that in the former the externalization of trauma can only be achieved by first releasing the affects that have been strangulated in traumatic fixations whereas the latter is based on an ascetic ideal of stoicism where it is silence—the refusal to speak one's pain—that drives a wedge between the self and its traumatic experience. As we saw above, Nietzsche advocates a "decision" to forget, a resolute shutting out of traumatic experience, a refusal to allow this experience to dominate one's consciousness.

Living next to trauma

Freud understands better than Nietzsche that such a "decision" is usually powerless against acute forms of traumatization. Yet the concept is perhaps not always entirely alien even to those who have experienced extreme violence. Listen to Holocaust survivor Charlotte Delbo:

> Auschwitz is so deeply etched into my memory that I cannot forget one moment of it.—So you are living with Auschwitz?—No. I live next to it. No doubt, I am very fortunate in not recognizing myself in the self that was in Auschwitz. To return from there was so improbable that it seems to me I was never there at all. . . . I live within a twofold being. The Auschwitz

> double doesn't bother me, doesn't interfere with my life. As though it weren't I at all. Without this split I would not have been able to revive. (2–3)

Delbo reports that even though Auschwitz is so thoroughly etched into her memory that she cannot for one moment forget about it, she does not live "with Auschwitz" but rather "next to it." That is, Delbo describes a process of dissociation whereby she is able to separate herself—who she is in the present moment—from the person who was incarcerated in Auschwitz. The self who was in Auschwitz, Delbo claims, does not interfere with her life because it is as though "it weren't I at all." Our therapeutic culture (like Kleinian psychoanalysis) tends to pathologize such processes of dissociation, of splitting, yet Delbo makes it clear that if she had not been able to create a division between her past and present selves, she would not have been able to go on living; sometimes dissociation is the only way to survive.

Discussions of trauma tend to imply that one is either "within" it—unable to forget, acting out, repeating patterns, having flashbacks, and paralyzed by it—or "beyond" it, in a place where the trauma has been worked through, overcome, or at the very least integrated (metabolized) into the current of life. Most clinicians and trauma theorists of course recognize that working through is an ongoing and open-ended process, one that is never definitively "done." Nevertheless, the dominant either/or paradigm conceals the fact that many trauma survivors ultimately end up living neither "within" their trauma nor "beyond" it.

Well before I encountered Delbo's statement about living "next to" her trauma, I thought that one way to survive trauma is to learn to live "to the side of it" rather than in the midst of it. On a basic level, this is the message I hear in Nietzsche's statements regarding forgetting. His message seems to be that given that you cannot banish trauma, that you cannot transcend it, perhaps the best you can do is to learn to live in such a way that you exist to the side of it rather than in its disorienting vortex. Admittedly, such a strategy may be more effective in instances of traumatization that are less devastating than that of Delbo, that are a breed of the microtraumas that erode the quality of everyday life. In the case of such microtraumas, it is possible that silence, withdrawal, reticence, and discretion might rebuild one's resources—including one's capacity to invent new forms of life—faster than the incessant resuscitation of trauma.

This way of looking at things raises concerns about the insistence with which trauma survivors are sometimes asked to recall the past (and not only in therapeutic settings). The confessional ethos of our culture valorizes the curative value of remembering so strongly that it can make forgetting difficult even for those who genuinely would like to. While it is the case, as I acknowledged above, that acts of remembrance frequently carry a tremendous ethical force, there are also situations where the injunction to remember becomes intrusive, where it becomes a means of—explicitly or implicitly—questioning the ethical virtue of those who would rather forget.

On the one hand, as I have stressed, there are pasts that are impossible to forget for the simple reason that they are too excruciating. On the other, there may be something to be said for the survivor's desire to not be constantly reminded of them; there may be something to be said for the recognition that remembering is not always and in every situation the most productive thing to do. Our therapeutic culture teaches us that working through trauma via narrativization is healing. But there may be situations where working through is actually too painful. Against this backdrop, forgetting could be interpreted as a refusal to submit oneself to this agonizing process; it could be said to be a way of pushing old griefs to the margins of one's life.

It may also be worth asking who has the leisure or the capacity to linger in suffering. I suspect that there are many who cannot afford to dwell on their misery because they must focus on survival instead. In saying this, I do *not* mean to imply that severely traumatized individuals are somehow self-indulgent in being unwilling to brush off their trauma. I hope to have made it clear that I believe that there are situations where such a brushing off is absolutely impossible. Moreover, there are also situations where doing so would depoliticize—privatize—a deeply political problem, such as rape. I am merely referring to the possibility that for some people lingering in trauma can be overagitating to the point of being unbearable.

Whenever this is the case, people might be driven to seek out the kinds of compromised forms of agency that I described in Chapter 4 in the context of affect theory and particularly Berlant's notion of lateral agency: coasting along, disengagement, addictions, the distractions of entertainment, and so on. Some of these activities are more self-destructive than others but all of them can offer the kind of temporary oblivion that allows one to forget. While it may be easy to cast judgment on such activities, for many people they are the only way to proceed without letting traumatic memories swallow them; they are a way to forget, if not in the Nietzschean sense of creating an opening for existential vitality, then at the very least in the more fragile sense of creating a bit of breathing space in a life that might otherwise lack it altogether.

Are we all traumatized?

Distractions such as these may appear depoliticizing in the sense that they fulfill—temporarily at least—the dreams of escaping, losing oneself, getting away, and leaving it all behind that I outlined in Chapter 4. But it is also possible that a constant emphasis on the importance of remembering may be equally depoliticizing. More specifically—and to revisit my reservations about bad feelings having become the virtuous feelings of progressive theory, particularly affect theory—I want to propose that when the rhetoric of traumatization becomes so generalized that it seems to apply to more or less everyone, including the most privileged members of the global elite, it loses some of its political edge. For instance, as much as I admire Berlant's examination of cruel optimism as a means of grasping the ideological underpinnings of post-Fordist society, her accent on the ordinariness of trauma, on the general attrition of life under neoliberal capitalism, sometimes seems to level out distinctions between different forms of traumatization in ways that make it sound like trauma is an unavoidable component of everyday life.

If one adopts the Lacanian ontological perspective, this is obviously true: as I have argued all along, for Lacan, the subject's foundational trauma of having to leap from nature to the signifier, its constitutive lack-in-being (or "deformation," to return to Eisenstein and McGowan's wording), is a universal condition of human existence. But this type of ontological traumatization is not what Berlant means when she refers to trauma as a commonplace feature of contemporary life. Rather, she views trauma as a more or less inevitable consequence of post-Fordist social organization, of specific sociohistorical conditions, which is why she explicitly distances herself from trauma theorists, such as Cathy Caruth, who portray trauma as an extraordinary moment of injury. I have demonstrated that Berlant's analysis of quotidian traumatization is powerful insofar as it reveals that trauma can be systemic and prolonged ("slow") rather than an exceptional and shocking perforation in the fabric of life. However, I am more skeptical of her claim that, in the post-Fordist era, we have entered a stage of history where precariousness is pervasive and somehow more acute than during earlier eras.

Berlant is aware that her critics might respond to her reasoning about the ordinariness of trauma by saying that "precarity is existential" (2011, 11). On some level, this is exactly what I am saying without thereby trying to imply that existential precarity is the only kind of precarity in the world. On the one hand, I have emphasized that I do not wish to stop at the Lacanian lack-in-being, that I recognize the importance of more circumstantial genres of negation. On the other, I cannot help but feel that Berlant's relentless focus on "dissipated subjectivity"—on the kind of impoverished subjectivity that lives the impasse of "crisis ordinariness" as a pervasive failure of fantasies of "upward mobility, reliable intimacy, and political satisfaction" (9–10)—at times veers too close to replacing existential (or ontological) precarity with the idea that we are all victims of the *unique* insidiousness of neoliberal society. This impression of epidemic context-specific traumatization is particularly pronounced when Berlant shifts her analysis from the marginalized to subjects who used to believe that their lives would be secure but who now, partly due to the collapse of welfare states, find themselves faced with various specters of looming insecurity.

Berlant boldly proposes that "a spreading precarity provides the dominant *structure* and *experience* of the present moment, cutting across class and localities" (2011, 192). And even though she wonders what it means to talk about a new global class called "the precariat," she appears to take the existence of this class for granted: "This emergent taxonomy raises questions about to what degree precarity is an economic and political condition suffered by a population or by the subjects of capitalism generally; or a way of life; or an affective atmosphere; or an existential truth about the contingencies of living, namely, that there are no guarantees that the life one intends can or will be built" (192). Berlant here once again admits that precarity may be an existential condition. However, she pushes her argument beyond the existential (or ontological) when she asserts that neoliberalism mobilizes "instability in *unprecedented* ways . . . with its efficiency at distributing and shaping the experience of insecurity throughout the class structure and across the globe" (192–93; emphasis added).

To a degree, I agree. Following McGowan, I have conceded that capitalism exploits the structure of human desire. Likewise, I have argued that neoliberalism manipulates human resilience, asking for ever-increasing levels of flexibility, adaptability, and elasticity—for the capacity to cope with rapidly shifting circumstances. And it may even be true, as Berlant claims, that the managerial classes of the West "have recently been forced to enter a new historical phase" characterized by the "shattering of the expectations, rules, and norms of reciprocity that govern life across diverse locales and statuses" (2011, 193); it may be true that neoliberal subjectivity is characterized by "the increasing corrosion of *security* as a condition of life for workers across different concentrations of economic and political privilege" (193).

Unquestionably, Berlant offers a nuanced, and for the most part strikingly accurate, sketch of contemporary everyday life. But where I begin to hesitate is in the face of her assertion that, under the neoliberal regime, life has gotten more precarious for everyone so that even "the relatively privileged now are . . . living the affective life of those who had never been economically and institutionally secure": "adaptation to a *sense* of precarity dramatizes the situation of the present" (2011, 195). The ordinary, in short, has shifted toward a crisis: "What makes the present historical moment a situation is not just that finally the wealthy are experiencing the material and sensual fragilities and unpredictability that have long been distributed to the poor and socially marginal. It is that adaptation to the adaptive imperative is producing a whole new precarious public sphere, defined by debates about how the rework insecurity in the ongoing present" (195).

According to Berlant, this is a situation in which the answer to the question of "whether better futures are even imaginable" remains uncertain at best, for people are no longer able to disavow "the living precarity of this historical present" (2011, 195–96). In addition, Berlant believes that for the more privileged, "the increase in vulnerability appears to produce more confusion than optimism about what kinds of adjustment to prefer": "For what defines this pressing situation is the problem of living in the ongoing now of it. The enduring present that is at once overpresent and enigmatic requires finding one's footing in new manners of being in it. The haunting question is how much of one's creativity and hypervigilant energy the situation will absorb before it destroys its subjects and finds a way to appear as merely a steady hum of livable crisis ordinariness" (196).

Berlant makes the statements I have just quoted in the context of her interpretation of two films by Laurent Cantet—*Resources humaines* (1999) and *L'emploi du temps* (2001)—so that it is at times hard to know to what extent her commentary remains confined to these films and to what extent she means it to apply to the neoliberal condition more generally speaking. Yet the impression her analysis gives is that we are living in an unusually unstable, contingent, messy, and demanding politico-affective moment that is eroding the security of even those who used to feel secure.

Again, it is impossible to deny that on some level Berlant is right: her account is evocative of a volatile restlessness that seems specific to the neoliberal world. This is why I referred to the list of "nervous-system symptoms" that Berlant lifts from Vassilis Tsianos and Dimitris Papadopoulos in the context of my analysis of anxiety in Chapter 3. I grant that the hectic lifestyles of present-day workers on every level of the socioeconomic ladder imply a noticeable shift in affective states. "This instability," Berlant claims, requires "embarking on an intensified and stressed out learning curve about how to maintain footing, bearings, a way of being, and new modes of composure amid unraveling institutions and social relations of reciprocity" (2011, 197).

True enough. However, I am not entirely convinced that present conditions among the more privileged are intrinsically more demanding, more traumatic, than they might have been during earlier time periods. That is, I am not sure that the kinds of slow-burning, slow-moving crises (ordinary crises) that Berlant describes are new. Instead, what is new is our ability to analyze them and in some instances perhaps even our choice to see them as crises.

I remain wary of the tendency of progressive theory—particularly of its Foucauldian inflections—to suggest that neoliberal capitalism is exceptionally traumatizing, that social conditions have never been as destabilizing as they are now. In other words, I remain skeptical of the portrait of contemporary society as an ongoing crisis where everyone, including the most privileged, is terribly broken, derailed, and oppressed. It is true that democracy is in shambles; that millions of people are displaced; that the climate is in chaos; that global poverty, hunger, and violence have reached astounding proportions; and that few people's livelihoods are secure. But I am not sure that we can cast everyone as a victim—a precarious creature whose survival is threatened by a host of malign forces—without diluting the concept of victimization to the point that it loses all theoretico-political meaningfulness. Although I do not think that we should stop being critical of biopolitics or cruel optimism, I fear that the intensity of the critique can lead to the propensity to find traumatization even in places that are relatively devoid of it.

It is indeed the case, as I have posited, that neoliberalism demands inhuman levels of performance, productivity, and positive thinking. Yet the more privileged of us usually have a choice about the degree to which we are willing to respond to this demand. For some of us, our eagerness to play the game is habitual rather than essential to our survival, which is why I am not certain that precariousness is the appropriate term to describe our predicament. There was a time when it felt that spending my summers writing books was the precondition of forging a meaningful life: the only means to prevent the emotional disaster of being kicked out of the North American continent. But by now it is a preference in a way that my mother's job at the factory never was. I do not want to lose track of the difference. And I do not want to fall into the Foucauldian-Butlerian trap of insisting that I am unable to break my psychic and affective investment in my stressful life. The fact is that I could accomplish this break. I just choose not to.

It seems to me that the universalization of quotidian trauma—the emphasis on the ordinariness of trauma—can result in the kind of flattening of distinctions that affect theorists and other post-Foucauldian critics have often accused Lacanians of being guilty of. Yet the Lacanian discourse of universal lack-in-being and alienation remains frankly ontological: it does not pretend that there is something unusually traumatizing about our current social world. In contrast, the universalization of quotidian—biopolitically induced—trauma neutralizes our ability to differentiate between social contexts that are precarious and others that are merely customary, the consequence of the kind of psychic or affective conditioning that could in principle be undone.

Suffering may not be extraordinary. But it is not entirely ordinary either. Moreover, there is arguably something bizarre about the fact that even though much of progressive theory complains about the precarity of contemporary life, it simultaneously elevates the ability to cope with insecurity, irresolution, fragmentation, and decentering to an ethical virtue. This is a deeper contradiction than it might at first appear: if precarity is so terrible, caused by the biopolitical exploitation of our resilience, why is it so necessary for our ethical viability that we remain capable of withstanding it? Why should we not be doing everything in our power to stabilize our lives?

Recall, for instance, Butler's argument—discussed in Chapter 2—that attempts to recenter subjectivity are not just ethically problematic but *evil*. The question that this argument raises for me in the present context is the following: if being decentered is a condition that is forced upon us not just by the ontological insecurities of life but also by an overly taxing neoliberal system that causes crisis to be ordinary and anxiety to be an almost unavoidable state of being, why should we not try to recenter our lives, to make them less insecure, irresolute, fragmented, and decentered? And why not admit that this is exactly what most of us actually strive to accomplish? So why valorize the opposite? Why, for example, valorize bad feelings in the way that some of affect theory does? Here Kristeva—who has been accused of all manner of conservatism—seems more honest: she admits that melancholia is nothing to aspire to. And as one of my undergraduates told me after having been hospitalized for depression and self-cutting, "feminine" masochism (Halberstam's darling of an idea) is not necessarily something to aspire to either.

Is suffering an event?

Freud and Nietzsche also recognize that turning suffering into an aspiration would be damaging, which is why both seek to devise strategies for alleviating it. I have proposed that even though their strategies on the surface seem diametrically opposed to each other—with Freud advocating remembering and Nietzsche advocating forgetting—in reality both aim at a situation where the ability to forget creates space for new life. The point of psychoanalysis, even of Lacanian analysis, is to undo psychic and affective fixations so as to release energy (life, vitality) that then becomes available for less painful usages. Nietzsche in turn believes that forgetting is a conduit to new passions. But it is also worth noting that, from a Nietzschean perspective, the converse is equally true: our ability to become genuinely passionate about something new extinguishes memories not only of old passions but also of old grievances. In this sense, it is only by developing ardent passions that we become capable of forgetting in the first place.

Consider the well-known fact that it is often only when we find a new lover that we are finally able to let go of the one we have lost (and that we are usually able to forgive our lost lover for the pain that he, she, or they may have caused us). In such instances, a new passion erases the memory of the old, or at the least neutralizes the power of that memory to cause pain. Likewise with other preoccupations. In this sense, it is not merely that we need to forget the past in order to bring about a new present but also, and equally, that we forget about the past when we become so passionate about, so committed to, something about the present that our surplus passion crowds out the concerns of the past.

Stated otherwise, the crystallization of energy demanded by a new passion pushes aside what is irrelevant to the moment—including traumas that belong to the past—so that it becomes possible for us to step into the present. In this sense, the best way to overcome the pain of the past is to become so passionate about something in the present that the past—including what was painful about this past—fades into oblivion. This is what Zupančič has in mind when she claims that "it is the pure surplus of passion or love (for something) that brings about this closure of memory" (59). In the absence of such passion, the reigning reality principle becomes the only possible form of reality, preventing the kinds of events, acts, or ruptures that might open a path to a different future; that is, the absence of passion closes off the space of creativity.

One of the many tragedies of acute traumatization is that it makes it difficult for the traumatized subject to experience passion: because passion is agitating and derailing, because it asks the subject to dwell within the rupture in the sense that Eisenstein and McGowan describe the process, it can be too destabilizing for those who have already been deeply destabilized. One of the (less obvious) violences of traumatization is that it renders subjects cautious and vigilant; it makes them look over their shoulder in ways that prevent the type of oblivion that Nietzschean creativity demands. I do not mean to imply that traumatization neutralizes the capacity for creativity. Sometimes the very opposite is the case. But it can certainly complicate it.

This may on some level be the goal of the perpetrator of violence: he or she may want to rob the victim of his or her capacity for creative living, for the capacity to move in the world freely and with relaxed shoulders. Even daily microabrasions such as street harassment compromise the subject's ability to do this, stiffening its demeanor and forcing it to pay attention to its surroundings in ways that impede the fluid movement of the imagination. And drastic forms of traumatization, such as what happened to Delbo, can all but extinguish the spark of creativity. This spark can be—and often is—reignited, but this demands psychic and affective renewal. This is why I believe that (acute) suffering is an event: something that alters the course of one's life, usually irrevocably, replacing the subject that used to exist with a new kind of subject.

I am not here talking about existential (ontological) lack or alienation. Nor am I indiscriminately talking about the kinds of ordinary crises that Berlant analyzes, though some of them certainly qualify for the point I am making. I am talking about deep suffering without thereby wanting to suggest that it needs to be sudden or fleeting. Prolonged suffering—such as the suffering caused by quotidian racism—can be just as much an event as a single derailing incident. Either way, my point is that no one emerges from acute traumatization unaltered, which suggests that traumatization should logically count as an event in the sense that Badiou gives the term.

At the beginning of this chapter, I argued that Badiou does not acknowledge suffering as an event because it is an experience that we would like to betray as fast as possible by forgetting it. Yet I have also shown that even if forgetting suffering is an ideal for Nietzsche, and perhaps even for Freud in a different sense, this task is extremely difficult to accomplish, so that it may even be that suffering is an event in the purest Badiouian sense: unlike Badiou's (actual) events, suffering is hard to betray because it is virtually impossible to forget, replace, transcend, or render unimportant. Or is it perhaps the case that, like the American dream, what Badiou calls fidelity to the event is supposed to be difficult to accomplish? Does he dismiss suffering as an event because our faithfulness to it comes too easily?

For Badiou, the event is supposed to have positive consequences, which traumatization on the surface does not have. Yet like Badiou's events, it might have unforeseen, and sometimes even enriching, ones. Badiou (2001) looks down on traumatization because he deems the victim of trauma to be incapable of true subjectivity, reduced to a "mere" animal incapable of transcending its "situation." But what Badiou overlooks is the fact that many victims—survivors—do eventually transcend their situation. The moment of being raped, of being tortured, of being racialized may be one where subjectivity in Badiou's sense—that is, subjectivity as a site of inspiration—is annulled. But the aftermath of that moment may be when subjectivity in this precise sense comes into being.

Throughout my earlier work I have proposed that those who have suffered tend to be more multifaceted than those who have not. In making this argument, I am not denying that there are times when suffering crushes the subject; there is no way to refute the mortifications of suffering. Yet there is also no reason to insist—as Badiou seems to do—that the new subject that suffering engenders is less interesting, capable, or creative than the old one.

This brings me back to my reservations regarding Berlant's leveling of the distinction between extraordinary and ordinary trauma. Although I do not want to glorify acute suffering, let alone prescribe it as a means of enriching a life, I do want to note that the type of quotidian malaise that Berlant (sometimes) groups under traumatization rarely augments a life. It is often simply what life is made of: it does not render any of us very interesting, as is obvious from attending dinner parties where people complain about how dreadfully busy they are, how overwhelming their professional lives are, how often they have to travel for work, how hard it is to find the time to cook, how complicated their children's sports schedules are, and how many emails they have to deal with. I myself engage in this type of complaining all the time, especially about too many emails. But I also know that my life would not collapse if I stopped reading all of them.

This, once again, is why I think that the distinction between quotidian malaise and more severe forms of suffering ultimately comes down to whether or not I have a choice: I can choose to work less, travel less, cook less, forgo having children, and blow off some emails; but I cannot choose not to get sick, get raped, get tortured, get displaced by war, get stuck at an unwelcoming border, or get tormented as a child. Many people also cannot choose to work less. This is why I do not want to pretend that because my subjectivity has been permeated by neoliberal ideals, I am leading some sort of an extra-precarious life. I am just leading a life. At least for now.

Can an event be planned?

I have suggested that low-grade suffering, even the kind that is not necessary, can become an enduring habit, which is one reason that Nietzsche hates such habits. In contrast, Badiou's events—as I have argued—are somewhat paradoxical in the sense that they are supposed to shatter the reigning status quo (the reigning habits) at the same time as they are supposed to give rise to a new status quo (new reigning habits). It seems to me that the only way out of this dilemma—the problem of events giving rise to enduring habits—is to keep replacing old events by new ones: even events that result in a positive outcome, such as the introduction of Galileo's scientific breakthroughs, need to be challenged by new events lest they solidify into life-arresting configurations of habitual thought and action.

I have noted that Badiou seems to admit this when he argues that the subject is always living "between" events. Furthermore, I have stressed that he believes that an event, such as Beethoven's symphonies, remains a genuine event even when it is replaced by a new one: the arrival of John Cage on the music scene did not nullify the genius of Beethoven. This seems undeniable. Yet I am not certain that Badiou's reasoning holds in every instance. I am, for instance, not convinced that the events that caused the collapse of the Berlin Wall had no impact on the event of the Russian Revolution, that the legacies of this revolution were not tarnished by the toppling of Eastern European communism. It is true that we now live in a world that has forever been altered by the Russian Revolution, but surely the glow of that revolution has been dimmed by subsequent events.

Interestingly, it is once again the amorous event as the odd one out in Badiou's lineup of events that puts most pressure on his entire theoretical edifice. We have seen that Badiou (2012) insists that a new amorous event does not betray an older one, that he claims that he will always love every woman he has once loved. But as I mentioned in Chapter 2, I am not sure I trust this line of thinking. It seems to me that a love event is irrevocably betrayed when it is supplanted by a fresh event of the same genre: when a lover falls in love with a new person, she automatically violates the pact of love she had with the previous beloved; she replaces what is supposed to be irreplaceable, thereby putting into question the event-status of the original event.

I do not see any way around the fact that a new love event reduces the luster of the preceding one. John Cage may not diminish the sparkle of Beethoven, but my falling in love with a new person does diminish the sparkle of my former lover; if it did not, I might just as well stay with the first one. Granted, it would be possible to argue that the different objects of my love are equally sparkly for different reasons. Granted, it would also be possible to argue that they are equally irreplaceable to me at different stages of my life, so that the person I loved at the age of twenty, in the larger scheme of things, remains as indispensable as the one I love at the age of fifty.

Yet somehow this reasoning does not seem right: it feels that the person I love at fifty pushes the person I loved at twenty into oblivion in a manner that John Cage does not push Beethoven into oblivion. Things might be different if I am the one left behind: I might stay madly in love with my first partner even after I find a new one if my first partner abandons me; I might never love anyone else as much. But if I am the one who experiences a new amorous event, surely I dent the previous one. Maybe I am just not as virtuous as Badiou is.

Alternatively, maybe the idea that the amorous event is by definition betrayed by a new event in the same category raises the possibility that the betrayal of the previous event is *always*—even in the case of Badiou's political, scientific, and artistic events—to some degree built into the very structure of the event: while John Cage did not eclipse Beethoven, he did arguably steal some of the latter's thunder. In this sense, perhaps there cannot, after all, be an event that does not on some level betray preceding events.

Why, then, is the notion of the event so seductive? When I teach Badiou, the most common question I get from students is whether an event can be planned: it seems like my students would like nothing more than to be able to conjure one into existence in order to spice up their lives. If they saw suffering as an event in the manner that I do, they might change their attitude. But as long as their understanding of the event is confined to Badiou's original formulation, they cannot help but hope, perhaps cruelly optimistically, that they might find a way to will one into being.

Badiou himself is emphatic about his conviction that an event cannot be planned: we cannot plan the amorous encounter that derails our life any more than we can plan a scientific discovery. However, it seems plausible that it may be possible to cultivate a life that increases the likelihood of events. For instance, a fairly arduous training is usually the prerequisite of a scientific event. At the very least, we can try to clear the ground for events by participating in political, scientific, artistic, or amorous activities. An event of any kind—except maybe the event of suffering—is unlikely to arise if we spend our days watching television; a certain openness to events seems like a precondition (though not a guarantee) for their appearance.

In this context, it may be helpful to recall Nietzsche's complicated attitude toward habits. On the one hand, as we have seen, Nietzsche despises "enduring habits," the kinds of habits that have solidified into lifeless, boring modalities of being. On the other, Nietzsche recognizes that the robustly original can usually only emerge from within meticulously cultivated habits of thought, action, and practice. Consider, for example, that a new style of philosophy—such as Nietzsche's own eccentric brand of thinking—does not normally spring out of a philosophical vacuum but demands years of dedicated study of previous styles: Nietzsche's philosophy, like Freudian psychoanalysis, may have represented a break from preceding systems of thought, but neither would have been possible without the foundation laid by these systems. Generally speaking, every event that flees from an established system (a habit) could be said to presume this system as its disavowed ground. No one grasps this better than Nietzsche who repeatedly refers to the relationship between creativity and asceticism: the Nietzschean creator knows that the price of freedom (the event) is a tireless engagement with the (sometimes harsh) limits imposed by preexisting habits.

Still, the best we can do in relation to events is to foster a mode of life that provides a clearing for them; they cannot be planned per se. From this perspective, maybe suffering is not an event in Badiou's sense because, unlike his inspiring events, it *can*—in many of its more quotidian forms at least—be "planned" with much less complexity than what I just said about Nietzsche's understanding of creativity. I can "plan" to have my heart broken by entering into a terrible relationship. I can "plan" to experience the sting of disappointment by messing up my job so badly that I get fired. I can "plan" to get into a car accident by driving after drinking a bottle of vodka. And I can even (within reason) "plan" to get sick by leading the least healthy lifestyle I can conjure into being. In this sense, our quotidian habits of suffering are easier to plan than to betray. And perhaps these habits are also too predictable, unlike the Haitian Revolution, the discovery of general relativity, the invention of Picasso's cubism, or even the moment of meeting the love of your life at the local café.

Nevertheless, I want to end this book by proposing that for many of us, suffering in its intense—acute rather than habitual—modulations ends up being the event of events, the event that transforms our life beyond recognition, that makes it impossible for us to return to our previous life, and that we absolutely cannot take back (like we might be able to take back a scientific discovery by burning our data, notes, and evidence). Suffering is the event that we cannot forget even if we want to, even if we would be willing to make a deal with the devil to be able to do so. It alters not just our present but also our past and future, so that our entire life gets filtered through its distorting prism.

Many of us want one of the other events: we want to be part of a political revolution, a scientific discovery, an artistic innovation, and—because our society tells us that this is the event that in the end makes up for all of our misery—we want to fall deeply in love and stay so. Suffering, in turn, is not an event that any of us want. Unfortunately, it is probably the one that many of us are more likely to experience than any of the others. As tempting as it is to try to offer a more sanguine conclusion to the distillation of ideas that this book has attempted to accomplish, I cannot end on a polite lie. I know that if falling in love is an event, losing that love is no less so.

BIBLIOGRAPHY

Adorno, Theodor, and Max Horkheimer (2002). *Dialectic of Enlightenment: Philosophical Fragments*. Trans. Edmund Jephcott. Stanford: Stanford University Press.

Ahmed, Sara (2010). *The Promise of Happiness*. Durham: Duke University Press.

Ahmed, Sara (2014). *Willful Subjects*. Durham: Duke University Press.

Allen, Amy (2008). *The Politics of Our Selves: Power, Autonomy, and Gender in Contemporary Critical Theory*. New York: Columbia University Press.

Allen, Amy (2013). "Feminism, Foucault, and the Critique of Reason: Re-reading the *History of Madness*," *Foucault Studies*, #16: 15–31.

Allen, Amy (2017). *The End of Progress: Decolonizing the Normative Foundations of Critical Theory*. New York: Columbia University Press.

Badiou, Alain (2001). *Ethics: An Essay on the Understanding of Evil*. Trans. Peter Hallward. London: Verso.

Badiou, Alain (2012). *In Praise of Love*. Trans. Peter Bush. New York: The New Press.

Badiou, Alain (2013). *Philosophy and the Event*. Trans. Louise Burchill. Cambridge, UK: Polity Press.

Badiou, Alain, and Slavoj Žižek (2009). *Philosophy in the Present*. Trans. Peter Thomas and Alberto Toscano. Cambridge, UK: Polity Press.

Barthes, Roland (1977). *A Lover's Discourse: Fragments*. Trans. Richard Howard. New York: Hill & Wang.

Bataille, Georges (1986). *Eroticism: Death and Sensuality*. Trans. Mary Dalwood. San Francisco: CityLights.

Berlant, Lauren (2011). *Cruel Optimism*. Durham: Duke University Press.

Berlant, Lauren, and Lee Edelman (2014). *Sex, or the Unbearable*. Durham: Duke University Press.

Bersani, Leo, and Adam Phillips (2008). *Intimacies*. Chicago: University of Chicago Press.

Brown, Wendy (2005). *Edgework: Critical Essays on Knowledge and Politics*. Princeton: Princeton University Press.

Butler, Judith (1990). *Gender Trouble: Feminism and the Subversion of Identity*. New York: Routledge.

Butler, Judith (1997). *The Psychic Life of Power: Theories in Subjection*. Stanford: Stanford University Press.

Butler, Judith (2004). *Precarious Life: The Powers of Mourning and Violence*. New York: Verso.

Butler, Judith (2005). *Giving an Account of Oneself*. New York: Fordham University Press.

Butler, Judith (2009). *Frames of War: When Is Life Grievable?* New York: Verso.

Butler, Judith (2012). *Parting Ways: Jewishness and the Critique of Zionism*. New York: Columbia University Press.

Butler, Judith, and Athena Athanasiou (2013). *Dispossession: The Performative in the Political*. New York: Polity Press.

Butler, Judith, Ernesto Laclau, and Slavoj Žižek (2000). *Contingency, Hegemony, Universality: Contemporary Dialogues on the Left*. London: Verso.

Caruth, Cathy (1996). *Unclaimed Experience: Trauma, Narrative, and History*. Baltimore: Johns Hopkins Press.

Cheng, Anne Anlin (2001). *The Melancholy of Race: Psychoanalysis, Assimilation, and Hidden Grief*. Oxford: Oxford University Press.

Cobb, Michael (2012). *Single: Arguments for the Uncoupled*. New York: New York University Press.

Delbo, Charlotte (1985). *Days and Memory*. Trans. Rosette Lamont. Marlboro, VT: The Marlboro Press.

Deleuze, Gilles, and Félix Guattari (2009). *Anti-Oedipus: Capitalism and Schizophrenia*. Trans. Robert Hurley. New York: Penguin.

Derrida, Jacques (2001). *On Cosmopolitanism and Forgiveness*. Trans. Mark Dooley and Michael Hughes. New York: Routledge.

Derrida, Jacques (2006). *Specters of Marx: The State of the Debt, the Work of Mourning, and the New International*. Trans. Peggy Kamuf. New York: Routledge.

Edelman, Lee (2004). *No Future: Queer Theory and the Death Drive*. Durham: Duke University Press.

Edelman, Lee, and Lauren Berlant (2014). *Sex, or the Unbearable*. Durham: Duke University Press.

Ehrenreich, Barbara (2009). *Bright-Sided: How Positive Thinking Is Undermining America*. New York: Picador.

Eisenstein, Paul, and Todd McGowan (2012). *Rupture: On the Emergence of the Political*. Evanston, IL: Northwestern University Press.

Foucault, Michel (2000). *The Essential Works of Michel Foucault*. Ed. James Faubion. New York: The New Press.

Foucault, Michel (2006). *History of Madness*. Trans. Jonathan Murphy and Jean Khalfa. London: Routledge.

Foucault, Michel (2008). *The Birth of Biopolitics: Lectures at the Collège de France, 1978-1979*. Trans. Graham Burchell. New York: Picador.

Freud, Sigmund (1910). *Five Lectures on Psychoanalysis*. Trans. James Strachey. New York: W. W. Norton & Company.

Freud, Sigmund (1914). "On Narcissism: An Introduction." In *The Standard Edition of the Complete Psychological Works of Sigmund Freud, Volume XIV*. Trans. James Strachey. London: Hogarth Press, 1957: 73–102.

Freud, Sigmund (1917). "Mourning and Melancholia." In *The Standard Edition of the Complete Psychological Works of Sigmund Freud, Volume XIV*. Trans. James Strachey. London: Hogarth Press, 1957: 239–60.

Gurewich, Judith (2017). "Understanding the President's Reality: A Psychoanalytic Contribution to Public Life," *The Immanent Frame: Secularism, Religion, and the Public Sphere*, March 15.

Halberstam, Jack (2011). *The Queer Art of Failure*. Durham: Duke University Press.

Harari, Roberto (2002). *How James Joyce Made His Name: A Reading of the Final Lacan*. Trans. Luke Thurston. New York: Other Press.

Hardt, Michael, and Antonio Negri (2011). *Commonwealth*. Cambridge, MA: Harvard University Press.

Huffer, Lynne (2010). *Mad for Foucault: Rethinking the Foundations of Queer Theory*. New York: Columbia University Press.

Huffer, Lynne (2013). *Are the Lips a Grave? A Queer Feminist on the Ethics of Sex*. New York: Columbia University Press.

Kristeva, Julia (1989). *Black Sun: Depression and Melancholia*. Trans. Leon Roudiez. New York: Columbia University Press.

Kristeva, Julia (2002). *Intimate Revolt: The Powers and Limits of Psychoanalysis*. Trans. Jeanine Herman. New York: Columbia University Press.

Lacan, Jacques (1954–1955). *The Seminar of Jacques Lacan, Book II: The Ego in Freud's Theory and in the Technique of Psychoanalysis*. Trans. Sylvana Tomaselli. New York: W. W. Norton & Company, 1991.

Lacan, Jacques (1959–1960). *The Seminar of Jacques Lacan, Book VII: The Ethics of Psychoanalysis*. Trans. Dennis Porter. New York: Norton & Company, 1992.

Lacan, Jacques (1960–1961). *The Seminar of Jacques Lacan, Book VIII: Transference*. Trans. Bruce Fink. Cambridge, UK: Polity Press, 2015.

Lacan, Jacques (1962–1963). *The Seminar of Jacques Lacan, Book X: Anxiety*. Trans. A. R. Price. Cambridge, UK: Polity Press, 2014.

Lacan, Jacques (1964). *The Seminar of Jacques Lacan, Book XI: The Four Fundamental Concepts of Psychoanalysis*. Trans. Alan Sheridan. New York: W. W. Norton & Company, 1981.

Lacan, Jacques (1966). *Écrits: The First Complete Edition in English*. Trans. Bruce Fink. New York: W. W. Norton & Company, 2007.

LaCapra, Dominick (2001). *Writing History, Writing Trauma*. Baltimore: Johns Hopkins University Press.

Laclau, Ernesto, Judith Butler, and Slavoj Žižek (2000). *Contingency, Hegemony, Universality: Contemporary Dialogues on the Left*. London: Verso.

Levinas, Emmanuel (1998). *Entre Nous: On Thinking-of-the-Other*. Trans. Michael B. Smith and Barbara Harshav. New York: Columbia University Press.

Mahmood, Saba (2011). *The Politics of Piety: Islamic Revival and the Feminist Subject*. Princeton: Princeton University Press.

Marcuse, Herbert (1974). *Eros and Civilization: A Philosophical Inquiry into Freud*. Boston: Beacon Press.

McGowan, Todd (2013). *Enjoying What We Don't Have: The Political Project of Psychoanalysis*. Omaha: University of Nebraska Press.

McGowan, Todd (2016). *Capitalism and Desire: The Psychic Cost of Free Markets*. New York: Columbia University Press.

McGowan, Todd, and Paul Eisenstein (2012). *Rupture: On the Emergence of the Political*. Evanston, IL: Northwestern University Press.

Mullen, Gary (2016). *Adorno on Politics After Auschwitz*. Lanham, MD: Lexington Books.

Muñoz, José (2009). *Cruising Utopia: The Then and There of Queer Futurity*. New York: New York University Press.

Nelson, Maggie (2015). *The Argonauts*. Minneapolis, MT: Graywolf Press.

Ngai, Sianne (2005). *Ugly Feelings*. Cambridge, MA: Harvard University Press.

Nietzsche, Friedrich (1973). *Beyond Good and Evil*. Trans. R. J. Hollingdale. New York: Penguin Books.

Nietzsche, Friedrich (1974). *The Gay Science*. Trans. Walter Kaufmann. New York: Vintage Books.

Nietzsche, Friedrich (1989). *The Genealogy of Morals*. Trans. Walter Kaufmann and R. J. Hollingdale. New York: Vintage.

Nobus, Danny (2002). "Illiterature." In *Re-inventing the Symptom: Essays on the Final Lacan*. Ed. Luke Thurston. New York: Other Press.

Puar, Jasbir (2007). *Terrorist Assemblages: Homonationalism in Queer Times*. Durham: Duke University Press.

Ruti, Mari (2009). *A World of Fragile Things: Psychoanalysis and the Art of Living*. Albany: SUNY Press.

Ruti, Mari (2012). *The Singularity of Being: Lacan and the Immortal Within*. New York: Fordham University Press.

Ruti, Mari (2015a). *The Age of Scientific Sexism: How Evolutionary Psychology Promotes Gender Profiling and Fans the Battle of the Sexes*. New York: Bloomsbury Press.

Ruti, Mari (2015b). *Between Levinas and Lacan: Self, Other, Ethics*. New York: Bloomsbury Press.

Ruti, Mari (2017). *The Ethics of Opting Out: Queer Theory's Defiant Subjects*. New York: Columbia University Press.

Ruti, Mari (2018). *Penis Envy and Other Bad Feelings: The Emotional Costs of Everyday Life*. New York: Columbia University Press.

Sedgwick, Eve (2003). *Touching Feeling: Affect, Pedagogy, Performativity*. Durham: Duke University Press.

Spivak, Gayatri (1988). "Can the Subaltern Speak?" In *Marxism and the Interpretation of Culture*. Eds. Cary Nelson and Larry Grossberg. Champaign: University of Illinois Press.

Stewart, Kathleen (2007). *Ordinary Affects*. Durham: Duke University Press.

Woolf, Virginia (2008). *A Room of One's Own*. Oxford: Oxford University Press.

Žižek, Slavoj (2005). "Neighbors and Other Monsters: A Plea for Ethical Violence." In *The Neighbor: Three Inquiries in Political Theology*. Eds. Slavoj Žižek, Eric L. Santner, and Kenneth Reinhard. Chicago: University of Chicago Press.

Žižek, Slavoj (2012). *Less Than Nothing: Hegel and the Shadow of Dialectical Materialism*. New York: Verso.

Žižek, Slavoj (2014). *Event: A Philosophical Journey Through a Concept*. New York: Melville House.

Žižek, Slavoj (2017). "Moebius Strip, Cross Cap, Klein Bottle: The Twisted Space of Subjectivity." Plenary Address at LACK II: Psychoanalysis and Politics Now, Colorado College, October 19–21.

Žižek, Slavoj, and Alain Badiou (2009). *Philosophy in the Present*. Trans. Peter Thomas and Alberto Toscano. Cambridge, UK: Polity Press.

Žižek, Slavoj, Judith Butler, and Ernesto Laclau (2000). *Contingency, Hegemony, Universality: Contemporary Dialogues on the Left*. London: Verso.

Zupančič, Alenka (2003). *The Shortest Shadow: Nietzsche's Philosophy of the Two*. Cambridge, MA: MIT Press.

INDEX